D1212678

Applying Qualitative Methods to Marketing Management Research

Also by the same editors

Organising Knowledge

Applying Qualitative Methods to Marketing Management Research

Edited by

Renate Buber

Johannes Gadner

and

Lyn Richards

BOWLING GREEN STATE UNIVERSITY DISCARDED LIBRARY

palgrave
macmillan

BOWLING GREEN STATE
UNIVERSITY LIBRARIES

Selection and editorial matter © Renate Buber, Johannes Gadner
and Lyn Richards 2004
Individual chapters © contributors 2004

All rights reserved. No reproduction, copy or transmission of this
publication may be made without written permission.

No paragraph of this publication may be reproduced, copied or transmitted
save with written permission or in accordance with the provisions of the
Copyright, Designs and Patents Act 1988, or under the terms of any licence
permitting limited copying issued by the Copyright Licensing Agency,
90 Tottenham Court Road, London W1T 4LP.

Any person who does any unauthorised act in relation to this publication
may be liable to criminal prosecution and civil claims for damages.

The authors have asserted their rights to be identified
as the authors of this work in accordance with the Copyright,
Designs and Patents Act 1988.

First published 2004 by
PALGRAVE MACMILLAN
Houndmills, Basingstoke, Hampshire RG21 6XS and
175 Fifth Avenue, New York, N.Y. 10010
Companies and representatives throughout the world

PALGRAVE MACMILLAN is the global academic imprint of the Palgrave
Macmillan division of St. Martin's Press, LLC and of Palgrave Macmillan Ltd.
Macmillan® is a registered trademark in the United States, United Kingdom
and other countries. Palgrave is a registered trademark in the European
Union and other countries.

ISBN 1–4039–1660–8

This book is printed on paper suitable for recycling and made from fully
managed and sustained forest sources.

A catalogue record for this book is available from the British Library.

Library of Congress Cataloging-in-Publication Data
Applying qualitative methods to marketing management research / editors
Renate Buber, Johannes Gadner, Lyn Richards.
        p.   cm.
    Includes bibliographical references and index.
    ISBN 1–4039–1660–8 (cloth)
    1. Marketing—Management—Research—Methodology.   2. Qualitative
research.   I. Buber, Renate, 1954–   II. Gadner, Johannes.
III. Richards, Lyn.
HF5415.13.A664 2003
658.8′007′2–dc21

                                                            2003056406

10   9   8   7   6   5   4   3   2   1
13   12   11   10   09   08   07   06   05   04

Printed and bound in Great Britain by
Antony Rowe Ltd, Chippenham and Eastbourne

Contents

Preface

In general the development of an appropriate research design starts with a discussion of the research problem. Marketing researchers, however, have to cope with the pressures of time and cost. Moreover because of the dynamic development of markets (for example as a result of globalisation) and increasingly unpredictable consumer behaviour, marketing researchers in both academia and practice are having to deal with growing uncertainty. One of the main aims of marketing research nowadays is to enhance our understanding of phenomena, situations and people. Therefore researchers have had to reconsider the traditional research methods and look for alternatives to surveys and questionnaires in order to ensure that the method used is appropriate for answering the research question. Controversial research paradigms or worldview issues make these decisions more difficult (Kuhn, 1970; Gummesson, 2000, p. 19; 2001).

A school of mixed methodology, which Tashakkori and Teddlie (2003, p. ix) call the 'third methodology movement', has evolved as a pragmatic way of combining the strengths of the quantitative and the qualitative approaches. In academic discussions this has coincided with the perceived trade-off between high-quality research and quick results. Gummesson (2000, pp. 14–17) identifies three challenges for researchers: (1) access to reality, (2) preunderstanding (the researcher's input) and understanding (the research's output) and (3) quality (reliability, validity, objectivity, relevance and so on).

In the literature considerable emphasis has been put on the commercial side of qualitative market research (see for example Imms and Ereaut, 2002; Chrzanowska, 2002; Desai, 2002; Ereaut, 2002; Chandler and Owen, 2002; Wardle, 2002; Lillis, 2002), but very little effort has been made on the scientific discussion of applying qualitative research methods to marketing management research and market research. But if the recent marketing literature is looked at very carefully, themes relating to qualitative methods can be seen in a more favourable light. In addition, scientists from disciplines in which qualitative methods have been very widely used in research try to approach business and marketing management researchers and argue that 'It is singularly unhelpful to all concerned if disciplines become tightly classified and circumscribed according to styles of research. It is too easy to assume that disciplines like economics or psychology are exclusively characterised by quantification and positivist epistemologies' (Atkinson *et al.*, 2001, p. 6). According to Ereaut *et al.* (2002, p. xiii), 'Initially it was marketers who began to recognise that meeting consumer wants and needs required a level of understanding of people's motivations, usage and attitudes that went beyond measurement of the "simple, hard facts" accessible to survey methods.' Consumer behaviour is one of the core issues in marketing research and analysis (Foxall, 2001) and this demands qualitative approaches. Meanwhile qualitative research methodologies are gaining greater acceptance in both academic and business circles (Gummesson, 2000). The dynamics and complexity of markets, the growing value of marketing to business, changes in consumer behaviour and the new concepts and applications of marketing, to name but a few, demand deeper and more meaningful insights than quantitatively based information can usually deliver. Marketing has to cope with these phenomena, and marketing managers have to understand them. The contribution that qualitative research methodologies can make in this respect is immense (Carson *et al.*, 2001), in that 'Qualitative research generally attempts to make sense of and interpret phenomena in terms of the meanings people bring to them' (Ereaut *et al.*, 2002, p. viii).

At the beginning of a study the researcher has to reflect on general research issues and paradigms, formulate the research problem and decide on the research design, methodology and means of data collection. Then he or she has to decide on appropriate ways of analysing and interpretating the data and communicating the results to the client (the research report). This book is organised in accordance with the steps of an ideal research process (Churchill and Iacobucci, 2002, p. 56) and consists of four parts.

Part I focuses on methodological aspects of qualitative marketing management research. Marketing management theory, case-based research, paradigms in marketing theory and the use of appropriate software tools are discussed.

In Chapter 1 Evert Gummesson considers the practical value of marketing management theory. He presents a critical discourse on marketing management textbooks and their presentation of general marketing theory, and claims that marketing management has become stereotyped on a derelict foundation in commodity-like textbooks. The chapter ends with guidelines on how research in marketing could reinvent itself to the benefit of both academics and practitioners.

In Chapter 2 Lyn Richards discusses qualitative software tools. She points out that all qualitative researchers confront a dilemma between the need for thorough and convincing research results and the demand for speedy results. She explores the degree of fit between the various goals of marketing research and the tools of qualitative computing. She concludes that appropriate software offers substantial support for the data required, the methods used and the analyses sought by researchers in marketing.

Scientific paradigms and case research in marketing is the focus of Chapter 3. Chad Perry starts saying that paradigms are coherent views of the world that scientists use to guide their research decisions. He distinguishes three types of 'world' that underlie these paradigms and argues that the positivism paradigm is usually inappropriate for marketing research, as are the common alternatives of constructivism and critical theory. He claims that the realism paradigm should be used for much marketing management research and demonstrates how that can be done in case research.

Part II considers ways of generating and presenting data. In qualitative research data is usually obtained from in-depth interviews and focus groups and is therefore available as text. Working with textual data demands a thorough reflection on the purpose of the study and the expectations of the client. In practice most clients are not used to dealing with qualitative data.

In Chapter 4 Andrea Kurz, Walter Aigner and Dieter Meinhard discuss the problems involved in presenting the results of qualitative research. Even if the client agrees to a qualitative study and the research team sticks to all applicable standards of quality control, presenting the results can be problematic. It must be done in a way that is concise but adequate for the complexity of the topic, to an audience that is typically not ready to accept emotional comments, and to listeners who tend to treat critical statements with disbelief. When generating qualitative data, researchers have to consider the client's lack of experience in 'thinking qualitatively'.

More pragmatically, in Chapter 5 Astrid Spranz's aim is to offer marketing managers an insight into their customers' shopping experience, focusing on the decision-making process. Her decision to use mixed methods was based on a general demand for better understanding of consumers' buying behaviour in food retail outlets. The use of thinking aloud protocols, qualitative interviews and observation as means of generating data are discussed, as is the analysis of textual data with the assistance of NVivo. Some suggestions for marketing managers are offered.

Chapter 6 describes a somewhat unusual method of generating data, namely convergent interviewing. Sally Rao and Chad Perry discuss a study on the impact of Internet use on interfirm relationships, in which interviews were conducted with marketing managers and business consultants from 10 Australian service companies. Besides the results, the process and strengths of convergent interviewing are discussed.

Focus groups are a research technique for revealing customers' perceptions of new or planned products. In Chapter 7 Arthur Sweeney and Chad Perry present the results of a study on the use of focus groups to investigate Internet-facilitated relationships in a regional financial services institution. Four focus groups were conducted with customers of the 'Reward Bank' in a non-metropolitan region of Australia. Details of the procedures are described, and examples of the findings are provided to show how the focus group sessions were successful in revealing customers' perceptions. The research demonstrates the power of focus groups to investigate emerging issues of major concern to marketing managers.

In Chapter 8 Doris Ohnesorge discusses an important aspect of generating qualitative data: Coding. She illustrates coding issues using textual data from an intercultural study and presents the steps of a coding process following the GABEK method. The central aim of coding is to identify essential themes from the interviewees' point of view, but the process is vulnerable to mistakes, misperceptions and misinterpretation, and therefore needs a careful approach. The method presented leads to hierarchically connected summaries of textual data that are generated via coding. In general, these summaries are highly suitable for presentation to the client.

Part III is devoted to theoretically and practically oriented questions of mixed models, methods and methodologies in research in general and marketing management in particular. Several forms of qualitative data analysis – content analysis, the GABEK method, cognitive mapping and action research – are presented in detail.

In Chapter 9 Pat Bazeley concentrates on the mixing of qualitative and quantitative approaches to research. That mixed-method studies have become trendy again after a time in the wilderness does not mean that the controversy such methods provoked has gone away. Definitional, paradigmatic and methodological questions continue to be raised when researchers write about mixed methods, while problems with design, sampling, analysis and reporting, plus the strong demands on researchers' skills, finances and time, are faced daily by those involved in mixed-method studies. Mixed-method researchers, in bringing together the benefits of qualitative and quantitative approaches to research, often claim that greater validity of the results is the reason for their methodological choice, but without adequate consideration of the issues involved such validity may be more imagined than real.

In Chapter 10 Renate Buber, Johannes Gadner and Bernhart Ruso develop a mixed-model research design to investigate consumer behaviour in recreational areas of shopping malls. The hypotheses presented are based on (1) an evolutionary psychological model of key factors that affect individual behaviour and (2) a behavioural psychology model that is widely used in consumer behaviour research. While the quantitative approach produces data on how people react to different environments, the qualitative approach generates data on why people react to environments in certain ways. Moreover the study combines two epistemological positions: positivist and interpretivist. The use of mixed models and mixed methods is aimed at gaining a better understanding of specific behavioural processes and the motivations of consumers in different settings.

In Chapter 11 Gerhard Wührer explores cognitive mapping, a simple but powerful technique that can help managers to identify routines that are central to an organisation's success. First the elicitation of cognitive maps and the advantages and drawbacks of various approaches are explained, and then an exploration of export managers' cognitive maps is described. Qualitative and quantitative data are obtained by means of a mixed-method approach. Some quantitative tests are carried out to analyse the correlation between the parameters of cognitive maps and managers' demographic variables.

In Chapter 12 Christine Vallaster discusses action research and internal branding. The latter is a means of creating powerful brands. It allows an organisation to align its internal processes and culture with those of the brand. Yet there is little understanding of how the process of internal branding should be managed so as to create and maintain a unified understanding of a brand's core values among employees. This is because the majority of current marketing research methods and techniques are inappropriate for capturing dynamic processes. The chapter argues that action research is an appropriate method of studying internal branding.

In Chapter 13 Tine Adler focuses on the development of an internal marketing concept using two methods of data analysis. The chapter is based on a case study of internal marketing processes in a not-for-profit organisation. Interviews were conducted with staff members of a geriatric rehabilitation clinic in Germany. When the verbal data were analysed the results were not convincing, so a second analysis using the GABEK method was conducted. This supported the main themes of the actual situation more systematically and in greater detail.

Part IV consists of studies predominantly carried out for practical use. In Chapter 14 Petra Kuchinka illustrates the development of a measurement scale for firms' level of corporate globalisation, which is an important variable in global customer relations and firms' overall performance. The objective is to provide a tool to help companies adapt their strategies as they increasingly deal with global customers.

Thomas Haller's primary aim in Chapter 15 is to show how focus groups can help to develop a statement battery for determining customers' involvement with electricity supply and services. It is shown that a qualitative approach is a very productive alternative to the usual way of developing items for tests. A quantitative analysis examines and corroborates the quality of the chosen method and procedure. However the results should not be seen as a definitive guide to test development. Their actual task is to illustrate the capabilities and limitations of focus group interviews for such purposes.

In Chapter 16 Thomas Reutterer and Andreas Mild investigate the suitability and limitations of collaborative filtering methods when only binary respondent information is available. Using shopping basket data (consumers' choices/non-choices from product categories in a grocery assortment) with very similar characteristics as 'pick-any' data encoded from qualitative interviews, the authors investigate the effects of similarity measures, available data points per respondent and the number of recommended items or categories on the relative predictive performance of a memory-based collaborative filtering algorithm. Based on various measures for evaluating predictive ability, some recommendations for the proper parameterisation of such systems when applied to qualitative marketing research data are offered.

RENATE BUBER
JOHANNES GADNER
LYN RICHARDS

References

Atkinson, P., Coffey, A. and Delamont, S. (2001) 'A debate about our canon', *Qualitative Research*, vol. 1, no. 1, pp. 5–21.

Carson, D., Gilmore, D., Perry, C. and Gronhaug, K. (2001) *Qualitative Marketing Research* (London, Thousand Oaks and New Delhi: Sage).

Chandler, J. and Owen, M. (2002) *Developing Brands with Qualitative Market Research* (London, Thousand Oaks and New Delhi: Sage).

Chrzanowska, J. (2002) *Interviewing Groups and Individuals in Qualitative Market Research* (London, Thousand Oaks and New Delhi: Sage).

Churchill, G. A. and Iacobucci, D. (2002) *Marketing Research. Methodological Foundations* (Australia, Canada, Mexico, Singapore, Spain, UK and US: South Western).

Desai, P. (2002) *Methods Beyond Interviewing in Qualitative Market Research* (London, Thousand Oaks and New Delhi: Sage).

Ereaut, G. (2002) *Analysis and Interpretation in Qualitative Market Research* (London, Thousand Oaks and New Delhi: Sage).

Ereaut, G., Imms, M. and Callingham, M. (2002) 'About Qualitative Market Research', in M. Imms and G. Ereaut, *An Introduction to Qualitative Market Research* (London, Thousand Oaks and New Delhi: Sage), pp. viii–xiii.

Foxall, G. R. (2001) 'Foundations of consumer behaviour analysis', *Marketing Theory*, vol. 1, no. 2, pp. 165–99.

Gummesson, E. (2000) *Qualitative Methods in Management Research* (Thousand Oaks, London and New Delhi: Sage).

Gummesson, E. (2001) 'Are current research approaches in marketing leading us astray?', *Marketing Theory*, vol. 1, no. 1, pp. 27–48.

Imms, M. and Ereaut, G. (2002) *An Introduction to Qualitative Market Research* (London, Thousand Oaks and New Delhi: Sage).

Kuhn, T. S. (1970) *The Structure of Scientific Research* (Chicago, Ill.: University of Chicago Press).

Lillis, G. (2002) *Delivering Results in Qualitative Market Research* (London, Thousand Oaks and New Delhi: Sage).

Tashakkori, A. and Teddlie, C. (eds) (2003) *Handbook of Mixed Methods in Social and Behavioral Research* (Thousand Oaks, London and New Delhi: Sage).

Wardle, J. (2002) *Developing Advertising with Qualitative Market Research* (London, Thousand Oaks and New Delhi: Sage).

Notes on the Contributors

Tine Adler was formerly a tutor in social policy at the Katholische Stiftungsfachhochschule in Munich and lecturer on education at the Katholische Universität Eichstätt in Munich. In 1991 she became a freelance consultant for non-profit organisations. Between 1993 and 2000 she was a specialist in project coordination. In 1999 she was awarded a scholarship to study in South Africa. In 2001 she graduated from the Vienna University of Economics and Business Administration with an MAS in social management, and she completed her doctoral studies at the Ludwig-Maximilians-Universität in Munich (pedagogy, managerial psychology and intercultural communication) in 2002. In 2001 she became managing director of innot gmbh (interdisciplinary crisis management and training) in Munich.

Walter Aigner holds a doctoral degree in business administration and has more than 17 years of teaching and research experience at university level and in management training. In 1998 he cofounded HiTec Marketing and since then has served as its managing director. In HiTec Marketing's research team he fosters the commercialisation of new technologies via action research and the team of practitioners, consultants and researchers produce new knowledge on emerging technologies and strategies. Qualitative methods are the main tools for interviewing and interpretation.

Pat Bazeley provides research training and consultancy (through her company, Research Support) to academics, graduate students and practitioners from a wide range of disciplines in universities and government departments in Australia and elsewhere. Since graduating in psychology she has worked in community development, project consultancy and academic research development. As a consequence she has gained considerable experience of research design and methodology throughout the social sciences. Her particular expertise is helping researchers to make sense of their data and to manage it with the help of computer programs. In her own work she explores tools and techniques for integrating qualitative and quantitative data and the methodological implications of doing so.

Renate Buber is Assistant Professor of Marketing at the Vienna University of Economics and Business Administration (VUEBA). She holds a PhD in marketing and an MBA in business pedagogy from VUEBA, as well as a diploma in psychology from the University of Vienna. In January 2003 she became member of the visiting faculty at the Institute for International Studies, Rhamkhamhaeng University, Bangkok, Thailand. Besides a strong interest in qualitative research methodologies, her major research and teaching interests are consumer behaviour, sales management and not-for-profit management. At present she is heading a two-year research project on consumer behavior in the recreational areas of shopping malls, funded by the Austrian National Bank.

Johannes Gadner studied philosophy, anthropology and psychology at the University of Vienna, the Free University Berlin and University College London (UCL). In 1997–98 he worked as a research assistant at UCL and the Anna Freud Centre in London. In 1999 he won a PhD in philosophy from the University of Vienna. From 1999 to 2001 he worked as a researcher at the Department of Philosophy, Leopold Franzens University, Innsbruck. Since 2001, as one of the founders, he has worked as a researcher at and secretary of the Institute of Knowledge Organisation. He is also a secretary of the Club of the Green Party in the Austrian Parliament, which enables him to communicate to the public the relevance of science and research in society. His main research interests are knowledge organisation, cognitive science, epistemology and hermeneutics.

Evert Gummesson is Professor of Management and Marketing at the School of Business, Stockholm University, Sweden. His research is directed towards relationship marketing, customer relationship management and quality management, with a particular emphasis on services. In 1977 he published the first book on services marketing in Scandinavia and was instrumental in establishing a new school of thought in management, the Nordic School of Services. In 2000 he received the American Marketing Association's Award for Lifelong Leadership in Services Marketing. He has authored more than twenty books and numerous articles in journals such as the *European Journal of Marketing*, the *Journal of the Academy of Marketing Science*, the *Journal of Marketing Management*, *Management Decision*, *Long Range Planning* and *Service Industry Management*.

Thomas Haller is a faculty member of the Department of Retailing and Marketing at the Vienna University of Economics and Business

xvi *Notes on the Contributors*

Administration (VUEBA). He holds a master's degree in marketing and business administration from VUEBA. Before he started his doctoral thesis on the marketing of commodities he worked as a consultant with Simon-Kucher & Partners, where he carried out projects in new product planning and pricing, as well as strategy-focused projects in general. Among his clients were Aventis, Apogepha, EnBW, Kelag, T-Mobile, N-ERGIE AG, Procter & Gamble, Siemens, Steweag, UFA and Zumtobel.

Petra Kuchinka began her studies in business and economics at the Johannes Kepler University, Linz, in 1995. Her diploma thesis dealt with relationship marketing. In March 2003 she completed her PhD thesis on corporate globalisation and global customer management. Since 2000 she has worked as an assistant at the Department of Marketing, Johannes Kepler University, Linz. Her research interests are customer relationship marketing, global account management and networks. Since 2001 she has taught students and researchers the basics of the qualitative software program NVivo.

Andrea Kurz is a senior researcher at HiTec Marketing, a non-profit research institution in the field of marketing technological innovations. She holds an MBA and an MSc in chemistry, and has been involved in several international technology projects. Her research focus is the analysis of research networks and knowledge management. She was a contributor to 'Inventory of the current COST (European Co-operation in the Field of Scientific and Technical Research) Actions in which Austria participates', a study conducted for the Austrian Federal Ministry of Transport, Innovation and Technology.

Dieter Meinhard is a senior researcher at HiTec Marketing and a member of the executive board of the Austrian Institute of Navigation. He has conducted market assessment and technology transfer studies in several international research projects and provides marketing coaching to non-commercial expert communities. His research focus is the analysis of location-based, value-added services and practice in research networks. Qualitative methods of interviewing and interpretation are his main tools of analysis. He graduated from a technical school (electrical engineering) and also holds an MBA.

Andreas Mild is an Assistant Professor at the Department of Production Management, Vienna University of Economics and Business Adminis-tration (VUEBA). He holds a master's degree and a doctoral degree in business administration from VUEBA. His current research focuses are new product development and data mining techniques. Articles about his earlier research have been published in *MIS Quarterly, the Journal of Targeting, Measurement and Analysis for Marketing, Lecture Notes in Computer Science* and *Management Science*.

Doris Ohnesorge is a graduate of Leopold Franzens University, Innsbruck, Austria. During her studies in business administration she specialised in cross-cultural management. She wrote her diploma thesis on cross-cultural management and interactions and transactions between Austrian and Thai managers. She spent one year in an international programme at Chulalongkorn University, Bangkok, Thailand, organised by Michigan State University. During her studies in Thailand she conducted empirical research on cross-cultural management. She has practical experience in the field of accounting and controlling, and has been involved in a number of projects. She has attended conferences on qualitative and cross-cultural research in Europe, Australia, the United States and various Asian countries.

Chad Perry retired in December 2002 from his position as Professor of Marketing and Management at the Graduate College of Marketing and Management, Southern Cross University, Gold Coast, Queensland, Australia, where he was involved in the college's MBA, DBA and PhD programmes. His main research interests are relationship marketing and qualitative research methods. He has written or cowritten three text-books, eight book chapters and more than 100 journal articles and conference papers. Articles by him have been published in international journals such as *the European Journal of Marketing, Qualitative Market Research: an International Journal, International Business Review, the Journal of Business and Industrial Marketing* and *the Asia Journal of Marketing and Management Science*.

Sally Rao is a lecturer in marketing at the School of Commerce, University of Adelaide, Australia. She has a special interest in relationship marketing, services marketing and marketing research. She has published in several journals, including *the Journal of Business and Industrial Marketing, the European Journal of Marketing, the Australasia Journal of Marketing* and *Qualitative Market Research: an International Journal*. One of her papers won the best paper award at an International Services Marketing Conference.

Thomas Reutterer is Assistant Professor at the Department of Retailing and Marketing, Vienna University of Economics and Business Administration (VUEBA). He holds an MA and PhD in marketing and business administration. His research interests include business applications of marketing and management science methodology. In 2000 he served as visiting professor at the University of Sydney, Australia, and in 2002 he worked for an international marketing and strategy consulting company. Some of his research reports have been published in *Computers & Operations Research, Industrial Marketing Management, the Journal of Retailing and Consumer Services* and *Lecture Notes in Computer Science.*

Lyn Richards is Director of Research Services at QSR International. As a sociologist she taught qualitative methods at the undergraduate and graduate levels, and wrote four books based on qualitative family research projects. These led to the development, with computer scientist Tom Richards, of the NUD*IST research project, (on ways of handling non-numerical unstructured data by indexing, searching and theorising). The resulting software is now in its sixth version and has been joined by a partner software package, NVivo. Lyn is the author of *Using NVivo in Qualitative Research, Using N6 in Qualitative Research* (with Pat Bazeley), *The NVivo Qualitative Project Book* and *Readme First for a User's Guide to Qualitative Analysis* (with Jan Morse). She has taught qualitative methodology and the use of qualitative software to some three thousand researchers in fourteen countries.

Bernhart Ruso studied anthropology and ecology at the University of Vienna and the University of Manchester, and commodity science at the Vienna University of Economics and Business Administration (VUEBA). In 2000 he won a master's degree from the University of Vienna. His thesis was on artificial environments and consumer behaviour. He is currently working as a research assistant at VUEBA. He also teaches landscape perception at the Department of Landscape Architecture, Vienna University of Technology.

Astrid Spranz first studied at the University for Veterinary Medicine, Vienna, and the University of Vienna (sociology and communication science), and then went on to study international business administration at the Vienna University of Economics and Business Administration (VUEBA). Her VUEBA course and her diploma thesis focused on marketing research. In 2000/1 she spent six months at the Libera Università degli Studi Sociali Guido Carlì in Rome. In 2003 she graduated from

VUEBA with a master's degree. Her main interests are sociological phenomena in the zoological and anthropological fields.

Arthur Sweeney holds a PhD from the University of Southern Queensland, Australia. His specialist field is Internet-facilitated relationships in regional financial services institutions. Since January 2000 he has been a lecturer in marketing at the Charles Sturt University, Australia. During the course of 30 years he has gained practical as well as theoretical experience in large service, consumer and industrial environments in Australia and elsewhere. He has developed and taught Internet marketing, project management and international marketing.

Christine Vallaster won a doctoral degree in marketing from the Leopold Franzens University, Innsbruck, Austria, where she researched and lectured for more than two and a half years before becoming a research and teaching fellow at the Marketing Department, IAE, Universidad Austral, Argentina. At the Center for Management Research in Latin America and at the WHU Otto Beisheim Graduate School of Management, Germany, she researched internal brand-building processes, culture and leadership. In August 2002 she was granted an Alexander von Humboldt research fellowship in Germany. She has received several awards, including a doctoral dissertation award by the Academy of Marketing Science, and was a runner-up for the Gunnar Hedlund Award.

Gerhard Wührer worked in the marketing department of a travel agency in Salzburg, Austria, and Stuttgart, Germany, before studying management science and technology at the University of Stuttgart, where he became Assistant Professor in the Department of Management. After completing his PhD thesis he worked as a consultant and marketing researcher at Roland Berger Consultants in Munich. In 1988 he became Assistant/Associate Professor in the Department of Marketing and International Management, University of Klagenfurt. In 1990 he served as a visiting professor at University of Northern Iowa, Cedar Falls/Waterloo, Iowa. In 1994 he became Professor and Head of the Department of Marketing, Johannes Kepler University, Linz, Austria. His interests include international marketing, strategic marketing management, relationship marketing, marketing research and research methodology.

Acknowledgements

This book is the outcome of a long-standing collaboration between the three editors. It started out as brainstorming on a train-ride somewhere in Austria, continued with a thrilling conference in Vienna, and ended reading and discussing the ever so many interesting papers. It was an extraordinary experience meeting all the contributors as well as our audiences, who generated the discussions and the momentum to go ahead with the book. The presentations, discussions and informal conversations about qualitative methods for knowledge organisation and their application to marketing management research laid the foundation-stone for this book. Keith Povey and his team's efforts to review and make positive suggestions elegantly put the finishing touches to it.

The editors and publishers are grateful to StudienVerlag, Innsbruck, to John Wiley & Sons, and to Blackwell Publishing Ltd, for permission to reproduce copyright material in this book. Every effort has been made to contact copyright-holders, but if any have been inadvertently omitted the publishers will be pleased to make the necessary arrangement at the earliest opportunity.

JOHANNES GADNER
RENATE BUBER
LYN RICHARDS

Vienna and Melbourne

Part I

Marketing Management Meets Qualitative Research

1

The Practical Value of Adequate Marketing Management Theory*

Evert Gummesson

Introduction

This chapter presents a critical discourse on marketing management textbooks and their presentation of general marketing theory. These books claim to be general, complete and up-to-date, even though they are based on consumer goods mass marketing, which is a minority marketing pursuit compared with services and business-to-business marketing (B2B). Seminal developments over the past decades in services marketing, quality management, relationship marketing and customer relationship management are treated as special cases, despite being relevant to all types of marketing. This chapter claims that marketing management has become stereotyped on a derelict foundation in commodity-like textbooks. It ends with guidelines on how marketing research could reinvent itself to the benefit of both academics and practitioners.

The need for marketing management theory

Vedic philosophy treats knowledge as a blend of three interacting elements: the process of knowing (methodology), the knower (the researcher) and the known (the results). All three are needed in knowledge generation. An article by Gummesson (2001, p. 23) deals with the process of knowing and offers a synthesis of several methodological approaches under the

---

* This is a revised version of Gummesson, Evert (2002), 'Practical Value of Adequate Marketing Management Theory', *European Journal of Marketing*, vol. 36, issue 3, pp. 325–49. Published with permission.

name of interactive research. The object of this chapter is the 'known' in the form of marketing theory on a high general level. A limited number of themes in marketing theory are discussed. They are all concerned with the validity, generality and practical applicability of marketing as presented in textbooks.

It is my contention that the value of good theory is underrated by both academics and practising managers. The demand that marketing research be immediately applicable to please industry is sometimes practical, sometime impractical. It stimulates short-term thinking – which is also a necessity – but surfing on the waves of today's currents and winds does not tackle the generic properties of marketing. Basic research takes time and its hallmark is uncertainty about future yields. It challenges the very core of the mainstream research paradigm: its axioms, methods, techniques and research topics.

Marketing textbooks offer a smorgasbord of dishes, and handbooks and anthologies offer even more. There is a need for these types of book as they have something for everybody, but they leave the reader to compose the meal and provide a context. Handbooks are popular among practitioners as they are able to look up an issue of interest without bothering about the rest. While extended checklists can be very helpful in practical situations, the smorgasbord text offers minuscule context. If a plate is filled to the brim from the smorgasbord, it can look quite messy. The texts do not interlink phenomena in a deeper sense, although they may offer a framework. A continuous building of core variables to an increasingly more general level is not offered. For that, basic scholarly research is required. Marketing is such a captivating, confusing and rich field that no one has been able to sort out its constituent elements and their links at a higher conceptual level, that is, to suggest a more general and systemic theory. Much of marketing therefore stays on a descriptive level, with traces of analysis and conceptualisation but remaining closer to substantive data than to a general theory. Research in marketing too often regresses to simplistic surveys without in-depth reflection on the mechanisms being studied.

The more general the theory the better our ability to understand major changes in market conditions (such as new consumer attitudes and the effects of the European Union), and the usefulness of technological advances (such as the Internet and mobile communication). Apart from theory being helpful in understanding the new, the new sets new conditions that pose a challenge to theory, either for refinement or for a paradigm shift. This does not mean that at some point we shall find a complete and general theory and live happily ever after. It is a road to be travelled and the destination is not defined and static, but if we never set off on the road no progress will be made. Scholars are Flying Dutchmen who are doomed to travel and are not allowed to dock in a harbour.

It is contended here that relationship marketing can offer the beginnings of a general theory, using relationships, networks and interaction as its core variables (see also Gummesson, 2002). These variables have kept appearing in the marketing developments in which I have been involved during the past thirty years, and have reappeared more often than any other variables. It is not my intention to prove that I am right but to draw attention to the fragile scaffolding of marketing and make this discourse interesting and credible by discussing what could (1) add to a more general theory or (2) impede progress.

The staggering amount of research and practical experiences offered today in reports, articles, books, dissertations, conferences, TV and the Internet show that marketing is a bewildering field. There is no chance for anyone to spot and extract the most seminal contributions from these sources. In that sense marketing is production-oriented, storing new knowledge but not managing to reach out. Consequently there is waste of brainpower and talent. When something has attracted a critical mass, such as services marketing in the 1980s and relationship marketing in the 1990s, there is no tradition of lifting it into general marketing theory, either to support old theories or to replace them. Instead the new is presented as a special case and an add-on. The development of general marketing theory requires the integration of new lessons on a higher conceptual level than the existing theory, or to change the foundation of marketing theory.

We have more data in marketing than we can handle. On a business level, data warehouses contain an overwhelming amount of customer data that can only be converted into an implementable marketing strategy if meaningful patterns can be found through data mining. In business practice this is a task for customer relationship management (CRM), but CRM is also in need of general theoretical assistance. Theory offers context and patterns. Theory can emerge inductively through the sensitive and open analysis of data, or, deductively, existing theory can help us to sort out a puzzling reality. Theory includes concepts and categories in which homeless data can be offered a much more meaningful and comfortable habitat than mere storage in large warehouses. Unfortunately, for want of better alternatives or out of convenience, old marketing concepts and categories are used routinely, and research has become an exercise of trying to squeeze new data into old structures, or missing or discarding data because there is no accommodation available.

A theory–reality gap

My interest in scholarly research arose from my experience of the huge gap between the marketing textbooks I read and the reality I encountered as a marketing manager and management consultant. Constant comparison between my own experience and the literature has become my scholarly destiny and it accompanies me like a faithful dog.

In analysing the shortcomings of marketing management theory, the mission of this chapter is to present a state-of-the-art review of the marketing discipline in a conceptual, readable and inspiring format. Although a tremendous amount of experience, observations and scientific knowledge has accumulated, textbooks do not live up to their mission. They are caught in reminiscences from the 1960s and patched like a pair of old jeans, presenting fragments of theory, models and research findings together with examples, cases, success stories and quotes from journal articles, books and news media. Textbook theory is structured around a series of phenomena, among them the 4P marketing mix, and it embraces product, pricing, sales management, advertising, channel management, marketing strategy, market research, marketing planning, organisational buying behaviour, international marketing, marketing organisation and so on. How they relate to each other and to the bottom line is unclear. It is a 'theory mess'.

Prior to relationship marketing, with its credo of long-term interactive relationships and win–win situations, theory was clearly manipulative and management-centric. It was not customer-centric as it focused on anonymous statistical masses. Unfortunately there are relationship marketing proponents who see long-term relationships as another 'P' to be used to manipulate the consumer in the marketing management tradition. This is apparent in expressions such as 'managing the customer', 'owning the customer' and 'locking in the customer'. If we apply a marriage metaphor – managing, owning and locking in your spouse – such strategies stand out as less than desirable.

In discussions of the development and future of general marketing theory, the US standpoint dominates the global arena. However discussions are also ongoing in other countries. In Europe, recent contributions include a review of the historical evolution of marketing at the international level by Baker (1999a), and fierce and unorthodox attacks in the postmodern spirit, especially that by Brown (1998, 2000). The intention here is not to list all the contributions over the years but to focus on the present situation. Furthermore the chapter is limited to efforts in which I have been involved for three decades, often referred to as the Nordic School. Despite all the attempts to redefine and renew marketing, nothing much seems to have happened in basic research and the generation of general marketing theory. To mention just two landmark contributions out of many, Alderson's (1957) general theory of marketing may have been too elaborate even for academics to handle – which is a pity, but perhaps the time is ripe five decades later? Zaltman *et al.* (1982) submitted an eclectic and audacious review of theory-generation processes that failed to become part of mainstream research in marketing. There is reason to wonder whether publications and conferences push marketing ahead or if there is a mystical force – perhaps an evil conspiracy – that controls what really happens.

With all the marketing wisdom that is available, is it not a folly to add to the literature? Feeling obliged to read up on everything before one speaks out and trying to find a 'story-line' for developments in marketing (is there one?) has a choking effect; there is no oxygen left for one's thoughts. As the things that strike me as important are not well communicated in textbooks, which set the standard in respect of which areas to master and prioritise, there should be scope for more literature. There are pivotal questions to ask. Why is it that services, quality and relationships are not easily identified in the wealth of marketing literature? Why is it that trivial contributions based on simplistic survey techniques are quickly accepted by journal reviewers as long as the script is neatly crafted? Why is it that we cannot say that general marketing theory is moving ahead?

The Nordic School has broadened its initial services marketing domain to merge services marketing with the network approach to B2B marketing, traditional marketing management and other management disciplines (such as quality), resulting in a generalised approach in which relationships, networks and interaction are central concepts (Gummesson, 1994, 2002; Gummesson *et al.*, 1997; Grönroos, 1997, 2000; Edvardsson and Gustafsson, 1999). Researchers in Sweden who work in what is usually referred to as the IMP (industrial marketing and purchasing) tradition were quick to observe the heavy emphasis on networks in B2B marketing practice and the lack of theory to explain it (for a review see Håkansson and Snehota, 1995). These approaches are mainly conceptualisations from inductive and comparative research and not the outcome of surveys and other statistical techniques favoured in the marketing research literature. Nordic researchers soon linked up internationally. Through organisations such as the European Academy of Marketing (EMAC), the American Marketing Association (AMA) and individual contacts, networks were established in the 1970s and three decades later are thriving, with new generations constantly joining in.

The United States is popularly seen as being the thought leader in marketing, but considerable contributions have come from other countries. A major bone of contention for Europeans is that the top US journals are practically closed to non-US authors whereas European journals are open to US authors (Danell, 2001). Furthermore European academics read US journals but US academics rarely read European ones. European researchers – out of modesty, lack of confidence or ambition, or an inability to promote themselves, often reinforced by language barriers – succumb to US hegemony. They unnecessarily clone themselves on US icons instead of enriching marketing with original knowledge from their own cultures. Nordic researchers have continued their efforts to contribute to theory and ally with the Americans and the British, but also with other European countries and Australia and New Zealand.

Marketing management, as presented in textbooks and taught at universities, suffers from two major weaknesses: (1) it lacks a general, theoretical foundation and therefore offers a poor context for conceptual understanding and the development of contemporary phenomena; and (2) it is pedagogical and easy to grasp, sometimes driven by a desire to make the text attractive and therefore offering unfortunate simplifications, sometimes more aligned with media hype than profoundly addressing core variables and their links. Claims such as 'competition is global', 'everything changes faster and faster', 'Internet shopping will take over', 'technology is good and only delayed by customer inertia' are present-day mantras. Many such claims are founded on scattered observations or wishful thinking and become overexposed for a fleeting period. Some of them are no doubt true in certain cases but do not necessarily deserve a place in the sustainable development of general theory.

Yesterday–today–tomorrow: a balancing act

It is contended here that the foundation of marketing management and the theoretical fragments contained in textbooks need to be replaced. It is, however, no simple feat to determine whether history and established research and theory provide a stage for the future, or whether they cement the next generation to the bottom of the sea. Baker (1999b, p. 817) points out the risk of reinventing the wheel, as in many texts no citation is more than ten years old. This is an important observation as marketers are incessantly exposed to old phenomena dressed up in new clothes. Repeatedly reverting to the 'classics' can also turn into a mental prison. When studying the sociology of science, one learns both from the literature and from one's own experience that scientists with great promotional abilities receive much more attention than others, and that this does not necessarily bear any relation to their true scientific contribution. Once a concept, model or reference has reached a critical mass and appeared in the *Journal of Marketing* it will appear everywhere, both for serious study and for celebrity name-dropping in reference lists. Less well known authors who publish in less highly ranked journals and in languages other than English will not be noticed internationally, especially if they present novel ideas, even if these are seminal. Science has become a commodity on the market, and just as with new products it is difficult to get a foothold in markets dominated by an oligopoly of powerful players. The original mission of science – to discover the truth about reality and offer solutions – is pushed aside. The belief that if the new has substance it will compete its way to eventual recognition is wishful thinking.

Scholars can be inventors or interpreters. The inventor finds something genuinely new or conceptualises a piece of reality that has previously not been observed or communicated to larger audiences. Being an interpreter is probably the more common role for a scholar. He or she describes what is already in progress and lifts it conceptually, thus making it explicit, or repositions and reconceptualises the old and known to fit a contemporary context.

In a recent book published by the American Marketing Association (Fisk *et al.*, 2000) ten established contributors to services marketing present personal and subjective accounts of how service research has evolved over the past few decades. The advantage of such an approach is that it does not tell *the* history of services marketing but *ten* histories. The researchers have different perceptions of the past, the present and the future and are inspired by different sources and events, but there is also overlap and consensus. The histories show progress. We have learnt that goods and services are partially different; that the interactive service encounter includes the customer in partially simultaneous production, delivery and consumption processes; that customer-to-customer interaction is important; that customers evaluate service quality in the service encounters; that all offerings consist of both goods and services; that goods and services can be both substitutes and supplements; that the service content of manufacturing firms is often higher than the goods content; and more. The future includes such concerns as service quality and how to take advantage of e-services. Unfortunately it can already be seen that services marketing is partially stuck in some early and illusory models, with some being perpetuated in the literature as though no real progress had occurred.

It would have been ideal if this knowledge had become an integral part of more general and upgraded textbook theory and not been added as a special case. Just as the informed, reflective and constructive historian can be beneficial in putting events into perspective, the destructive researcher can be detrimental to theory generation. I have encountered three archetypes of the latter.

Prosecutors

The attitude of 'prosecutors' is: 'If you have a new idea then prove to me, beyond all doubt and with rational arguments and evidence (that is, what I recognise as rational and as evidence), that you are right. I am the prosecutor and the judge and you are the defendant.' It would take prosecutors decades to accept the wheel if it were invented today. No discipline can develop on courtroom premises; it is inherently impossible as theory development is a creative process based on intuition, individual reflection and observation, and often circumstantial evidence in the early stage.

Warners

Norwegian-Danish author Aksel Sandemose is best remembered for his conception of the Jante Law. Jante was a town ruled by ten paragraphs of the law, all designed to keep people down. The first one is 'Do not believe you are somebody', and the tenth 'Do not think you can teach me something'. Researchers who constantly warn against false prophets – that is, everybody outside their clique and paradigm – are exemplary citizens of Jante. This is as detrimental to progress as reinventing the wheel. We heard these warnings in the 1970s in respect of services: 'Don't think services are special!' We heard them when we became involved in quality management in the 1980s: 'Quality is not new. We have always worked with quality, but of course nothing is so good that it can not be made better.' We heard them in the 1990s: 'Marketing management stands on solid ground. Relationships are just another component that could fit in under the third P (promotion) as a sub-category of communication.' Behind this is conservatism and fear of the new, especially if it is complex and ambiguous. This was illustrated in an opinionated commentary in *The Times Higher Educational Supplement*

(2000). Underpinning the theme of the commentary was reverence for the established and frustration over the novel where realistic complexity and ambiguity is laid bare. It also included a patronising portrayal of students and practitioners as unable to embrace much more than the 4Ps. The simplistic and fragmented Ps are easy to remember and therefore should not be extended.

Fad-and-fashion researchers

The opposite of the prosecutors and warners are those who are carried away by trends promoted by the media, companies, consultants and professors. The recent hype on dotcom, home shopping and Internet banking is a case in point. Researchers in marketing jumped on the bandwagon and until 2000 it was dangerous for your reputation ('You are too old to understand') to claim that IT would not totally and instantly reshape marketing and replace the old. When relationship marketing became a buzzword, fad-and-fashion proponents stepped forward and presented simplistic messages about customer loyalty and the blessings to be had from keeping customers for life. Suddenly the acronym CRM caught on, but nobody really knew what it was and how it could be practised. When this is presented as eCRM – electronic customer relationship management – it is the coolest of the cool. This is not to say that dotcoms, e-services, relationship marketing and CRM are the emperor's new clothes; they are also objects of scholarly analysis (Carlell, 2001; Eggert and Fassott, 2001; Lennstrand, 2001; Frostling-Henningsson, 2003). The problem arises when shallow analysis, overexposure and eagerness to find a quick fix erect a cosmetic facade at the expense of insights into the nucleus of the new.

I once listened to the demands for proof and rigour, the warnings and the fad-and-fashion proponents because I thought one could learn from listening. I now realise that I listened too much, probably out of insecurity and lack of self-confidence, but also because I naively thought that famed professors, high-profile speakers and authoritative news media such as *The Times* were dedicated to innovative thinking and reflective analysis, all in the name of knowledge enhancement.

Do not fool yourself into believing that knowledge is cumulative and that new knowledge should arrange itself neatly on the foundations of traditional science and textbooks. New knowledge with a different vantage point is the essence of a paradigm shift. Services, quality and relationships are phenomena that should play leading roles in the third millennium. Old knowledge should be used whenever it qualifies for use – it should never be discarded because of age, but equally it should never be justified by age; the old economy does not die because of the new economy. As the same time, do not fool yourself into believing that everything presented as new is new, or that hyped media messages are either right or wrong. This sounds difficult – and it is. History, the present and the future are all characterised by uncertainty.

Marketing as the science of missing the obvious

Among the spectacular misses that did not surface in research in marketing until the past two or three decades are services, quality and relationships. These phenomena are eternal and basic to human life and society, just as basic as air, earth, water and fire. Why, then, did they go practically unnoticed in general marketing theory until lately and are still considered as special cases? Babies instinctively understand them. Babies are the most demanding and outspoken consumers of services, quality and relationships. They are selfish and their feedback is instant and clear. They know what service is; they cry when they are hungry or uncomfortable. They demonstrate their perception of quality by spitting out food they do not like. They know what relationships are before they can walk and talk, and a close physical relationship with the mother is considered an essential precondition for a good life. Services, quality and relationships will occupy their days until they die.

Despite their omnipresence and importance, in marketing these phenomena remained virtually unnoticed by academic researchers, educators and textbook writers. And they still have not earned a place in general marketing theory; they have merely been added to the top of the old marketing cake: a strawberry for services, a cherry for quality and a slice of kiwi fruit for relationships. They are treated as just a few among a plethora of factors in marketing. The following subsections consider each of them in turn to show that they are of paramount importance to general marketing theory.

Services

Services are provided by private firms, governments and voluntary organisations, and they are part of family and working life. Until the late 1970s they were considered to be unimportant to Western economies, all in the spirit of Adam Smith and Karl Marx. Services were second rate compared with goods. They were invisibles, intangibles and residuals. However goods and services always appear in tandem; there are always goods (things) and always services (activities), a tenet that is accepted but has never been adequately sorted out. Goods and services are partially substitutes, partially supplements. From the customer's point of view there is no such thing as a service sector and a manufacturing sector; these categories are superimposed on the economy by producers, who are product-oriented, not customer-oriented. Unfortunately official statistics perpetuate these obsolete categories and do not even mirror the reality of the old economy. Nor do statistics mirror the reality of the new economy, as some of its major drivers, such as IT and knowledge, have been given no proper categories.

In older textbook theory, goods were tangible offerings, manufactured in large factories with smoky chimneys. Goods were macho and services were sissies. If services were noted at all it was in connection with servicing machinery, or with industries such as banking and transportation, but they were not conceptually elevated to a more general level. One of the major service industries – goods distribution through wholesaling and retailing – was treated as a logistical problem of moving and storing goods, with scale economies and reduced costs being key factors. It was not treated from a customer service and revenue perspective. Textbooks claimed that services marketing was the same as goods marketing.

However services are now beginning to be understood by academics. As shown above, services have specific properties that affect marketing. Furthermore it is at last acknowledged that services dominate employment – 70–90 per cent of all employed people (the ratio depending on the definition) are working in services. One group of services that is not treated properly even in the service literature consists of essential life-support services, which to a large extent are government-operated but are increasingly being deregulated, privatised or run as government and private-sector partnerships. Striking a balance between what is best operated by the government and what is best offered by the private sector is very difficult. As a regulator, competition works well to a point but its benefits are eventually exhausted, something that is rarely discussed in textbooks. In the meantime the competition axiom continues to hold that companies with satisfied customers will survive and those with bad services and dissatisfied customers will not. Among the essential life-support services are health care, education, legal services and utilities such as water – services that are available to some but not to others, where there are often long waiting times, highly variable quality and often scarcity. This is in contrast with the common claim that there is a surplus of everything in the wealthy economies of the United States and Western Europe. It is true that there is no shortage of varieties of yoghurt and potato crisps – with very dubious nutritional value – but there is a shortage of natural foods. The entire food sector is a political sector, heavily regulated and subsidised. Competition exists as one of several dimensions, but it is not an overriding aspect of the food market. The same goes for the essential services of life.

Services are perspectives rather than categories. So it is never goods versus services; it is always services with goods. Services first, because it is value-enhancing services that we are looking for, irrespective of the medium that carries them – a thing or an activity.

Services are still treated superficially in general textbook theories. As noted above, service research has taught us a number of fundamental lessons but we still do not know how to define services generically or how to define goods. Rather we settle for listing them in traditional production-centric categories: hotels, banks, potatoes, tomatoes. We do not understand their atoms, molecules, electrons and genes. In short, we are still scratching the surface. If geologists and people in the iron industry knew as little about rock and iron as we know about goods and services, there would be no roads and no cars. In this regard the industrial society and the service society correspond to the Stone Age and the Bronze Age. And now we have e-services (perhaps indicating an Iron Age) which move so fast that we barely have time to tickle their skin before they are gone or have entrenched themselves.

Is there not a need to merge services into general textbook theory?

Quality

Quality was long considered to be so self-evident and trivial that it was hardly mentioned in marketing textbooks. When it was, it was said to be important and that companies should strive for the highest possible quality. They could not improve quality too much, however, because it would be so outrageously costly and demanding of resources that customers would not be willing to pay for it. Quality was defined by the 'knowledgeable' expert in the design and engineering department, not by the 'ignorant' user and customer. Quality was an issue for operations management, not for marketing and sales. Quality was handled on the shop floor, not by top management.

Gradually the quality of goods and services in Western industrialised countries contracted a cough, which then turned into chronic bronchitis and lethal pneumonia. The complacency of the UK and US car industry, for example, was breathtaking. According to US car manufacturers, customers did not want safety or fuel-saving engines, they wanted big cars and fashion, and they obviously loved to bring their cars in for repair and maintenance. Accidents were explained as 'driver error', not as the consequence of faulty engineering, design and manufacturing. The Japanese seized the initiative and not only conquered the car industry but also invaded every corner of the manufacturing sector. Meanwhile established corporations in Europe and the United States continued to chant 'We are the best!'

One aspect of quality – customer satisfaction – has established itself at the very top of the marketing agenda, but it long went unnoted by the quality discipline, with its operations management focus. So marketing has contributed to the modern quality concept, although other aspects of quality, including service quality, have been ignored by marketers, and the quality management discipline alike. However all consumers know that service quality is bad. As consumers we spend every day of our lives in a service setting, a genuine field laboratory. We have all had our share of late trains and aircraft, overcharging taxi drivers, hotels that can find no record of our reservation when we arrive, sloppy plumbers, unreliable car mechanics and unpleasant waiters in restaurants. Everybody knows that government agencies often do not treat people well, making them queue interminably, being unhelpful to them on the phone, sending them unintelligible letters and behaving condescendingly. Everybody knows that hospital services, day and residential care for the elderly, police services, the services of the legal system and education constitute major problems and are often in short supply. The concepts of customer satisfaction, customer-perceived quality and value, and links to the bottom line and long-term survival are at last being discussed (Oliver, 1997; Johnson and Gustafsson, 2000), and the axiom that satisfied customers will repurchase and become profitable to retain is being questioned. What do companies really know about customer satisfaction – and how much do they care?

Through prestigious quality awards we have become aware that quality should be inherent in every function of a company, including marketing. ISO 9000 has taught companies in B2B that they must satisfy a minimum quality requirement in their processes and operations and become certified; without the ISO stamp they will not be added to the list of potential suppliers. The new 2000 version of ISO will be even more demanding.

One of the tenets of total quality management is continuous improvement. This is in line with the scholarly spirit in which continuous theory development transforms into theory testing and justification in an endless spiral.

Relationships

Until 1990, relationships and their close companions – networks and interaction – were hardly mentioned in general marketing textbooks or training courses. They still have not made a substantial impact on general textbook theory, although texts are gradually including more cases and examples of relationship marketing and CRM, and relationship marketing is sometimes awarded its own chapter at the end of textbooks.

Despite the slowness of marketing theory to include relationships, you do not have to work long in business before experience tells you that your network of relationships and your ability to interact are instrumental in success. Social skills must be applied to commercial purposes in organisations and markets. If you are in marketing and sales, relationships with customers are in focus. When studying relationship marketing it also becomes apparent that you need other market relationships: relationships with your suppliers, intermediaries and competitors. You need mega-relationships with the media, local governments, the EU and others. You need nano-relationships inside your organisation; as a marketing manager you need good working relationships with colleagues in manufacturing, accounting, personnel and other specialist functions. This multilevel approach to relationship marketing adds theoretical context to relationships, networks and interaction (Gummesson, 2002).

It is embarrassing that it took so long to understand the very trivial fact that society is a network of relationships. If society is a network of relationships and if business and marketing are subsets or properties of society, then these must also be networks of relationships. This is clearly stressed in Castells' (1996) treatise on the new economy, where human and electronic networks form the core. If society is a network of relationships but marketing only recognises this in a footnote to or subgroup of some other classification, something is fundamentally wrong and a paradigm shift is called for. But this should not be an isolated paradigm shift. It should be part of changes everywhere, in organisations, technology, the environment and other areas. It should be supported by modern natural science and a shift from a mechanistic and linear paradigm to a paradigm characterised by complexity, chaos and non-linear, systemic interdependencies: 'the basic pattern of life is a network pattern' (Capra, 1997, p. 290).

Comment

For almost three decades researchers have been actively involved in the fields of services, quality and relationship marketing. These are all ancient phenomena. Traditional marketing management with the 4Ps or more is of course important, as are a lot of other elements, but research in the past decades indicates that they are one or two levels down the hierarchy of variables. Relationships, networks and interaction are more justified as subcore variables under the general core variable of relationship marketing. The special cases of services, quality and relationships are not so special. It is the allegedly general that may actually be the special case.

Intersubjective axioms

All science – social and natural alike – is built on axiomatic assumptions that are intersubjectively approved among peers. The assumptions are subjective and qualitative. Good assumptions are transparent and reasoned and can be relaxed; they are not protected like a holy shrine. Bad assumptions are the opposite; they are malignant like a cancer. Their purpose may be mainly to facilitate the design of beautiful equations and the quantitative processing of data, or for political, value-laden advocacy, not to offer valid explanations and understandings of reality. Ritual has taken over at the expense of result. Ritual also offers a comforter for the insecure because a ritual can be distinctly laid out and regulated, while entrepreneurial, innovative research is for risk-takers, often without a lifeline. Mainstream researchers are bureaucrats, but true scholars should be entrepreneurs. In the next subsections four types of axiom are considered: axioms in economics, in survey research methodology, in categorisation and official statistics, and the core axiom of marketing management, the 'marketing concept'.

Axioms in economics

The main reason why microeconomics has made no contribution to marketing during the past decades – marketing partly arose from microeconomics – is that economics has continued to defend carcinogenic assumptions. Unfortunately economists are awarded Nobel Prizes because the Nobel Committee members do not represent the economic sciences – as it should do, according to its statute – but almost exclusively economics, including finance. Econometricians are at the top of the pecking order, they are *so* scientific. Now there are also micro-econometricians, and two of them shared the Nobel Prize in 2000.

Economic theory is an axiomatic system: the conclusions are contained in the assumptions, the axioms, as you can only get responses to the hypotheses you define, the questions you ask and the categories you investigate. In a textbook used in Stockholm University undergraduate economics courses (Schotter, 2001) the following are all assumed: perfect competition, perfect information, a large number of customers where the individual customer has no influence over the market, a large number of suppliers, equilibrium of supply and demand, easily divisible products, homogeneous products and homogeneous customers. The items in the index do not include services, quality, relationships, networks, interaction, branding, intellectual capital, the Internet, B2B, B2C (barriers-to-consumer marketing), C2C (customer-to-customer marketing) or M2M (machine-to-machine marketing), the last of which is a new and growing practice, especially in B2B marketing (Gatarski and Lundkvist, 1998). The producer and the consumer are still considered as separate entities, whereas in marketing their roles are intertwined, particularly in services and B2B. These realities of marketing are too mushy and woolly to be considered; they mess up the rigour and beauty of received categories, equations and graphs.

Other 'typical' markets are also described, such as monopoly and oligopoly, but they are very crude categories. They are deviations from the ideal model; in fact the ideal model is nothing but a very special deviation. Tagging the most frequent cases as 'deviations' is neither scientific nor the epitome of common sense. Rather it reminds one of George Orwell's book *1984*, in which words have been manipulated to mean the opposite: freedom meants slavery, democracy means dictatorship.

Axioms in survey research

The use of survey data is loaded with consensus between the reigning trendsetters in market research. Yet surveys abound with problems. One is the increasing non-response rate, which for B2B surveys can amount to 80–90 per cent. Nonetheless the handful of replies are used for advanced statistical processing. Efforts have been made to investigate non-responses and some methods have been established, but they are often difficult to apply with any certainty. Instead report writers make flat statements such as 'There is no reason to believe that the response rate has affected the results'. I have even been told that 'It is difficult to get business managers to reply so we have to accept a low response rate.' While it is indeed difficult, accepting a low response rate is nonsense if the study is to be used as quantitative evidence and not only for idea generation. If the sample is divided into cells there might be very few observations in each. Why then engage in random sampling?

Another vexing weakness of surveys is the shallowness of the questions and answers. It is an onerous task to find valid categories and concepts that fit a simple scale, and to interpret the aggregated outcome. It might be possible to draw sweeping conclusions about majorities and averages, but it is not possible to predict the behaviour of an individual consumer, although relationship marketing and CRM instruct us to think in terms of one-to-one and not masses.

The choice of method is wrong from the very beginning if respondents do not respond, so some other method should be chosen. When surveys are justified and properly managed they have their place in marketing, but they are no cure-all with automatic legitimacy.

The axiom of size

One example of slow or no development in textbooks is the preoccupation with huge companies where profit, growth and stock price rule supreme. The self-employed and small family businesses are given little attention, although entrepreneurship has gradually entered the agenda.

Official statistics on size are shaky to say the least, probably because it is not feasible to define business operations within the paradigm of the statistical tradition; the statistical community is on a ghost hunt. What these statistics are used for, apart from academic exercises, and what conclusions can be drawn from them is an enigma. Let me offer one observation about the importance of small business that is not considered in textbook theory. According to official statistics, Britain has 3.5 million companies, most of which are small family businesses that will remain small. Lowe's (1988) study of the survival of hotels in Scotland supports a known fact that profit maximisation, growth and becoming a public company are rarely on small companies' agendas; the driving forces are survival and preferred lifestyle. Definitions of 'company' are fuzzy and arbitrary and vary between countries; the phenomena they try to capture entail so much diversity. Despite the insignificant attention these businesses are given in marketing textbooks, they provide at least 50 per cent, and perhaps even 60–70 per cent, of all employment. Sweden has 800 000 companies, of which 600 000 are one-person operations and most of the others employ just one or two people (Hult *et al.*, 2000). Ericsson is one of Sweden's major global companies with about 100 000 employees in 2000, a third of them in Sweden. However the small operations alone employ 600 000 people – six times the number employed by Ericsson on a global scale and 18 times the number of its employees in Sweden.

The point is that small companies are underrepresented in textbook theory. Furthermore the whole concept of small, medium-size and large is obsolete. In the new economy, where companies are recognised as networks of internal and external relationships, the number of employees

tells a misleading story that is only relevant for the hierarchical manufacturing company of the old economy. In today's markets companies
do not compete with companies, rather networks compete with networks.
In certain cases IT allows a single person to operate a global business.
The impact of IT can be seen everywhere but official statistics.

Is the marketing concept an adequate axiom?

Most people base their work in marketing on the marketing concept,
declaring that satisfying customers' needs is the best way to make
money. This is a benign axiom worthy of pursuit. It has stood out as
practical and ethical, defining a route from production orientation to
marketing orientation. It emerged from traditional marketing management but is more in harmony with relationship marketing and CRM.
It translates as customer focus, customer satisfaction, customer-perceived
quality and customer retention. But is it really lived, or is it merely
rhetoric? My conclusion is that it is both, but that it is not general and
valid enough to form a solid ground for marketing theory. Other driving
forces are often more important. Consider the following cases.

First, retail banking is driven by bankers' traditions, legal subtleties
and technicalities, one-sided contracts, pseudo competition, merger
mania, IT and short-term shareholder value. Perhaps most important is
the lack of transparency for the consumer and the small business. The
banking system can always doctor a win–lose situation by manipulating
interest rates, fees, commissions and stock market prices, and 'borrow'
consumers' money for free by delaying transactions. Who needs satisfied
customers?

Second, hospitals are driven not by influential medical consumers but
by the medical establishment, comprising doctors and the pharmaceutical and hospital equipment industries. Because of the way in which the
free market operates, pharmaceutical companies rarely make a cent out
of curing people; instead they make money from long-term relationships
in which customers become prisoners. The ideal medication is one that
relieves pain or other symptoms but is needed continuously over a long
period, preferably a lifetime. Medical research is dependent on industry
and the government for research grants and chairs. Western medicine is
based on a narrow paradigm that includes only a few research techniques, with reference to evidenced-based medicine and scientific rigour. It rejects knowledge obtained through the broader scientific
paradigm of 'alternative medicine', a collective name for a large number
of diverse therapies. If a patient does not fit into the parochial view
of reality embraced by established medicine – that is, when hospitals

fail – there is a beautiful excuse to save face: the patient is classified as a victim of the placebo effect (the silly patient is imagining things) or a case for the psychiatrist.

Third, the biotech industry is driven by professional interests and financial gains. The products of genetic manipulation have been given the euphemistic label 'genetically modified', and the unobtrusive acronym GMO (genetically modified organism) is used to make manipulated food sound harmless, even beneficial, to the consumer. The methods of marketing GMOs are not the marketing mix and the 4Ps; rather it is marketing on a mega level. It is elaborate lobbying to infiltrate political and administrative decision-making processes; rewarding scientists who support the industry by giving credibility to the quality of products that research results do not justify; gradually smuggling GMOs into the food store so that there can be no return; confusing the issue, knowing that if people fall ill and a GMO is suspected there will be long drawn out legal proceedings and difficulty with laboratory methods to establish the cause and effect link between the GMO and an individual's disorder.

Similar strategies have been used before, to the benefit of many companies and the detriment of individual consumers or entire populations, for example the fluoridation of water to protect teeth, unsafe nuclear plants and the health hazards of cigarette smoking. At a conference held by the American Association for the Advancement of Science in February 2001 it was established that 'scientific experts' demand that consumers trust them and not question what they are doing. The biotech industry has launched the concept of 'substantial equivalence', which sounds very scientific to the layperson but only means that a genetically manipulated food product, such as the American Flavr Savr tomato, is essentially, but not quite, the same a natural tomato. This is a traditional, production-oriented, arrogant and consumer-unfriendly attitude.

Finally, the IT industry is driven by technology and enthused hackers, and its axiom is that all new technology is a blessing to mankind. Since the 1960s the path of IT development has been paved with unfulfilled promises, with costs being loaded onto customers and society. Despite the slogan 'customer friendly', users have often found computers unfriendly, and still do. Microsoft Word's 870-page manual can now be found in the software itself, but it is still difficult for ordinary users to find what they are looking for. Most companies have problems with their Websites, especially if a site is designed as a marketplace for ordering; customers quickly grow tired of not being able to find pertinent information. An important marketing strategy is to make hardware and software obsolete, for example by expanding the need for memory capacity and thus making it impossible to use three-year-old hardware for new software. Furthermore it can be difficult for a user to obtain help when features do not work and bugs and viruses play games.

The above cases cover two of the largest service sectors – the financial and medical sectors – and two of the largest growth industries, biotechnology and IT. The customer-unfriendly side of their activities has been highlighted in the descriptions but they also add value to the customer: they lend money, treat medical disorders and facilitate data processing and communication. However none is primarily driven by customer needs, although many of the people who work in these sectors are no doubt committed to their customers and are convinced that what they do is beneficial to welfare. The strongest driving forces are probably technology, professional interests, competitive instincts, a thirst for domination and power, financial rewards and frequently excessive greed. Interacting in a network of relationships with politicians, legislators, scientists, investors and the media – that is, on a mega level above the market – is the first priority for marketing; the 4Ps and other tools of marketing management are used for lower-level strategies.

A crucial question is whether the marketing concept is at all realistic, given the way human beings are. The conclusion is that the marketing concept does not serve well as a general foundation for marketing. It needs to be replaced or accompanied by another concept that recognises that there are and will be other driving forces than customer needs and customer satisfaction. In a similar vein, Doyle (2000) is concerned that marketing has not had the impact on board members that it deserves. One reason for this could be that a customer focus is not believed to enhance shareholder value: 'Marketers can no longer afford to rely on the untested assumption that increases in customer satisfaction ... will automatically translate into higher financial performance' (ibid., p. 310).

Marketing management: science or art, theory or theatre, commodity or progress?

The logo of the Royal Institute of Technology in Stockholm, Sweden, carries the inscription 'Science and Art'. How can that be? We are taught that the natural sciences and technological research are firmly grounded in facts that are systematically collected, processed and tested by means of rigorous and objective methods. This is the image that universities and their professors peddle on the market, usually with success. The mantras 'science', 'scientifically proven' and 'there is no scientific evidence to support the fears of consumers' deceive not only the audience but also the professors themselves.

When scientific research in marketing has as its foundation subjectivity and intersubjectivity, expressed as qualitative assumptions that are appointed axioms, there is obviously something else than statistical rigour that matters. The great Russian film director Andrey Tarkovsky offers a connection. He asks 'Who needs art?' and gives a number of answers. He quotes Alexander Block, who said that 'the poet creates harmony out of chaos', and Pushkin, who believed that poets have the gift of prophecy (Tarkovsky, 1986, p. 36). Tarkovsky concludes: 'And so, art like science, is a means of assimilating the world, an instrument for knowing it in the course of man's journey towards what is called "absolute truth"' (ibid., p. 37).

As marketers we fantasise about order in chaotic and rapidly changing markets and the ability to predict and find absolute truths, the super-strategy that will make the fairy tale come true. According to Tarkovsky:

> it is perfectly clear that the goal for all art – unless of course it is aimed at the 'consumer', like a saleable commodity – is to explain to the artist himself and to those around him what man lives for, what is the meaning of existence. To explain to people the reason for their appearance on this planet; or not to explain, at least to pose the question. (Ibid., p. 36)

Marketing also needs to understand the reason for its being, and to explain it to the world. Deductively posing questions from existing theory is one starting point for understanding reality. Another is inductively to prompt reality to come up with answers to questions that have yet to be asked, and thus to reinvent marketing theory. It is somewhat like the popular TV quiz Jeopardy, in which a statement is made and the contestant has to find a question to match it. The exception to art is the saleable consumer commodity, to which we shall return later.

The words 'theory' and 'theatre' have the same Greek roots. Good theory puts a phenomenon into context and makes it comprehensible. Good theatre conveys a message through a variety of media: speech, music, costume, gesture, action, decor and light, performed on stage or screen.

True science – scholarship – is art; research is handicraft. Scholars are architects; researchers are carpenters. Science and art both include theory generation, innovation, paradigmatic breakthroughs and entrepreneurship.

Good art needs handicraft; a good actor interprets his or her role with empathy and personality, but must engage in systematic training and rehearsals to become skilled in communicating a message. A good scholar crafts his or her presentations and publications so that they are comprehensible, even exciting.

Universities should deliver both science and art, but are mainly delivering and remunerating handicraft. Marketing professors – with few exceptions – seem scared of the art part, the scholarship. It is safer to stick to peer-approved methodologies and techniques – the hammer and the saw – and the axioms of the current mainstream.

Tarkovsky (1986) asks 'Who needs art?' We could ask: 'Who needs business schools?' Professors and administrators, or students, the business community and society? If you practice business you soon learn that you have to sell at a higher price than you bought, that it is easier if you are the sole provider, and that if you are likeable customers will like you more and be more likely to come back. You also learn that customers are not often aware of their own best interests, for example they may pay more attention to the colour and taste of food than to its nutritional value. Therefore you can swindle them without their noticing, for example by using cost-saving additives, artificial colours and flavours, and incomprehensible – but scientific-looking – lists of ingredients on the package. According to Blumberg's (1989) extensive study this type of fraud is practised everyday in industry.

What, then, can business schools offer that is of unique value? What distinguishes universities and higher education colleges from other types of learning institution is that faculty members engage in scholarly research and are able to convey scientific knowledge to students. However basic research and theory are not priorities in business schools, where popularity and quality ratings provide an incentive to adhere to the traditional and add a gloss by including media-hyped issues in commodity-like textbooks, courses and research proposals.

The craft of writing and editing textbooks is well developed and the pedagogical standard is high. Therefore the important issue is not form but content. Should research and education in marketing be commodities or continuous progress? The textbook has become a supermarket product, branded by its title and the name of the author. It has all the properties of a mass marketed product; it offers a can of consumer behaviour, a six-pack of conjoint analysis, a bottle of CRM. The financial outcome depends on the number of copies sold and the longevity of the book, including intermittently revised editions. For the textbook writer and course producer this may be absolutely right.

A reason for the failure to keep up with developments and integrate new knowledge into current textbook theory has been suggested to me by a successful textbook writer: 'Marketing professors are very conservative.' They do not want their ground shaken by an earthquake registering seven on the Richter scale; they only want a slight tremor. They want to recognise the taste of the textbook Big Mac or Coca-Cola. Let us return to the film director Tarkovsky and his remark about art being a saleable commodity. He continues:

> All manufacture . . . has to be viable in order to function and develop, it has not merely to pay for itself but to yield a certain profit. As a commodity, therefore, a film succeeds or fails and its aesthetic value is established, paradoxically enough, according to supply and demand – to straightforward market laws. . . . As long as cinema remains in its present position, it will never be easy for a true cinematic work to see the light of day, let alone become accessible to a wider public. . . .
>
> Of course the yardsticks by which art is distinguished from non-art, from sham, are so relative, indistinct and impossible to demonstrate, that nothing could be easier than to substitute for aesthetic criteria purely utilitarian measures of assessment, which may be dictated either by the desire for the greatest possible financial profit or from some ideological motive. . . . Either is equally far from the proper use of art. (Tarkovsky, 1986, p. 164)

I would like to add the same for business school research in marketing. The real basic and independent research is also essential.

Interactive research: a note on the process of knowing

Although this chapter focuses on the known – the results of research in the form of more adequate theory – the process of knowing is intimately linked to the known. My interest in theory has gradually brought me closer to qualitative methods and the philosophy of science, as expressed in hermeneutics, phenomenology and the humanities, and away from the quantification and positivism of traditional natural sciences. This transition is the consequence of limitations experienced in quantitative research and the complacent attitude of marketing academics that statistical studies are *the* key to the truth, *the* superior approach, *the* cure-all. During my time as a producer of surveys, a buyer of market research and a user of marketing data I have seen research deliver only in special cases. By giving preference to highly deductive, survey-based approaches, researchers are exhibiting chronic myopia. Opportunities to get closer to the 'real reality' and thus secure validity are pushed aside by a fascination with the intricacies of research techniques, mistaking the outcome for a valid image.

In saying this I am not condemning quantitative research as such, just claiming that it is overused and overrated as a tool in decision making in business. An ingenious concept, category or theory provides much more guidance than survey distributions, standard deviations, staples and random samples. Together with experience, tacit knowledge and intuition, theory gives a structure and a framework, a context. (My stance is further explicated in Gummesson, 2000.)

One area of deep concern is analysis and interpretation. Here science and art have another rendezvous. When complex and ambiguous phenomena such as marketing are studied, completely explicit and systematic analysis is usually not feasible. Intuition is also required as it is often impossible to know exactly how to process data and how one should arrive at conclusions. Intuition as a concept goes back to the fifth century and has been a topic for philosophers ever since (Larsson, 1892). Intuition is often called non-scientific and irrational, but philosophers define intuition as 'complete knowledge of reality', 'the ability to quickly draw conclusions' and 'the instantaneous perception of logical connections and truths' (Matti, 1999, pp. 5–7). Genuine intuition is not a whim of the moment but an elaborate synthesis of huge amounts of data, processed in a nanosecond. It is not testable in the sense that the commonly used criteria of reliability and replicability demand. However this can be offset in many ways. The most important way, whenever feasible, is to apply research results to business practice and see how they work. Another way is to treat science as a journey and to make continuous improvements, just as total quality management recommends. Continuous theory generation means a continuous challenge to received theory and continuous justification of new theory. During this iterative process, credibility can be reinforced by offering rich descriptions and discussions as well as alternative interpretations.

Over time my methodological favourites have gradually become case study research (recognising wholeness, complexity, chaos, ambiguity and the need for in-depth understanding), grounded theory (generating theory by letting reality emerge and become gently conceptualised without forcing), anthropology and ethnography (emphasising the importance of being where the action is), action research (where the researcher is involved in both making things happen and detached reflection) and narrative research (which makes reality come alive and move nearer to art).

A package of these methodological strands led to my current preferred methodology: interactive research (Gummesson, 2001). The choice of label originates from the conviction that interaction and communication play a crucial part in all stages of research. On an abstract and general level, life has already been described as networks of relationships within which interaction takes place. Instead of searching for straightforward and partial causality, the scholar searches for a systemic whole that consists of individual and complex patterns of interactive relationships. 'Interactive' is the core property of this type of research.

The elements of interactive research are various interactions, such as between the researcher and the object of study and its actors; between the researcher's consciousness and qualities of his or her inner self; between substantive data and general concepts; between the parts and the whole; between words, numbers, non-verbal/body language and tacit language; and between data collection, analysis, interpretation and conclusions treated as concurrent, non-linear and dynamic elements of scholarly inquiry.

My addition to interactive research includes interaction with audiences and computers. By presenting concepts, ideas and tentative results, we test our ability to interact with different target groups: students, professors, practitioners. Encounters with audiences do not mark the end of a research programme and an attempt to sell our findings. They are an integral part of the whole research process. They force us to express ourselves and transfer knowledge to others. They offer dialogue and learning opportunities.

Presenting research is demanding. To make slides understandable we are forced to structure, condense, conceptualise and generalise substantive data. PowerPoint gives us the option of playing with words, diagrams, drawings, scanned pictures, colours, photos, animation and sound to make our message attractive. These aids do not rule out close human contact and informal dialogue. Lectures and seminars can be interactive stage performances. Theory and theatre merge, and presenting research becomes one of the performing arts. The computer also offers interaction between researchers and their text as it allows them to write, draw, edit and print in a technically almost effortless, non-stop process. The text comes alive and speaks back as it neatly appears on the computer screen, much like the film screen tells us a story. The Internet and e-mail extend the opportunities for interaction beyond the physical.

In interactive research, theory generation and theory testing are not consecutive stages. It is not a matter of boning up on the literature, then doing exploratory, conceptual and qualitative pilot studies, and eventually 'doing the real thing and going empirical' by testing hypotheses with numbers. Through iterative theory generation we build a never-ending helix in the search for knowledge. We go from preunderstanding to understanding and then to a new level of preunderstanding and so on, and from descriptions of specific substantive data to concepts that serve as vehicles to reach more general theoretical levels. In certain phases, statistical deductive testing can be used, but the strategy is continuous theory development, where improved or completely changed theories constitute the test results.

Guidelines for future theory generation

This chapter has claimed that general and valid marketing management theory is in short supply; there is a gap between theory and practice. Most of the concepts in current marketing textbooks, among them the 4P marketing mix, date back to the 1960s, although new ones have been added over time. It has become a 'theoretical mess' and there has been little effort to formalise marketing theory on progressively higher levels. Textbooks, which form the worldview and mindset of marketing students, have become lists or encyclopaedias of a fragmented mainstream: concepts, models, partial theories, cases and experiences edited to be palatable to educators and students – those who choose books for courses and those who buy the books. Today's textbooks are branded products, sitting on shelves among fizzy drinks and mayonnaise. To improve the situation the following guidelines are suggested.

First, we need basic research to arrive at (1) more valid theory and (2) more general theory. Academe could contribute here; in fact that is its unique domain. It should not only apply research – consultants and companies can do that just as well – but also provide the long-term basic research that consultants and companies rarely attempt. This would include reflective choice of marketing axioms.

Second, new developments in marketing are not being integrated into general theory; they are merely expanding the smorgasbord. Services, quality and relationships, which are generic traits of life and society, are among these developments and have been at the centre of attention in this chapter. A good theory offers a context in which data can be placed and interpreted. The numerous models and partial theories of marketing – which may be excellent *per se* – do not provide an overriding context that helps us acquire a systematic view of marketing. An ideal would be for textbooks to present a synthesis of marketing knowledge rather than an edited menu of available dishes.

Third – and here is a dilemma and paradox, but not an oxymoron – (1) we need theory for guidance but not for obedience; we should go back to the classics to obtain a perspective, but in terms of application most of the classics are in need of upgrading or replacement; and (2) we must propose more valid and general theory, discarding extant theory when this is deemed necessary, irrespective of its standing in the academic community. We need to save the cake, eat the cake and bake a new cake all at the same time. We should not put the new on top of the old, but blend the two together.

Fourth, we need to strike a better balance between the deductive and the inductive, and be more inductive and open to reality and practice, and less deductive and committed to approved theory and research techniques. We need to use all our capabilities, including tacit knowledge, reflection, intuition, experience and common sense.

Fifth, received theory can cause us to exclude information that does not fit its axioms, concepts, categories and research methods. We need to take seriously the strategies offered by methodologists for avoiding this trap. Kuhn (1962) points out that knowledge is only cumulative to a point, and then a paradigm shift is required to provide a fresh scientific foundation. Glaser and Strauss's strategies to generate grounded theory (Glaser, 2001) tell us not to get stuck in the mud of received theory, but to let theory be grounded in reality and be generated and tested through continued and sensitive comparison. Similarly Feyerabend (1975) urges us not to be trapped by methodological rituals.

Sixth, if scholarly research is viewed as a continuous journey guided by an open, sensitive and reflective mind, theory will be generated and it will test itself during the course of the journey. Our conceptualisations should move continuously towards more and more inclusive, dense and general categories. A key strategy is to gain intimate access to the real phenomenon and not a proxy. If close access, validity and continuous search are applied as key strategies, reliability and replicability will not be an issue. Unfortunately that is not how the scientific community necessarily sees it. Instead of being offered supporting guidelines we are exposed to inhibitory and bureaucratic rules and regulations.

Seventh, waiting for *the* general and high-validity theory may be like waiting for Godot, whose presence is felt throughout Samuel Beckett's play but he never manifests himself physically. There are likely to be several theories that could strive towards generality and validity.

Relationship marketing, with its core variables relationships, networks and interaction, offers one way of arriving at a more inclusive general theory.

Eighth, while it is essential to follow the progress of knowledge and technology it is important to be inspired rather than hyped up by the media and the icons of the IT industry, such as Bill Gates of Microsoft and Jeff Bezos of Amazon.com.

Finally, we need to pose a crucial question for the future: which phenomena that are fundamental to marketing are we neglecting at the moment, and what can we do to avoid such neglect in the future?

References

Alderson, W. (1957) *Marketing Behaviour and Executive Action* (Homewood, Ill.: Irwin).

Baker, M. J. (1999a) 'Marketing – philosophy or function', in M. J. Baker (ed.), *Encyclopedia of Marketing* (London: Thomson), pp. 3–17.

Baker, M. J. (1999b) 'The Future of Marketing', in M. J. Baker (ed.), *Encyclopedia of Marketing* (London: Thomson), pp. 816–31.

Blumberg, P. (1989) *The Predatory Society* (New York: Oxford University Press).

Brown, S. (1998) *Postmodern Marketing Two* (London: Thomson).

Brown, S. (2000) 'The Three R's of Relationship Marketing: Retroactive, Retrospective, Retrogressive', in T. Henning-Thurau and U. Hansen (eds), *Relationship Marketing* (Berlin: Springer), pp. 393–413.

Capra, F. (1997) *The Web of Life* (London: Flamingo and HarperCollins).

Carlell, C. (2001) *Technology in Everyday Life* (Stockholm: School of Business Dissertation Series, Stockholm University).

Castells, M. (1996) *The Rise of the Network Society* (Oxford: Blackwell).

Danell, R. (2001) *Internationalization and Homogenization: A Bibliometric Study of International Management Research* (Sweden: Department of Sociology, Umeå University).

Doyle, P. (2000) 'Value-based Marketing', *Journal of Strategic Marketing*, vol. 8, no. 4, pp. 299–311.

Edvardsson, B. and Gustafsson, A. (1999) *The Nordic School of Quality Management* (Sweden: Studentlitteratur, Lund).

Eggert, A. and Fassott, G. (eds.) (2001) *eCRM: Electronic Customer Relationship Management* (Stuttgart: Schäffer-Poeschel).

Feyerabend, P. (1975) *Against Method* (London: Verso).

Fisk, R. P., Grove, S. J. and John, J. (eds) (2000) *Services Marketing Self-Portraits: Introspections, Reflections and Glimpses from the Experts* (Chicago, Ill.: AMA).

Frostling-Henningsson, M. (2003) 'Internet Grocery Shopping: A Necessity, a Pleasurable Adventure, or an Act of Love?' (Stockholm: School of Business Dissertation Series, Stockholm University).

Gatarski, R. and Lundkvist A. (1998) 'Interactive Media Face Artificial Consumers and Must Re-Think', *Journal of Marketing Communications* no. 4, pp. 45–59.

Glaser, B. G. (2001) *The Grounded Theory Perspective* (Mill Valley, CA: Sociology Press).

Grönroos, C. (1997) 'From Marketing Mix to Relationship Marketing: Towards a Paradigm Shift in Marketing', *Management Decision*, vol. 35, no. 4, pp. 322–39.

Grönroos, C. (2000) *Service Management and Marketing* (Chichester: Wiley).

Gummesson, E. (1994) 'Marketing According to Textbooks: Six Objections', in D. Brownlie, M. Saren, R. Wensley and R. Whittington (eds), *Rethinking Marketing: New Perspectives on the Discipline and Profession* (Coventry: Warwick Business School), pp. 248–58.

Gummesson, E. (2000) *Qualitative Methods in Management Research* (Thousand Oaks, CA: Sage).

Gummesson, E. (2001) 'Are Current Research Approaches in Marketing Leading Us Astray?', *Marketing Theory*, vol. 1, no. 1, p. 27–48.

Gummesson, E. (2002) *Total Relationship Marketing* (Oxford: Butterworth-Heinemann).

Gummesson, E., Lehtinen, U. and Grönroos, C. (1997) 'Comment on Nordic Perspectives on Relationship Marketing', *European Journal of Marketing*, vol. 31, nos. 1–2, pp. 10–16.

Håkansson, H. and Snehota, I. (eds) (1995) *Developing Relationships in Business Marketing* (London: Routledge).

Hult, E.-B., Liljeberg, U., Lundström, A. and Ramström, D. (2000) *Soloföretag* (Örebro, Sweden: Forum för småföretagsforskning).

Johnson, M. D. and Gustafsson, A. (2000) *Improving Customer Satisfaction, Loyalty and Profit* (San Francisco, CA: Jossey-Bass).

Kuhn, T. S. (1962) *The Structure of Scientific Revolutions* (Chicago, Ill.: University of Chicago Press).

Larsson, H. (1892) *Intuition: Några ord om diktning och vetenskap* (Stockholm).

Lennstrand, Bo (2001) *Hype IT* (Stockholm: School of Business Dissertation Series, Stockholm University).

Lowe, A. (1988) 'Small Hotel Survival: An Inductive Approach', *The International Journal of Hospitality Management*, vol. 7, no. 3, pp. 197–223.

Matti, G. (1999) *Det intuitiva livet* (Uppsala: Uppsala University).

Oliver, R. L. (1997) *Satisfaction* (Boston, Mass.: Irwin and McGraw-Hill).

Schotter, A. (2001) *Microeconomics: A Modern Approach* (Boston, Mass.: Addison-Wesley).

Tarkovsky, A. (1986) *Sculpting in Time: Reflections of the Cinema* (London: Bodley Head).

Times Higher Educational Supplement (2000) '30Rs that go a step too far', 25 February.

Zaltman, G., LeMasters, K. and Heffring, M. (1982) *Theory Construction in Marketing* (New York: Wiley).

2
Qualitative Software Meets Qualitative Marketing: Are These Tools the Right Tools?

Lyn Richards

Introduction

What do researchers want of qualitative software in marketing and management? What do qualitative software programs offer? And do these tools offer what is needed? All qualitative researchers confront a dilemma between the demand for thorough, convincing research outcomes on the one hand, and for speed on the other. The researcher's dilemma is clearest in 'real world' settings such as marketing and management. This chapter explores the degree of fit between the varied goals of marketing research and the tools of qualitative computing. To date software tools designed for academic research have been little used in more real-world contexts. But both the methods and the tools are changing. Nowadays specialist software offers substantial support for the data required, the methods used and the analyses sought by researchers in marketing. In so doing it both enhances research quality and speeds up slow processes. But the ability to do more can also cause delay. It is concluded that researchers must select tools and use software toolkits appropriately, and software development must attend to the needs of researchers who require rapid and convincing results.

This chapter is a result of what many would regard as an unlikely collaboration between a department of marketing (at the Vienna University of Economics and Business Administration) and a qualitative software developer (QSR International). More specifically, it is a result of the strong demand by marketers for both research quality and rapid outcomes, which confronts all qualitative research with dilemmas. The contribution of software to those dilemmas and their resolution will be evaluated in this chapter.

The methodological challenge

The widespread acceptance of, even requirement for, qualitative research in marketing and management is relatively recent. An international market research association that now runs conferences on qualitative research called a recent one 'Qualitative Ascending'. Nonetheless a leading author who conducted a search of the literature could find 'only one book on research in management subjects in which quantitative and qualitative methods are treated as equals' (Gummesson, 2000, p. 5). Whilst specialists who 'do qualitative' have found their way into many companies in recent years, for most observers market research remains synonymous with survey research. Yet researchers in marketing and management, perhaps more than other social researchers, study process. As Gummesson (ibid., p. 35) remarks, survey methods 'can be used only to complement the analysis of processes within a company'. Survey techniques lead to processes being examined in a 'fragmented and mechanistic manner' (ibid., p. 35). To understand changing behaviour, preferences and performances, the researcher requires different data, and the data require different methods of analysis.

So what is the problem? Business and market research demand convincing and rapid analysis. Qualitative data are inherently messy, so their analysis is inevitably time consuming and their outcomes are often inconclusive or impressionistic. The technical challenges of managing such data, and especially of managing it in a limited time, are immediately apparent. Manual methods involve typescripts and note-cards, often messily distributed over several tables and floors; plus heavy use of a photocopier in order to place copies of pregnant passages in as many category piles as necessary. Clerical overload, inadequate documentation and unsystematic access to data mean impressionistic outcomes. Typically, those who attempt to control such material are understandably driven to find a simple explanation and leave it untested because of the difficulties of assembling the data. This means that in the time- and cost-limited world of commercial research, qualitative projects are regarded with suspicion.

Marketing is of course not alone in confronting the need for such research and the unacceptability of its demands and outcomes. The same dilemmas face many areas of research into education or health behaviour (Richards, 2002b). In such fields, whilst the need for qualitative data is recognised there is concern that traditional formats and standards of empirical research cannot be met by qualitative work, and even if they could be the time required is too great. The study must be rigorous but it must also be cost- and time-efficient. It must be rapidly concluded, but the researcher still has to be able to claim that the results are adequate and suitable for management and marketing decisions. The report of this impossible study must be persuasive. Marketers or management researcher recognising the need for qualitative research are increasingly frustrated by the difficulty in reaching their high goals of research performance. So marketing researchers reach for sharper tools for tougher, faster research processes. For the software developer their dilemma offers a challenge.

The software tools

In this context the relevance of computers is obvious, yet software is currently little used (Ereaut, 2002). Qualitative computing is more than two decades old, but the software used was first developed for academic research. My own involvement dates to the first publication on the NUD*IST Project (Richards and Richards, 1981). In what follows we shall explore the relevance of software in marketing and management using as an example the software I know best – that designed by Tom Richards for my own research and later for researchers in over eighty countries. The current versions at the time of writing are N6 (the latest NUD*IST) and NVivo 2.0. (It is beyond the scope of the present chapter to describe fully the functionality of these software products. For more details, demonstration software and materials, the reader should go to the QSR website: www.qsrinternational.com.)[1]

These two packages offer related but different toolkits for different purposes since qualitative research covers many research modes. N6 offers ways of handling text data, primarily via coding and searching. Text can be rapidly imported and coded, with special methods of automating clerical work. The software can manage small or large amounts of data, ranging from focus group transcripts, Web-based documents to answers to open-ended questions in surveys, and outcomes can be purely qualitative or combine statistical and qualitative analysis (Bazeley, 2002).

The sister software, NVivo, is less code-based, handles rich text and multimedia files, and offers many ways of linking data and ideas. Designed for more fine-grained analysis, it supports annotation, linking and reflecting, modelling and theory building. This is a toolkit for analysing discourse and meaning, working, for example, with in-depth interviews, thinking-aloud protocols or focus groups (Richards, 1999; Bazeley and Richards, 2000).

Demands meet software: the researcher's dilemma

In the new dialogue between researchers and software developers, four very strong sets of demands are evident. Marketing and management research demands rigorous research (trustworthy and impressive), reliability (results that can be shown to be representative and adequate) and persuasive reports (quick and easily navigated). And it demands all these with speed.

Together these demands present a dilemma that is familiar in all qualitative research. Producing trustworthy outcomes from a thorough understanding of complexity is the challenge of any researcher working with the rich and messy records we call qualitative records. Producing them rapidly can seem impossible. In academic settings, where qualitative software was first developed, the dilemma was usually dodged by sacrificing speed. Qualitative research that is trustworthy and impressive has always been seen as taking time, sometimes a lot of time. Reliable results require painstaking theory development. And reports can be long and diffuse – a book or discursive paper rather than a bite-size punch line.

As qualitative methods were accepted in fields where rigor, reliability and speed were of equal importance the dilemma reappeared. As the chapters in this book clearly show, specific studies driven by the demands of their context can produce the outcomes sought in the required time. They do so by limiting the scope, design and goals of the research to precisely what is needed. In this they have been helped by qualitative software, but the use such tools is still in its infancy.

In this context, this chapter asks the following questions. What do the current tools for qualitative computing offer to researchers? What qualitative software techniques best serve the researcher's need for rigor, speed, reliability and rapid reports? Asking these questions raises future issues. What types of qualitative software could be developed to address the needs of marketing and management research? Will future software be able to address the qualitative researcher's dilemma? In the following sections we shall explore the dichotomy of rigor and speed through four aspects of qualitative research that software has dramatically changed: coding, managing ideas, searching, and presenting results. When software was first produced for qualitative research the most immediate result was rigorous coding, and given the right tools this in turn supported idea management, searches that enabled the rapid interrogation of data, and new ways of modelling and reporting (Richards, 2002a).

Computer-assisted coding

All qualitative researchers have a problem with their data. Rich, messy and unruly, it threatens deadlines, budgets and researcher control. Enter coding. Coding by topic was a time-honoured (and time-consuming) qualitative method of dealing with unruly data. Researchers needed to gather material on a topic or category, then to think about it and summarise it. All manual methods of gathering everything available on a topic were very time-consuming and researchers often saw them as untrustworthy. However it was done, by marking up text, cutting and pasting into files, or keeping notes on index cards, the task consumed researchers' time.

When specialist software programs were first developed for qualitative research they offered researchers the promise of control by coding. Software could do this much more efficiently than manual copy and paste methods. Specialist software programs brought computing to the code-and-retrieve model and changed it (Richards and Richards, 1994). Coding by sophisticated software addressed both horns of the researcher's dilemma. The researcher could now do a far more thorough interpretation and far more rapidly.

Both the software programs described here allow the researcher to select text, allocate it to a category, name the category and optionally define it, or to store a memo about it. Having coded, the researcher can review all the text that is coded there, read and reflect and jump back to the context to enrich interpretation. This entire process takes considerably less time than it would to copy the passage and file it. Software-assisted coding is therefore much more likely to do justice to qualitative data, representing its richness, maintaining interpretation and allowing flexibility. There is now no limit to how many times a rich passage can be coded, reflecting its multiple meanings, or to how many categories can be held, viewed, ordered and consistently and reliably accessed.

Coding with such facility is more akin to thinking aloud than to a clerical, onerous task. Qualitative coding requires easy category creation and the easy allocation of text to a category (Miles and Huberman, 1984). Neither is easily done on paper. But software can make both very rapid. In N6 the categories created are shown in responsive 'explorers' and selected text can be instantly coded there. The same task can be done with 'drag and drop' in NVivo, with displays showing text coding and the resulting categories (Morse and Richards, 2002).

With N6 and NVivo categories for thinking about data can be managed in hierarchical trees or catalogues, and as understanding grows they can be merged or their dimensions teased out. So the coding system responds to the emerging understanding of the data, and can be disciplined to contain just the categories needed to ask just the questions required.

What of the demand for reliability? Qualitative researchers rarely expect identical coding across coders or across time since the goal is to learn from the data. But differences, especially gross differences, in coding can now be displayed and discussed, offering a firmer basis for the claim that coding is reliable. One enhancement of traditional methods is computerised reliability checking. Software can locate these differences rapidly – a task that is almost impossible to do manually (N6 includes a process that automatically identifies areas of difference and similarity between two researchers' coding of the same document).

To return to the researcher's dilemma, have these advantages come at the cost of slowing the research process? Computer-assisted coding can certainly be easier and swifter. Moreover it is possible to harness the computer to a task that qualitative researchers could never attempt without software – automatic coding. If the text to be coded contains identifiable words, the software can code it automatically by means of a text search. Both the programs discussed here can find strings of characters with subtle pattern matching, and find them in specified data, such as only in interviews with managers, or only where innovation is discussed. Both programs can also return the required context – for example the whole answer to a question or just a paragraph. And both can code the findings, so the researcher can now ask another question, for example when 'trust' is mentioned by managers in the context of innovation, what do they say about training?

If the text to be coded is identifiable by the structure of the data, software can do better! A major development early in the NUD*IST program was the ability to write command files that could automate complex coding tasks, setting up projects in minutes by coding all the answers to each question, or everything said by one participant in a focus group. The latest version, N6, includes command assistant that writes the commands. Even easier is the automatic coding of such structured data with NVivo, since it can handle formatted rich text; it will automatically code questions or responses identified by subheadings.

Despite these benefits, software has been only slowly accepted in domains where speed is required, often because the software itself is seen as time-consuming. With barriers removed, researchers can do far more coding than their goals require. For inexperienced researchers in an academic setting, this can result in what I call 'coding fetishism' – overreliance on coding to the point where it stultifies insight (Seidel and Kelle, 1995; Richards and Richards, 1994). For researchers in areas where time is a more immediate constraint, this is a risk to be avoided.

The ability to do more with coding epitomises the dilemma of thoroughness versus speed. Possibly the most radical of the analysis tools in these packages is the ability to work within and beyond coded data (Richards, 1998). Whereas the filing cabinet offered pieces of paper with extracts, the computer can take researchers to all the material there is on a topic: they can view all the text coded at a category (including hyperlinked material, annotations and coding); they can jump to the original or see the context, coding extra text if needed or refine the coding; and by viewing and reviewing coded data they can revisit and reflect on a theme or topic, and code-on to a new and finer categorisation or dimensionalise a concept. Coding need never be the end of the analytical road. But the longer that road extends, the more challenging the deadline becomes.

To summarise, all of these advantages both enhance research and take time. But they also save time. To take just one example, the ability to browse coded material allows the rapid 'cleaning up' of coded text, or the resorting of data coded at a generic category. Returning to the original documents and clean up the coding might have taken weeks (but then, I hear you say, we would not have done the task!)

The management of data and ideas

The qualitative researcher's goals are never limited to coding original data. Many other sorts of knowledge must be stored and accessed. In particular, most projects require the storage of information, emerging ideas and thoughts. Both of the packages discussed here offer such storage.

Take simple information. What do we know about the respondents? With both software packages, in different ways, one can categorise data records by demographic and other factors in a form that is interchangeable with statistical or tabular data-processing packages, such as databases and spreadsheets. This means that data can be imported from a table in seconds. It also offers the possibility of fruitful interactions between the quantitative and qualitative aspects of a project as searching for patterns of coding by attribute is possible. (This may be a problem mainly for those who prefer alternative medicine, do they sound different?)

Combining qualitative and quantitative data is the next logical step, and one that is particularly relevant to the commercial world. The integration of qualitative and quantitative data can be done by data import, and also by exporting qualitative coding (expressed as the value of variables) to quantitative software. In N6 and NVivo, qualitative matrices can be viewed on the screen. Click on the cell of interest and the software will show all the data coded there. Flip the matrix to report the number of documents in each cell. When searching for a pattern, export it to a statistics package (Bazeley, 2002).

Recording thoughts is a different challenge, and researchers in commercial settings may be under too much pressure to move on to have time to record their reflections. Software facilitates the recording and storage of notes, reports, probings and so on. N6 has a provision for separate plain-text memos. In NVivo, memos are fully fledged documents within the project's database, available for coding and so on: the same as the primary field documents.

Finally, when it comes to managing ideas and categories, qualitative researchers generate categories at an alarming pace. With the first versions of NUD*IST, researchers gained the ability to store and sort coding categories in catalogues or 'trees', and in a way that made them easy to access and hard to lose. This permitted theorising and the clarification of related codes (Richards and Richards, 1994).

Searching and re-searching

Software of course does not offer to do the analysis, and if it should, would not be believed. For the researcher, reading and thinking still has to be done. The agency of the researcher in searching for the meanings and patterns is not replaced. The ultimate challenge then is for software to assist the researcher in the interpretative task, in doing it better and faster. It does so by integrating searches that draw not merely on the researcher's coding but also on information about the data and words that occur in the text.

From the filing cabinet I could retrieve all the material I had coded at a topic (for example everything about 'trust'). What even the earliest versions of NUD*IST added to this process were search tools for comparing and relating codes, and the passages they coded, to enable focused extraction of data that was relevant to a question or story. Given these tools, I could ask such complex questions as 'What text coded at trust is also coded at confidence in change?'

Now add access via information about the data, which was always hard to store and use in manual methods. Once the computer was able to store and access the attributes of people or sites, I could ask such questions as '*Who* talks about trusting managers, and is it the *older* staff whose accounts of trust are about authority?'

Text-search capabilities further expanded the scope of these searches. Text search could be used for any characters in data or memos – words from an original interview or added by me. So they integrated lexically based text handling ('Who uses that word, trust?') with the mark-ups of a researcher who responded more to the meaning, tone and intent of passages: for example inserting 'trust' where this could be detected and later use text search to gather all instances.

These three ways of searching – via your coding, what you know, and what occurs in the text – are integrated into the QSR software and the software automatically collects finds as coded data. Importantly, this means that it is possible to keep asking questions that build on previous ones in an iterative process that is referred to as 'system closure' (Richards and Richards, 1994). Thus questioning can be taken as far as the coding, information and texts can possibly take it. Suppose that I want to find out what women in clerical roles have to say about trust, and how this compares with the views of younger or older women. If I have given the program the coding and demographic attributes that underlie the nouns and adjectives in this example, I can now pose the question and gain access to the specific material that answers the request, and can read and think about what those women said. Then I can use text search to find occurrences of other words (such as 'faith') that have been used in that context.

Even before computing, of course, researchers searched data. Most commonly they searched via coding, accessing data that was high-lighted or filed according to topic. They pursued insights and hunches by rereading and rethinking the developing themes. And they still do. But these methods epitomised the researcher's dilemma. Often impressionistic, since the data could not be accessed with certainty, these processes were also time-consuming. Software assistance in enquiries such as the one just described offers new possibilities by providing and combining searches that were not previously available.

These possibilities are increased by software's ability to specify where a search will be conducted. The scoping of searches to focus on just the data asked about, just the cases of interest in the context in question, can now, with NVivo, be as finely tuned as wished and use any of the three ways of selecting data: coding, information or text. All that has to be done is to select the right scope, optionally 'assay' the scope to find just what is there, and then search exactly where you wish to ask the question.

This returns us to the researcher's dilemma. Working qualitatively always involves asking searching questions, and now the limitation on iterative, finely focused searches has been removed. Researchers can keep on asking questions until cases that do not fit are identified or a hunch is dismissed because it turns out to be unfounded. This is what many researchers have always tried to do – to go beyond coding to help researchers 'get up off' the data. These tools encourage researchers to engage: – complex and iterative interrogation using coding, information and text search. Rather than working directly with everything coded at a category researchers now work *from* there. Needless to say, this takes time.

Text search, a mechanical process, epitomises the ways in which speed and rigor can be combined. For researchers in a hurry, text search provides access to data required for illustration or examination. For researchers seeking validation of their accounts, text search provides it: *this* phrase was used only in *these* settings. But not doing so is even faster!

Showing results

Computer-based report-construction methods, plus computer-based delivery techniques, provide the opportunity to make a new art form out of reporting and displaying data. Good qualitative research cannot be reported in a little table of percentages. Corporate clients' expectations about what the consultant will tell them range from a quick summary and digest and unquestioning acceptance of the interpretation, to detailed reasoning about what the research data implies for their decision making. NVivo offers ways of progressively building theories as the project matures, keeping the theories as documents in the project and linking all aspects of a theory to evidential passages and justificatory arguments. Start an embryonic report document, after coding and analysing a first interview. As the project matures day by day, (or hour by hour in a rush job), edit and change that report, keeping it abreast of your current understanding. Elegantly formatted, it includes links to pictures, diagrams and tables. Code this report so that when you browse a code and review data on it, the relevant parts of your report will be there. Then when the client asks questions involving that code, any relevant parts of your report will be included in the results. Give the presentation, live, with all its links, to your client on a CD. The client can read the report as an executive summary, explore the evidential links and ask questions about the data. This is a new and richer way of reporting as it allows instant access to the data, without prior reduction, and offers a vivid encounter with supporting evidence.

Results can also be presented as a graphical model of the data and analysis. NVivo 2 offers a linked Show Tool and Modeller. Ask what documents are coded by this category (for example which documents have a coding for 'trust'?), they appear in the Show Tool and if you wish you can ask of any of those which other categories code them. Or start a model on the idea of trust, dragging onto the new model the code and all the documents it codes. Add ideas, documents or attributes at will, linking them and highlighting parts of the model with colour or emphasis. At this point a theory of trust in organisations is emerging? Layer the model so that each stage in building the theory, or each different picture from a different management setting, can be viewed individually, or all can be viewed together. A click of a mouse summons the data that lie behind the model, for example what senior managers say about trust. Then work on the screen in a team meeting, building the report in the model, and paste it into the paper for publication.

The researcher's dilemma is the developer's challenge

NASA adopted the mantra 'Faster, better, cheaper'. Engineers remark that you can choose any two. Perhaps it is also true that in terms of thoroughness and speed, the qualitative researcher can choose only one?

Undeniably, there is a tension between them. However (as any qualitative researcher or philosopher would remark), it depends what you mean. Speed is the easiest of these to achieve with computers. The removal of time-consuming clerical work has been a boon to all qualitative researchers. The ability to gain immediate access to data via automatic coding and searching techniques is invaluable. But the final result can be slower if the researcher is trapped into doing much more than is necessary, however rapidly it is done. Moreover rapid access offers far more the possibility of in-depth analysis, threatening slower results. How can this new manifestation of the old dilemma be avoided?

One answer is better training – especially training in research design – to assist researchers to identify and specify goals and work towards them. The control of coding is of high priority: software tools are only tools, to be used as appropriate for the goals of the researcher. The development of NVivo was partly a response to the challenge of coding: users can link data, model ideas, gather material in many ways and even complete a study without coding.

But the developers of software need to do more to put coding in its place as just one tool among many in the researcher's kit. As computer-assisted qualitative research has developed, coding has become the prominent, and sometimes only, mode of data handling for many researchers (Richards, 1998). In areas such as marketing and management, where there has never been time for all-encompassing coding, software that calls for detailed coding will be seen as unsuitable for a study with a one-month deadline.

Researchers need to drive not only their projects but also their software. Qualitative research earned a reputation for lack of rigor when researchers were buried in paperwork, access to data was inadequate and standards of evidence were pitifully low. Too often the search for something to illustrate a point was a hit-or-miss affair, and finding a counterexample, which is required by rigorous methodology, was largely impossible. With computer techniques that potentially offer total management of all data, qualitative researchers risk earning a new reputation for engaging in highly rigorous but totally impractical projects. Nothing needs to be lost or overlooked; the computer never says 'That's enough, I'm tired'. If it is coded and a counterexample lurks in some or other combination of coding, the right question will find it and the tools will tell you all you want to know about the context of the answer. Of course rigor alone is not enough, so qualitative researchers seek rigorous research that is also sensitive and insightful. And sensitivity is another time-devouring goal. 'Sensitivity' can mean close interrogation of data, a query scoped to just the relevant interviews, accurate identification of cases that do not fit, the pinpointing of categories associated with a problem and the profiling of all coding and attributes that accompany it. Computer tools strongly support such sensitive analysis, and puts considerable NVivo emphasis on it (Richards, 1998, 1999). But if sensitivity refers to the interpretation and subtle analysis of the human condition – the intellectual achievement that distinguishes a great novel from an airport thriller – this will depend, as do all intellectual achievements, on the researcher having time to reflect on all the available data; and if there is even more data, more ways of retrieving data and more patterns indicated in data, much more time will be needed.

Conclusion

Qualitative research cannot be reduced to a mechanical procedure so it will never be fully automated by software. However qualitative software can now handle complex qualitative research projects, and can support them at such a speed and with such comprehensiveness and rigor that obtaining professionally credible results is now achievable in a comparatively short time. This was never the case with manual methods or earlier generations of qualitative programs, which were largely confined to the luxurious years of postgraduate research. The tools described above certainly address the demands of researchers in marketing and management.

But are these tools the best tools? Producing good qualitative results still depends on the skill of researchers; they cannot be mechanised out of a job. And tools that perform the desired functions may not be appropriate for all researchers. Most researchers who use the new software products, including those discussed in this book, assert that they use few of the functions available.

Current software packages, including the two described here, are by design multifunctional. Aimed at the varied qualitative research that takes place in academia, they offer a wide range of linked techniques, far more than any researcher will need. Of course the same applies to the word processor, and most skilled users of word processors use only a tiny fraction of the available functions. But unlike the word processor, the qualitative software package is not part of the user's early training, rather is usually confronted just as a project begins. Researchers require time to learn, and this can be too much for researchers in commercial settings (Ereaut, 2002, pt 2).

Moreover all code-based tools rely on detailed coding by the researcher in order for interpretations to be made, patterns discovered and sophisticated searches brought into play. And coding is the most time-consuming of qualitative tasks. For many purposes in marketing and management it would be better for the researcher to by-pass coding and to use simpler methods of linking ideas to data.

Qualitative software offers efficient techniques to create and manage data, and to ask questions that are appropriate for, and quite specific to, qualitative data. This chapter has presented a sketch of these techniques and their often conflicting impact on the thoroughness and speed of research. It can be said that qualitative research technologies have reached the standard needed by market researchers and other types of social researcher, but marketers and management researchers need to harness these tools to their particular needs, and to drive software development by their demands.

Note

1. QSR International has developed the two products discussed in this chapter, and the author is a member of the development and support teams. NUD*IST

is an acronym for Non-numerical Unstructured Data Indexing Searching and Theorising – more recent versions are known only by their initial and revision number. N6 is the current version at time of writing. NVivo is a different software package for different purposes. Both are available, with information and teaching materials, at http://www.qsrinternational.com/. Readers who wish to know about the range of qualitative software are advised to go to websites and not to printed media, which are always out of date. The most recent authoritative review is Alexa and Zuell (1999). The CAQDAS website in the UK maintains links with most developers: www.caqdas.soc.surrey.ac.uk.

References

Alexa, M. and Zuell, C. (1999) *A Review of Text Analysis Software* (Mannheim: ZUMA).

Bazeley, P. (2002) 'Computerized data analysis for mixed methods research', in A. Tashakkori and C. Teddlie (eds), *Handbook of Mixed Methods for the Social and Behavioural Sciences* (Thousand Oaks, CA: Sage), pp. 385–422.

Bazeley, P. and Richards, L. (2000) *The NVivo Qualitative Project Book* (London: Sage).

Ereaut, G. (2002) *Analysis and Interpretation in Qualitative Market Research* (London: Sage).

Gummesson, E. (2000) *Qualitative Methods in Management Research* (Thousand Oaks, CA: Sage).

Kelle, U. (ed.) (1995) *Computer Aided Qualitative Data Analysis, Theory, Methods and Practice* (London: Sage).

Miles, M. and Huberman, M. (1984) *Qualitative Data Analysis: A Sourcebook of New Methods* (Thousand Oaks, CA: Sage).

Morse, J. and Richards, L. (2002) *Readme First: A User's Guide to Qualitative Analysis* (Thousand Oaks, CA: Sage).

Richards, L. (1998) 'Closeness to Data: the Changing Goals of Qualitative Data Handling', *Qualitative Health Research*, vol. 8, no. 3, pp. 319–28.

Richards, L. (1999) *Using NVivo in Qualitative Research* (London: Sage).

Richards, L. (2002a) 'Qualitative computing – a methods revolution?', *International Journal of Social Research Methodology*, vol. 5, no. 3, pp. 263–76.

Richards, L. (2002b) 'Rigorous, rapid, reliable *and* qualitative? Computing in qualitative method', *American Journal of Health Behavior*, vol. 26, no. 6, pp. 425–30.

Richards, L. and Richards, T. (1981) 'NUDIST: a computer assisted technique for thematic analysis of unstructured data', *La Trobe Working Papers in Sociology*, no. 59.

Richards, T. and Richards, L. (1994) 'Using Computers in Qualitative Research', in N. K. Denzin and Y. S. Lincoln (eds), *Handbook of Qualitative Research* (Thousand Oaks, CA: Sage), pp. 445–62.

Seidel, J. and Kelle, U. (1995) 'Different Functions of Coding in the Analysis of Textual Data', in U. Kelle (ed.), *Computer Aided Qualitative Data Analysis, Theory, Methods and Practice* (London: Sage), pp. 52–61.

3
Realism Also Rules OK: Scientific Paradigms and Case Research in Marketing

Chad Perry

Introduction

This chapter argues that at least three 'worlds' of marketing phenomena can be distinguished. For each world, scientists share a worldview or paradigm that is internally consistent, rational and logical. We shall consider each of these three worlds and their corresponding scientific paradigms (based on Magee, 1985; Guba and Lincoln, 1994):

- World 1 fits the *positivism* paradigm, consisting of objective, material things. Here, in essence, reality is a straightforward concept that is easy to measure.
- World 2 fits the *critical theory* and *constructivism* paradigms and consists of the subjective world of minds, that is, of meanings. Here, perception is reality.
- World 3 fits the *realism* paradigm and consists of abstract things that are born of people's minds but exist independently of any one person. The third world is largely autonomous, though created by us. Here, perceptions are a window to that blurry external reality.

The aim of this chapter is to show how the realism paradigm is appropriate for researching some marketing phenomena, especially marketing management phenomena, and to describe the use of case research within that paradigm. Essentially it is argued that marketers could use all four paradigms to investigate a range of phenomena, but the realism paradigm is especially appropriate for research involving cases of marketing management.

In the following section the three worlds are introduced and evaluated. Next the case research is described. Finally, theory-building research such as case research and theory testing research are contrasted and shown to be complementary.

The positivism paradigm

The positivism paradigm is the most widely used paradigm for business school research (Orlikowski and Baroudi, 1991) and implicitly or explicitly assumes that reality can be measured by viewing it through a one way, value-free mirror. Its World 1 assumptions are summarised in the left-hand column of Table 3.1. These assumptions are held by engineers, for example, when researching a physical science phenomenon such as a bridge.

However some studies show that these almost 'default' assumptions of business school research are inappropriate when researching social science phenomena such as marketing. For example replication research does not usually produce the same results as prior research, as one would expect in positivism research. In their study of the subject Hubbard and Armstrong (1994) found that only 15 per cent of replication studies in marketing fully confirmed the prior findings and only 25 per cent partially confirmed them. In other words 60 per cent of the replication studies produced results that conflicted with those of their predecessor. Indeed, of the few studies that supported prior research, over half were done by the researcher who had done the prior research (Hubbard and Vetter, 1996), suggesting that the research was not conducted in the value-free way that positivism declares.

Meta-analyses of positivism studies often confirm this picture. A meta-analysis compares several quantitative studies on a common scale. For example the correlations over many studies between customer satisfaction and these constructs cover a wide range of values that even spread across positive and negative values (Szymanski and Henard, 2000):

- Expectations: -0.13 to $+0.66$
- Disconfirmation: -0.24 to $+0.87$
- Performance: -0.37 to $+0.81$

The disappointing results obtained by using positivism as the default paradigm in management and marketing research is confirmed by Redding (1994). In a review of 30 years of research into the complex social science phenomenon of organisational culture, he concludes that the research

Table 3.1   Four scientific paradigms

| Element | Paradigm | | | |
	Positivism	Realism	Critical theory	Constructivism
Ontology	Reality is real and apprehensible	Reality is 'real' but only imperfectly and probabilistically apprehensible, and therefore triangulation from many sources is required to try to know it	'Virtual' reality shaped by social, economic, ethnic, political, cultural and gender values, crystallised over time	Multiple local and specific 'constructed' realities
Epistemology	Findings true	Findings probably true	Value-mediated findings – the researcher is a 'transformative intellectual' who changes the social world within which the participants live	Created findings – researcher is a 'passionate participant' in the world being investigated
Common methodologies	Experiments, surveys: verification of hypotheses, chiefly using quantitative methods	Case studies: triangulation, interpretation of research issues by qualitative methods and by the quantitative method of structural equation modelling	Action research	In-depth interviews, participant observation

Note: Essentially, ontology is 'reality', epistemology is the relationship between that reality and the researcher, and methodology is the technique used by the researcher to discover that reality.
Source: Based on Perry *et al.* (1999), which in turn was based on Guba and Lincoln (1994), from which the quotations come.

had uncovered little because most of it was positivist: 'This review of the major reviews leads to the conclusion that thirty years' work *has made little impression* on the immensely complex problem of cultures and organisational behaviour...The main body of work is clustered incompetently, unadventurously, but with comfortable conformity in the positivist . . . corner' (ibid., p. 331 emphasis added).

Thus it should come as no surprise that real world managers consider that most of the academic research that emanates from business schools is irrelevant. Porter and McKibbin's (1988) thorough investigation of senior managers, new MBA recruits into firms and their superiors and consultants found that business school research was definitely not useful to practicing managers:

> as far as we could tell, many key managers and executives *pay little or no attention* to such research and findings [of business academics] . . . the direct impact appears *nil* . . . not a single [manager] who was interviewed cited the research of business schools as either their most important strength or their major weakness. The business world is . . . ignoring the research coming out of business schools. (Ibid., p. 180, emphasis added)

In brief, I argue that using positivism as the default paradigm in marketing has led us nowhere in particular.

The constructivism and critical theory paradigms

The major alternative to positivism in the social sciences is postmodernism or interpretivism, which can be categorised within the paradigms of constructivism and critical theory. These two paradigms relate to World 2 in the introduction to this chapter and are summarised in Table 3.1. In essence they argue that the world is 'constructed' by people and that it is the latter's constructions that should be investigated in social science research. For example some people think that Levi jeans are the best available and are worth buying, even though tests conducted within a positivism framework by consumer magazines show that in terms of cloth, stitching and buttoning they are not as well constructed as other brands of jeans. Similarly people commit suicide because of the black world in which they perceive themselves to be, irrespective of whether or not that world is really as bad as they think it is. In other words a core element of these two paradigms is that individuals' constructed reality has such a powerful influence on their behaviour that any external reality is relatively unimportant. Moreover there is no way of comparing the multiple constructed realities of different people. But this incommensurability of perceptions – that is, the relativism at the heart of these paradigms – makes the two paradigms a *cul de sac* for scientific researchers. For example Hunt (1991, p. 318) asks how these paradigms could help with research into whether the Holocaust actually occurred in the 1940s – some people believe that it did occur and some believe that it did not, and this disagreement cannot be treated within the two paradigms of constructivism and critical theory:

> It is indeed true that one of the 'multiple realities' that some people hold...is that the Holocaust never occurred...An alternative 'multiple reality' is that the Holocaust did in fact occur...Which 'multiple reality' is correct? Sincere...advocates of reality relativism must stand mute when confronted with this question. (Ibid., p. 318)

One way out of this *cul de sac* would be for people with different constructed worlds to negotiate a shared understanding. But would such negotiations be possible? For example would burglars who perceive that taking the possessions of wealthy people is equitable, and wealthy householders who do not want their homes burgled, be able to negotiate a shared understanding? Pawson and Tilley (1997, pp. 16–21) answer that question with a clear 'No'. It is hard not to snigger when Guba and Lincoln (1994) talk about getting stakeholders to agree to and formally sign 'conditions for a productive hermeneutic dialectic'.

> [Their] hermeneutic dialectic circles (not surprisingly) go round in circles, rather than constituting a linear advance on truth. In particular, constructivism and critical theory are not especially relevant in research about marketing management, because marketing managers have to deal with a world that is external, that is out there and that does not particularly care about the perceptions of an individual manager: In marketing, the company's external environment is always more important than the internal. The real decisions are made in the world outside – among consumers, middlemen, competitors, politicians, legislators and trade organisations. The external environment is neither particularly knowledgeable nor interested in the company and its development. (Gummesson, 2000, p. 105)

In brief the subjective 'meaning' within constructed realities may indeed determine outcomes such as customers' choice of jeans, but not issues concerning the marketing management of those perceptions. Overall, constructivism/critical theory may be useful for research into important social science phenomena such as suicide, falling in love, family life and office power politics in big organisations, with slow or blurry feedback loops to the outside, political ideologies, racism and nationalism. But a lot of marketing management is merely about transactions in an external market place. In this sort of world, research has to be like a courtroom trial, where evidence is sought about the external reality of 'guilty or not guilty' that exists independently of what did or did not drive the person to commit the crime, even though that external reality can only be known imperfectly. We need a picture (even though it will be an imperfect one) of how marketers can manage the perceptions of the many customers in an external market, and at a profit. In short, constructivism and critical theory are a *cul de sac* for marketing management research.

The realism paradigm

We sometimes need to move away from Worlds 1 and 2 into World 3, with its paradigm of realism. The worldview of realism consists of abstract things that are born of people's minds but exist independently of any one person: 'the third world is largely autonomous, though created by us' (Magee, 1985, p. 61). This third world could be a country's legal system or the body of academic knowledge about segmentation, for example. A person's perceptions are a window onto the blurry external reality. Realism, which is summarised in the second column of Table 3.1, is about structural social mechanisms that do exist 'out there' (Easton, 1998; Pawson and Tilley, 1997). This world of mechanisms and their contexts is not as straightforward as the world in which physical scientists such as engineers work. An engineer knows that too much weight on a bridge will cause it to fall. But social science realists work with causal *tendencies* rather than causal certainties: A may cause B sometimes, but not always or even mostly. For example, whether installing lights a carpark will cause a reduction in car thefts may depend on the hours the carpark is used and its location. In other words lights may reduce crime or they may not, depending on the situation. Similarly, whether a marketing tactic is successful will depend on many contextual situations, such as a competitor's reactions. The imprecision of causal tendencies is exacerbated by the ability of people to change their behaviour after reflecting on it.

Rigorous case research methodology within the realism paradigm

We are now in a position to consider case research as an example of social science research within the realism paradigm. This discussion is based on the experience of many of my postgraduate research students who have successfully investigated areas as diverse as Internet marketing, customer service, home banking, international tourism, the exportation of high technology and business networks. Articles on this research are starting to be accepted by periodicals such as the *Journal of the Academy of Marketing Science*, the *European Journal of Marketing*, the *Journal of Travel and Tourism* and the *Journal of Services Marketing*. Case research is discussed in detail in Perry (1998a, 2001) and Carson *et al.* (2001).

The starting point for case research is to conduct a review of the literature in order to establish a theoretical framework and construct a set of related research issues to address the research problem. In effect these issues are the objectives that will guide later data collection and analysis. An example of a set of research issues can be found in Healy (2000):

- RI 1: What are the elements of the structure of a network?
- RI 2: What forces change that structure?
- RI 3.1: What is a network?
- RI 3.2: What roles do networks play in adaptation vs standardisation?

The next step is to justify the appropriateness of the realism paradigm for the research project. This justification usually focuses on the development of case-specific knowledge based on natural and social experiences to understand deeper structures and meanings in an external reality. Clearly, quantitative techniques from the positivism paradigm, which assume dependent variables with zero measurement error, are inappropriate. Moreover only causal tendencies can be found, rather than direct cause and effect relationships. In the epistemology of the realism paradigm, researchers are not objective and isolated from the research in the way that positivists are; unlike constructivists they are not involved participants who are passionately involved in creating the findings; and unlike critical theorists they are not concerned with transforming mental frameworks. Instead realism researchers are a value-aware part of the research process – they try to build a rapport with the participants to encourage them to share their perceptions of reality, but they do so in a way that minimises their influence (Perry, 1998a, 2001).

Within the realism paradigm the justification for using case research focuses on the assertion that the context and the phenomenon are not clearly distinct. The phenomenon is a complex situation that requires in-depth investigation, it is contemporary and dynamic, and the body of knowledge considered in the literature review has been shown to be 'preparadigmatic', so an inductive methodology such as case research is needed (Yin, 1994).

Case research usually involves two stages of data collection and analysis. The first is very inductive and uses methodologies such as convergent interviewing and focus groups to identify the core issues involved. The first stage facilitates the development of a theoretical framework from the literature that the second stage will set out to confirm or disconfirm. This second stage involves analytical generalisation rather than statistical generalisation (Yin, 1994), that is, it is concerned with the theory-building of realism rather than theory testing. Figure 3.1 illustrates these stages and shows how the level of prior theory is built up during the first stage. The level of prior theory is then held constant while the stage two cases are investigated, and a cross-case analysis is conducted using the answers to the same questions that were asked of all cases.

The data on the cases come from many sources but interviews are the most common source. Each interview conforms to an interviewer's guide with questions relating to each of the research issues. The process starts with a summary of the purpose of the research, the benefits to the interviewee and any ethical concerns, such as whether all identities will be disguised in the report. Then the interview begins with a general, non-threatening request such as 'Please tell me the story of your experiences with . . .' More detailed, probing questions are then asked if certain issues have not been included in the answers to the general question. Thus the interviews start as induction by the interviewee and the probing questions are deductions by the interviewer. The interviews

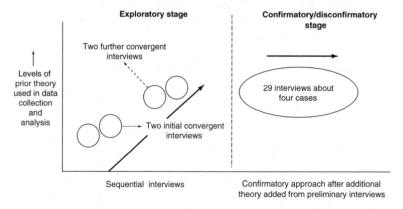

Figure 3.1   Levels of prior theory in the two stages of a research project
Source: Based on Hinkins (2000).

finish with questions about how things could be done differently with hindsight, who else could be interviewed and what other questions could have been asked. Finally, the interviewers are thanked for participating.

The data analysis concentrates on why things happen rather than on statistics because the cases were selected on a purposeful basis rather than a random one. That is, case research operates within the realism paradigm by searching for explanations of mechanisms within a context. Patterns in the data are looked for and codes are assigned to chunks of interview data that relate to the research issues. Matrices/tables that link themes and cases are drawn up, and appropriate quotations from interviewees are noted.

The validity and reliability of the research are ensured by the following (Healy and Perry, 2000):

- Ontological appropriateness: the research is about a social science phenomenon with reflective people.
- Contingent validity: context is incorporated into the selection of cases and the interviews, and causal tendencies are explored.
- Triangulation of interview data from other sources, such as Internet sites, other interviewees in the organisation, consultants and industry experts.
- Trustworthiness: a database of source materials is constructed, and matrices/tables and quotations are included in the report.
- Analytic generalisation/theory building, followed later by statistical generalisation/theory testing.
- Construct validity: incorporation of the literature into the initial theoretical framework, the above triangulation, and obtaining external reviews of draft reports.

The report finishes with a newly constructed theory about, say, how service quality and relationship development can be related.

We shall now consider the structure of a case research report for a thesis and for an article. A case research *thesis* has a five-chapter format (Perry, 1998b). In the first chapter the research problem is expressed as a 'How and why?' question. A preliminary theoretical framework and related research issues are presented at the end of a literature review in the second chapter. The methodology is described in the third chapter, including details of how the data was collected. The data analysis is presented in the fourth chapter. Finally, the conclusions are set out in the fifth chapter, together with the newly constructed theory.

Similarly a case research *article* is presented as follows:

1. The aim, expressed as a 'How and why' question.
2. A review of the literature, a preliminary theoretical framework and details of related research issues or objectives.
3. A description of how the data was collected and analysed, with details of the relevant steps, case research literature and justifications.
4. Analysis of the data, with matrices/tables and quotations.
5. The newly constructed theory.

This sort of case research has become quite popular with thesis examiners and postgraduate research students. For example two examiners have emphasised the method's rigour and appropriateness:

> This dissertation addresses an issue which is both contemporary and critically important for the prosperity of Australians...The candidate has adopted a most appropriate methodology of inquiry for this study...The conceptualisation and theoretical underpinnings are well chosen...I congratulate the candidate.

> The development and presentation of the research was first class. Seldom have I seen such a well organised chapter on paradigms and the justification for the one used...[was] thorough and well presented.

In turn the following comments by students emphasise the ability to learn about complex, real-world situations:

> A key benefit derives from the type of problem you can research... understand meanings rather just numbers.

> I learnt a lot from talking to the interviewees because we could discuss issues in depth. There was little prior research or theory in my area...[Case research was] a structured approach to understand and build theories about a changing complex situation within its context.

Case research within the realism paradigm lies in the middle of the theory-building/theory-testing continuum (Table 3.2). Alternatively theory-building from qualitative research and theory-testing quantitative research can be seen as two sides of the same coin. For example politicians can use a quantitative survey to discover what their popularity rating is – that is, the 'what' of their popularity – and then use qualitative focus

Table 3.2 Selected methodologies and their paradigms on a theory building and testing continuum

	Paradigm
1. Theory building: meaning	
Grounded theory	Constructivism
Action research	Critical theory
Focus groups	Constructivism/realism
2. Case-based research:	Realism
Survey and structural equation modelling	Realism
Survey and other multivariate techniques	Positivism
3. Theory testing: measurement	

groups to investigate the 'how and why' of their popularity. It is not necessary for one project team or one researcher to do both types of research, although those in a research programme may have to do so in order to obtain a full picture. A researcher merely uses the most appropriate method for his or her project.

Conclusion

In summary, science can investigate three types of 'world'. Scientific paradigms are coherent worldviews that are appropriate for studying these types of world. Of these paradigms, the realism paradigm is appropriate for much of marketing management research. That paradigm's ability to build theories about the complex reality of marketing management is especially appropriate, and rigorous case research within the paradigm is possible. The result is a picture that is necessarily imperfect but an improvement on the sketchy picture that existed in the literature when the research project began.

References

Carey, M. A. (1994) 'The group effect in focus groups: Planning, implementing and interpreting focus group research', in J. M. Morse (ed.), *Critical Issues in Qualitative Research Methods* (Thousand Oaks, CA: Sage), pp. 225–41.

Carson, D., Gilmore, A., Gronhaug, K. and Perry, C. (2001) *Qualitative Research in Marketing* (London: Sage).

Easton, G. (1998) 'Case research as a methodology for industrial networks: a realist apologia', in P. Naude and P. W. Turnbull (eds), *Network Dynamics in International Marketing* (Oxford: Pergamon), pp. 73–87.

Guba, E. G. and Lincoln, Y. S. (1994) 'Competing paradigms in qualitative research', in N. K. Denzin and Y. S. Lincoln (eds.), *Handbook of Qualitative Research* (Thousand Oaks, CA: Sage), pp. 105–17.

Gummesson, E. (2000) *Qualitative Methods in Management Research* (London: Sage).

Healy, M. (2000) 'Networks among Australian SMEs', PhD thesis, Toowoomba, University of Southern Queensland.

Healy, M. and Perry, C. (2000) 'Comprehensive criteria to judge the validity and reliability of qualitative research within the realism paradigm', *Qualitative Market Research – An International Journal*, vol. 3, no. 3, pp. 118–126.

Hinkins, S. (2000) 'Developing clinical management: an Australian health service perspective', DBA thesis, Tweed Heads (Australia), Southern Cross University.

Hubbard, R. and Armstrong, J. S. (1994) 'Replications and extensions in marketing: rarely published but quite contrary', *International Journal of Research in Marketing*, vol. 11, pp. 233–48.

Hubbard, R. and Vetter, D. E. (1996) 'An empirical comparison of published replications research in economics, finance, management and marketing', *Journal of Business Research*, vol. 35, pp. 153–64.

Hunt, S. (1991) *Modern Marketing Theory* (Cincinnati, Ohio: South-Western).

Magee, B. (1985) *Popper* (London: Fontana).

Orlikowski, W. J. and Baroudi, J. J. (1991) 'Studying information technology in organisations: research approaches and assumptions', *Information Systems Research*, vol. 2, no. 1, pp. 1–14.

Pawson, R. and Tilley, N. (1997) *Realistic Evaluation* (London: Sage).

Perry, C. (1998a) 'Processes of a case study methodology for postgraduate research in marketing', *European Journal of Marketing*, vol. 32, nos 9–10, pp. 785–802.

Perry, C. (1998b) 'A structured approach for presenting theses', *Australasian Marketing Journal*, vol. 6, no. 1, pp. 63–85.

Perry, C. (2001) 'Case research in marketing', *The Marketing Review*, vol. 1 (also available at www.themarketingreview.com).

Perry, C., Riege, A. and Brown, L. (1999) 'Realism's role among scientific paradigms in marketing research', *Irish Marketing Review*, vol. 12, no. 2, pp. 16–23.

Porter, W. M. and McKibbin, L. E. (1988) *Management Education and Development: Drift or Thrust into the 21st Century?* (New York: McGraw-Hill).

Redding, S. G. (1994) 'Comparative management theory: jungle, zoo or fossil bed?', *Organization Studies*, vol. 15, no. 3, pp. 323–59.

Szymanski, D. M. and Henard, D. H. (2000) 'Customer satisfaction: a meta-analysis of the empirical evidence', *Journal of the Academy of Marketing Science*, vol. 29, no. 1, pp. 16–35.

Yin, R. K. (1994) *Case Study Research Design and Methods* (Thousand Oaks, CA: Sage).

Part II
Generating Data

4

Presenting the Results of Qualitative Research to Public Research Administration Bodies

Andrea Kurz, Walter Aigner and Dieter Meinhard

Introduction

Even if a client agrees to a qualitative study design and the research team sticks to all the standards of quality control, the final step of the study can be difficult: presenting the results in a concise manner (but adequate to the complexity of the topic) to an audience that is typically not ready to accept emotional comments (for example verbatim statements from the field) and to listeners who tend to react to critical statements with disbelief. The material in this chapter derives from our presentation experiences with studies on the nature of international academic research networks, and some almost identical experiences by a team of policy consultants. The six critical factors that we have identified (complexity, stickiness, trust, practice, culture and use of results) are reflected upon in the light of selected literature.

A typical setting

Imagine you have been entrusted to investigate a European research network programme. Your client is the ministry that is managing Austria's participation in this programme. You conduct almost one hundred interviews with researchers involved in and people managing the initiative. You observe and cross-check your results. Eventually you are convinced you know how the network functions, you can imagine how the participants feel and what is really going on. And naturally you want your client to know as well. You sum up your findings and enthusiastically deliver your presentation. But alas the client is not at all responsive. This is true of most clients – as one said, 'If this is what participants do in this network, I just don't want to know.'

Statements such as that have prompted us to ask ourselves: What went wrong? Were the clients not prepared for the findings that a qualitative study produces? Was the description too explicit, too real? Obviously the clients had expected something else. Would simplicity be the solution? Then we observed that others, even experienced, well-known, successful business consultants, were confronted with quite similar reactions when presenting the results of a qualitative study.

Surprisingly this phenomenon has been scarcely touched on in the literature (Constas, 1992; May, 1997), although there are numerous hints on writing papers and reports even in the standard qualitative research literature (Miles and Huberman 1994, pp. 298–306; Rubin and Rubin 1995, pp. 257–74) and on the Internet (Massey, 1996). Oral presentations are only covered for academic settings – mostly PhD (Chenail, 1995; Morse, 1997). However books on presentation skills are of limited use as far as handling complex topics and rich descriptive data is concerned. Works on action research and policy consulting generally focus on interaction and acceptability issues (Constas, 1992; Rist, 1994; May, 1997) and tend to neglect the specific dynamics of a typical qualitative research design. The closest direct reference we have found is in Wigzell (1989). Wigzell rather harshly criticises the conduct and presentation skills of qualitative researchers in general, but unfortunately his own recommendations fall somewhat short of the mark: 'Check out the audience, mind the politics of the meeting, control the timing, paint a picture' (ibid., pp. 109 ff.).

The experiences of others and our team and the lack of literature prompted us to take a closer look at the problems encountered when presenting the results of qualitative research studies.

The problem in the light of six critical factors

Presenting the results of qualitative research is a challenging task. Presentations have to be made in a concise manner but adequate to the complexity of the topic. Delivering the insights gained in a format that is suitable for the audience is very demanding due to the context-dependence ('stickiness') of the subject matter. In policy consulting, public administration officials are typically unfamiliar with qualitative research methodology. Hence trust is an issue. Insight into practice (Brown and Duguid, 2000) seems to be of greatest relevance, but some results will be contrary to the organisational culture in public administration bodies. Also of concern are the excessive expectations that some qualitative researchers nurture in respect of the impact and use of their

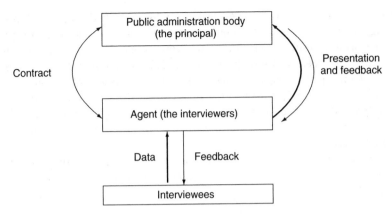

Figure 4.1 A typical relationship between qualitative researchers and a public administration body

results. In this chapter we shall focus on six critical factors, comment on them in the light of selected literature and offer preliminary conclusions and research suggestions.

The experiences that form the basis of this chapter occurred between 2000 and 2002 for our research group, and coincidentally during a project led by the head of the Austrian branch of an international business consulting agency (both come under 'Agent' in Figure 4.1). In all the cases discussed in this chapter the public administration bodies in question (referred to as 'Principal' in Figure 4.1) were engaged in research management and administration; some were international, some national.

As can be seen in Figure 4.1, a bilateral contract between a public administration body (the principal) and the agent typically forms the foundation of a study. The principal's aim is to find out something about the members of a community (the interviewees), their goals, assumptions and ways of communicating. This prepares the ground for intensified public support for the community in question.

Qualitative researchers conduct interviews, workshops and the like to gather data, which is subsequently analysed. The main conclusions are disseminated to the interviewees (feedback) and the principal. This chapter focuses on the oral presentation to the principal and the feedback from the principal. Presentation skills and the pros and cons of (electronic) slide shows will not be covered as these were not part of the core problem of the studies concerned. Nor shall we go into detail about the content of the presentation, but it can be taken for granted that we used the 'tricks of the trade' Becker (1998) described, and the tools suggested by Miles and Huberman (1994) for conducting a sound analysis and drawing relevant conclusions. We shall not discuss what might have been wrong with the contractual agreement and the process of setting up the project. Issues relating to organisational background and organisational change in the public administration body will also be ignored, although they might be a rewarding topic. Our focus will be solely on experiences that are unique to presenting the results of qualitative research.

Having described the setting and pointed out the limitations of our focus, we shall consider selected experiences and the critical factors revealed by them.

Complexity

When the results of qualitative research are presented the audience is frequently surprised at their complexity, although this factor is less predominant when the presentation is about survey results. The audience misses the commonly accepted statistical evidence, figures and correlations. At best they are given information on frequencies or distributions. Typically patterns, comparisons, pictures and metaphors are presented to the client; case-based reasoning is a primary approach (Miles and Huberman, 1994, p. 245 f.). The bottom-up approach – both in the fieldwork and during the pattern-seeking/interpretation stage (with the help of the software NUD*IST) – and the guiding concept of 'thick descriptions' add to the complexity of the report. In general, understanding qualitative results is more challenging than interpreting figures from quantitative surveys.

Stickiness

Another critical factor lies more predominantly with the agent. The presenter is enthusiastic about the findings of the pattern searching and thinks that the client deserves a full picture of the research. The critical factor that arises here is the transferability or 'stickiness' of information (von Hippel, 2001). Information may be sticky in the sense that there are findings that are difficult to convey to the principal by means of a presentation or written report, but the term can also be applied to the successful diffusion of new information (Gladwell, 2000). In the latter context stickiness (that is, easy to remember) helps new information to survive in a world of information overload.

Trust

The researcher may be convinced that the chosen method is the most appropriate for the research objectives, but the audience may denigratingly call metaphors and anecdotes 'interesting' and doubt their validity. Metaphors and stories collected during the fieldwork are particularly mistrusted as they look like individual shippets that are not relevant to the big picture. Here again the audience misses the familiar quantification: how can something as subjective as opinions and personal comments or feelings be turned into accurate and valid results? With quantitative surveys one is safe as clients tend to be familiar with criteria such as internal and external validity, reliability and objectivity. Therefore a vital task to be done is to promote trust in qualitative research. This should be a consolidated effort by the entire qualitative research community.

Practice

The audience can be uncomfortable with information on what is happening in practice, eventhough the purpose of the study was precisely to find out what was really going on. Remember the remark we highlighted at the beginning: 'If this is what they do, I just don't want to know.' Had the study been a survey this problem would probably never have come up. We shall call this critical factor 'practice' (Brown and Duguid, 2000).

Culture

The audience may fear the implications of the findings – the consequences may be too great or not part of their responsibilities. Furthermore the findings may seem to demand policy actions whose results will not be fully predictable, controllable or assessable (for example self-organising communities). Even mere knowledge of the findings could increase the pressure on policy makers. This was especially true of programmes and initiatives 30 or so years ago, when the evolution of practice was typically ahead of legally defined processes and structures. Crozier (2001, p. 148) puts it this way: 'The more knowledge we have, the less capable we are of controlling reality.' Growing environmental complexity and freedom of personal choice drives this paradox: our knowledge is and will always be a step behind reality. Therefore the audience tends to neglect critical statements or treats them with disbelief – strategies that are familiar to all of us for reducing dissonance. We shall call this critical factor 'culture'.

Use of results

This critical factor is mainly to do with the high expectations qualitative researchers have about the use of their results. They want their findings to be understood, accepted and disseminated. They want their clients to use them as the basis for decision making and implementation (Miles and Huberman, 1994, p. 305). Feedback is sought along the way and upon completion of the report. However public administration bodies often have a different perception of the role of a researcher/consultant. Their motive for commissioning a study may be to outsource tasks or share responsibility, and more often than not only symbolic use is made of the report (Doney and Armstrong, 1996).

Reflections on the critical factors in the light of the literature

Complexity

There is a need to differentiate between internal and external complexity. In qualitative research the researcher strives for a complete and vivid picture of reality – a 'thick description'. Since reality is complex, progress in the study will more often than not be accompanied by an increase in the complexity of the researcher's perception of the research topic (internal complexity). Reality as seen by the interviewee will always differ from the interviewer's perception. By increasing internal complexity it may be possible to arrive at a less distorted view. Becker (1998, p. 7) calls his 'tricks of the trade' 'ways to turn things around, to see things differently, in order to create new problems for research'. This is 'rewarding, because your picture gets more colourful, but [it is] lots of work'. In the meantime the degree of complexity expected by the client (external complexity) is usually significantly less than that sought by the researcher.

These considerations are summarised in Figure 4.2, which also depicts the different degrees of complexity observed in practice. As can be seen, empirical investigations are based on the views of the interviewees, (the far left of Figure 4.2; the arrows indicate perceived relationships between relevant constructs), offering a large pool of study findings. Based on the interviewees' ideas, the researcher constructs a picture that is as close to reality as possible. In order to make the findings vivid and comprehensible, during the presentation the researcher illustrates the findings by means of narrative. This is often asking too much of the client since he or she has not been directly involved in the generation of data. The degree of complexity expected by the

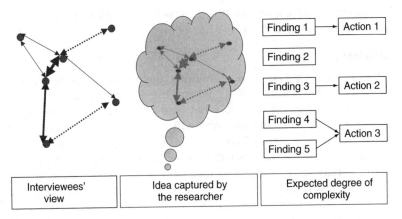

Figure 4.2 Internal and external complexity

client is merely a list of findings that are relevant to the proposed action plan.

Consulting agencies often live up to the client's expectations. We discussed an earlier version of this presentation with a study team in a multinational management and policy-consulting group. A senior policy consultant recommended the following:

- Stop being enthusiastic about what you have found out.
- Remember that policy consulting is not for missionaries.
- Be content to structure the topic in a way that will be accepted by the audience.
- Suggest future actions, but no more than seven.

For those who consider the management consulting approach a little too pragmatic, Crozier (2001) offers another solution. He advocates in favour of direct interaction of the administrators with the community they address. He proposes subsidiarity: decentralisation of planning, execution and control of politics and administration, made possible by a new culture of debate. Promising means of making such interactions happen are open space technology (Owen, 1997a, 1997b, 2000) and the methods used in action learning (Senge and Scharmer, 2001). Therefore in later projects we asked our clients to attend open space meetings with large sections of the communities studied. Such occasions enabled the clients to grasp many of the interpretative results of our interviews during the course of a whole day, instead of being restricted to a one-hour presentation of selected pages of the report[1].

Stickiness

Often a demanding and time-consuming interaction process is required to make qualitative information transferable and understandable to people with a completely different mindset (and at the same time to find a degree of complexity that is appropriate to the topic of the study). At the moment such personal contact and feedback is seldom sought. In Figure 4.1 it can be seen that there is no direct feedback between the public administration body and the community being studied. At best there are reports and surveys, which have to be completed in time but have no immediate consequences. Yet according to Lomas (2000, p. 140), both policy makers and the communities studied would benefit from a better understanding of each other's worlds. Ongoing contact between the two worlds is essential to such an understanding.[2] An 'action learning process' (Senge and Scharmer, 2001) would further the exchange of knowledge and allow for insights at more than the 'product' stage (when everything has been condensed into the final report).

Trust

One of the reasons for mistrusting the results of qualitative research is the absence of theories, facts and figures. Mixed-method approaches could help overcome this problem while maintaining the benefits of a qualitative approach. But if the research objective demands a purely qualitative design it might well be worth considering the following. According to Miles and Huberman (1994, pp. 263 ff.) numbers are important during the study process in terms of verifying a hunch or hypothesis, keeping the researchers analytically honest and protecting them against bias. Citing some of these numbers when presenting the results could help the audience to grasp the overall picture more easily. Nonetheless individual cases should continue to be reported in order to give credit to complexity.

In order to promote trust in qualitative research, researchers have to prove that their studies are methodologically sound. In this regard Lincoln and Guba (1985) stress the importance of credibility, transferability, dependability and confirmability. A number of authors offer strategies for putting these constructs into practice (Wallendorf and Belk, 1989, pp. 69 ff.; Miles and Huberman, 1994, pp. 263 ff.; Richards and Richards 1994, pp. 445–62; Morse and Richards, 2002). But there is a drawback to these quality indicators: they are specific to qualitative research. This is why they are unfamiliar to the audience and don't speak for themselves.

Nonetheless, methodological soundness is a technical prerequisite for building trust, but equally important is the social relation. Moorman *et al.* (1993, p. 81) have found that interpersonal factors such as 'perceived researcher integrity, willingness to reduce research uncertainty, confidentiality, expertise, tactfulness, sincerity, congeniality, and timeliness are most strongly associated with trust'. Astonishingly, Zaltman intensively researched issues of trust in market research settings and then with his 'metaphor elicitation technique' (Zaltman and Higie, 1993) broke with all the known standard quality measures and introduced a branded 'by Zaltman' research process. But we are not the renowned Zaltman and our principal was not a corporate management team. It was our first contract with this department and the department's first study contract on research networks. So when presenting really innovative, bottom-up research results for managerial decision-making purposes it is a good idea to have on board a renowned mainstream consultant who has an excellent reputation with the principal and has worked for him before.[3]

Practice

Brown and Duguid (2000) contrast process with practice in the typical management setting. They state that people who focus on processes look at a community or organisation from the outside. They take a business re-engineering point of view; they focus on functions and expect them to explain all that is going on. They regard people in the organisation as instruments to fulfil certain predefined functions, and they view lateral links among peers with suspicion.

Practice is different: 'communities of practice' draw heavily on lateral links. Because their activities take place in the same context, members share common routines, languages and stories, and have a common history. Spontaneity is a key element. Ideally there is collaborative problem solving and collective participation in the solution. Narration (storytelling) is a key approach, as is improvisation. Therefore life is much more complex in practice than is expected by those who focus on process. You may gather from the illustrations (Figure 4.3) where our preferences lie. For someone entrusted with management and control – such as public research administrators – life would be much easier if reality closely followed their view of process. If they are shown what reality is like they have to be prevented from taking re-engineering actions that will destroy much of the 'community of practice', together with its vitality and creative power.[4]

Practice	**Process**
	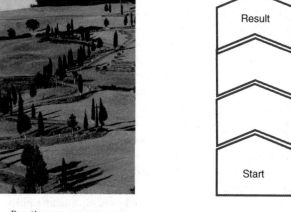

Figure 4.3   Practice versus process

Culture

Care is needed if the community being investigated differs from what the public administration body expects in terms of values and ways of doing things. According to Gibb (1999), government bodies look for accountability, information, clear demarcation, control measures, formal standards, transparency and hierarchy. In contrast the research communities managed by public administration bodies tend to be informal constructs requiring self-organised interaction processes and a great deal of freedom in order to generate, share and use knowledge successfully (Nonaka and Konno, 1998). In order to bridge the gap it is necessary to encourage interaction between the principal and the inter-viewees. There is no other way of gaining acceptance of the research results.[5]

Use of results

Qualitative researchers seem to draw a lot of their motivation not only from fieldwork, lengthy and collaborative interpretative work (that is never covered by tight project budgets) and 'thick' description but also from being in a position to voice what members of the com-munity think and feel. In particular, positive experiences with, and shortcomings of, the services delivered to the community by public authorities will be brought up. They are expected to further improve service offerings. Motivation also arises from accidental findings (serendipity) with a high information value to the principal. The commitment felt by the study team and the interviewees makes it especially difficult to cope with a principal's non-acceptance, negation or even dismissal of results.

This may even come down to a 'role conflict' for the qualitative researcher. The greater the bonding that takes place in the field, the more difficult it becomes for the researcher to convey that his or her findings are the result of sound analysis of data. Experience tells us that one should refrain from showing enthusiasm for the ideas generated since this will have a negative impact on your credibility when it comes to selling new information to public authorities.

Policy making is a multidimensional, multifaceted process that goes through interdependent cycles (Rist, 1994, p. 546). Activities are bounded and constrained by time, funds, political support and so on, and often do not come to a close. According to Rist (1994), choosing not to decide is a frequent outcome.[6]

Implications, conclusions and recommendations

As a result of our own reflections and discussions with members of the other study team and participants in a conference, plus the process of writing this chapter, we have come up with three sets of conclusions.

Documentation and research needs

There is little tradition of publicly documenting and sharing presentation experiences in principal–agent settings, but discussion and analysis of real presentation experiences is greatly needed. In order to address the practical issues involved in presenting qualitative research results, greater documentation of such events is required. Moreover details of less successful presentations would be of major help to the learning process.

Open space technology (Owen, 1997a, 1997b, 2000) deserves greater use in qualitative research – at present the discussion is mainly restricted to unresolved methodological questions about the validity of findings.

Issues to consider when doing a qualitative study in a principal–agent setting

First, case-based reasoning can lead to a role conflict for the researcher. He or she will be well advised to carefully balance neutral reporting of data (researcher's role) with suggesting improvements (the role attributed to a consultant).

Second, a single, knowledgeable, wise principal is an unlikely prospect. Public policy decision making is usually a multiperson process in which the complexity of your report is easily lost. In unfriendly settings (for example when these are conflicts of interest) a qualitative study runs a considerable risk of being devalued.

Third, the support of and full participation by the principal, preferably the head of department, is vital. It is important to ensure that there are plenty of opportunities for interaction. Otherwise your suggestions will be disregarded and, as the saying goes, 'the audience will have you for breakfast'[7]. Enthusiasm and partisanship are not necessarily ideal ingredients when it comes to selling new information, so it might be helpful to find audiences other than the principal to discuss surprising results, share your enthusiasm and maintain motivation.

Finally, the public authorities that govern research have the right to their own perceptions, interpretations and programme decisions – even if these are contrary to your research results.

Recommendations and warnings

Practice-oriented research is rewarding for the researcher but risky for the public administration body in question. The researcher should make sure that everybody is kept informed and offers feedback.

Everybody must understand what is being done. The job is to describe practice, not to evaluate somebody's management or administrative skills or the quality of a programme. (But if it is, say so as a matter of fairness.)

Organising joint meetings between members of the community studied and representatives of the principal can have a very positive effect on trust and the acceptability of the findings.

It pays for the researcher to strip his or her results to the point where it hurts. Before preparing the presentation the researcher should find out about the audience and their preferences as this will help to communicate the results in an appropriate way. It is probable that more than one presentation will be needed to cover all expectations.

We believe that the above suggestions will help to make Rist's (1994) optimistic statement come true: 'The policy community is, I believe, ready for ... anything those in the qualitative research community could offer, should they choose to make the effort to do so.'

Notes

1. For further details see Norris (1997), Mahon (1999), Braun (2001), Meinhard *et al.* (2002).
2. For further details see Brunner *et al.* (1993), Swanson *et al.* (1997), Aigner and Meinhard (2002).
3. For further details see Ducharme *et al.* (1995), Gummesson (2000).
4. For further details see Osterloh and Grand (1999).
5. For further details see Powel (1991).
6. For further details see Bakken (1993), Huber *et al.* (1995), Aigner *et al.* (2002), Kurz *et al.* (2002).
7. Lyn Richards (personal communication, 2000) puts it differently: 'Think twice about doing qualitative research in unfriendly settings.'

References

Aigner, W. and Meinhard, D. (2002) 'New and emerging good practice of regional innovation clusters to university–industry and university–government interaction. Reflections on findings from good-practice-cases documented for European Space Research and Technology Centre (ESTEC)', *The 4th Triple Helix Conference-Book of Abstracts* (Copenhagen: Department of Management, Politics and Philosophy, Copenhagen Business School), p. 160.

Aigner, W., Meinhard, D. and Berndorfer, J. (2002) 'How role perception and role attribution hinder successful university–industry and university–government interaction in cooperative research and development projects', *The 4th Triple Helix Conference-Book of Abstracts* (Copenhagen: Department of Management, Politics and Philosophy, Copenhagen Business School), p. 17.

Bakken, B. E. (1993) 'Learning and Transfer of Understanding in Dynamic Decision Environments', PhD dissertation, Sloan School of Management, Massachusetts Institute of Technology, January.

Becker, H. S. (1998) *Tricks of the Trade: How to Think About Your Research While You're Doing It* (Chicago, Ill: University of Chicago Press).

Braun, T. (2001) *Der komplexe Manager. Systemische Perspektiven* (Norderstedt: BoG).

Brown, J. S. and Duguid, P. (2000) *The Social Life of Information* (Boston, Mass.: Harvard Business School Press), pp. 95–7.

Brunner, K.-M., Jost, G. and Lueger, M. (1993) 'Kommunikative Informationsgewinnung in der Wirtschaft: Perspektiven qualitativer Sozialforschung', in R. Eschenbach (ed.), *Forschung für die Wirtschaft. Im Mittelpunkt: Der Mensch* (Vienna: Service Fachverlag), pp. 223–31.

Chenail, R. J. (1995) 'Presenting qualitative data', *The Qualitative Report*, vol. 2, no. 3 (http://www.nova.edu/ssss/QR/QR2-3/presenting.html).

Constas, M. A. (1992) 'Qualitative analysis as a public event: The documentation of category development procedures', *American Educational Research Journal*, vol. 29, pp. 253–66.

Crozier, M. (2001) 'The Crisis of Complexity', in R. Viale (ed.), *Knowledge and Politics* (Heidelberg: Physica), pp. 147–52.

Doney, P. M. and Armstrong, G. M. (1996) 'Effects of Accountability on Symbolic Information Search and Information Analysis by Organizational Buyers', *Journal of the Academy of Marketing Science*, vol. 24, no. 1, pp. 57–65.

Ducharme, M. K., Licklider, B. L., Matthes, W. A. and Vannatta, R. A. (1995) *Conceptual and Analysis Criteria: A Process for Identifying Quality Educational Research* (Des Moines, IA: The FINE Foundation) (http://www.iptv.org/FINELINK/publications/coutline.html).

Gibb, A. A. (1999) 'SME Policy, Academic Research and the Growth of Ignorance,' *International Small Business Journal*, vol. 18, no. 3, pp. 13–35.

Gladwell, M. (2000) *The Tipping Point: How Little Things Can Make a Big Difference* (New York: Little, Brown).

Gummesson, E. (2000) *Qualitative Methods in Management Research* (London: Sage).

Huber, G. P., Glick, W. H. and Waller, M. J. (1995) 'Functional background as a determinant of executives' selective perception', *Academy of Management Journal*, vol. 38, no. 4, pp. 943–74.

Kurz, A., Aigner, W., Berndorfer, J. and Stockhammer, C. (2002) 'On the usefulness of a GUI/Triple Helix framing when designing effective technology stimulation policies', *The 4th Triple Helix Conference-Book of Abstracts* (Copenhagen: Department of Management, Politics and Philosophy, Copenhagen Business School), p. 58.

Lincoln, Y. S. and Guba, E. G. (1985) *Naturalistic Inquiry* (Beverly Hills, CA: Sage).

Lomas, J. (2000) 'Connecting Research and Policy', *Canadian Journal of Policy Research* vol. 1, no. 1, pp. 140–4.

Mahon, C. J. (1999) *Charting Complexity* (Copenhagen: New Social Science Monographs, Institute of Organisation and Industrial Sociology, Copenhagen Business School).

Massey, A. (1996) 'Using the literature: 3×4 analogies', *The Qualitative Report*, vol. 2, no. 4 (http://www.nova.edu/ssss/QR/QR2-4/massey.html).

May, K. (1997) 'The politicking of research results: Presenting qualitative findings in the public arena', in J. Morse (ed.), *Completing a Qualitative Project: Details and Dialogue* (Thousand Oaks, CA: Sage), pp. 329–44.

Meinhard, D., Aigner, W. and Kurz, A. (2002) 'Marketing: European Models of Self-Organization of Networks and Innovation: Lessons from C.O.S.T.', *The 4th Triple Helix Conference-Book of Abstracts* (Copenhagen: Department of Management, Politics and Philosophy, Copenhagen Business School), p. 90.

Miles, M. B. and Huberman, A. M. (1994) *Qualitative Data Analysis: An Expanded Sourcebook* (Thousand Oaks, CA: Sage).

Moorman, C., Deshpandé, R. and Zaltman, G. (1993) 'Factors Affecting Trust in Market Research Relationships', *Journal of Marketing*, vol. 57 (January), pp. 81–101.

Morse, J. (ed.) (1997) *Completing a Qualitative Project: Details and Dialogue* (Thousand Oaks, CA: Sage).

Morse, J. and Richards, L. (2002) *Read Me First for a User's Guide to Qualitative Methods* (Thousand Oaks, CA: Sage).

Nonaka, I. and Konno, N. (1998) 'The Concept of "Ba". Building a Foundation for Knowledge Creation', *California Management Review*, vol. 40, no. 3, pp. 40–54.

Norris, J. (1997) 'Meaning through form: Alternative modes of knowledge representation', in J. Morse (ed.), *Completing a Qualitative Project: Details and Dialogue* (Thousand Oaks, CA: Sage), pp. 87–115.

Osterloh, M. and Grand, S. (1999) 'Praxis der Theorie – Theorie der Praxis: Zum Verhältnis von Alltagstheorien des Managements und Praktiken der theoretischen Forschung', in B. Schreyögg (ed.), *Organisation und Postmoderne* (Wiesbaden: Gabler), pp. 349–63.

Owen, H. (1997a) *Expanding our Now, The Story of Open Space Technology* (San Francisco, CA: Berrett-Koehler).

Owen, H. (1997b) *Open Space Technology* (San Francisco, CA: Berrett-Koehler).

Owen, H. (2000) 'Mission: control?', *The Journal for Quality & Participation*, February, pp. 26–9.

Powel, W. W. (1991) 'Neither market nor hierarchy: network forms of organization', in G. Thompson, J. Frances and R. Levacici (eds), *Markets, Hierarchies & Networks. The Coordination of Social Life* (Thousand Oaks, CA: Sage), pp. 265–77.

Richards, T. J. and Richards, L. (1994) 'Using Computers in Qualitative Research', in N. K. Denzin and Y. S. Lincoln (eds), *Handbook of Qualitative Research* (London: Sage), pp. 445–62.

Rist, R. C. (1994) 'Influencing the Policy Process with Qualitative Research', in N. K. Denzin and Y. S. Lincoln (eds), *Handbook of Qualitative Research* (Thousand Oaks, CA: Sage), pp. 545–57.

Rubin, H. J. and Rubin, I. S. (1995) *Qualitative Interviewing, The Art of Hearing Data* (Thousand Oaks, CA: Sage).

Senge, P. and Scharmer, O. (2001) 'Community Action Research: Learning as a Community of Practitioners, Consultants and Researchers', in P. Reason and H. Bradbury (eds), *Handbook of Action Research* (Thousand Oaks, CA: Sage), pp. 238–49.

Swanson, J., Durham, R. and Albright, J. (1997) 'Clinical utilization/application of qualitative research', in J. Morse, *Completing a Qualitative Project: Details and Dialogue* (Thousand Oaks, CA: Sage), pp. 87–115.

von Hippel, E. (2001) 'Perspective: User toolkits for innovation', *Journal of Product Innovation Management*, vol. 18, no. 4, pp. 247–57.

Wallendorf, M. and Belk, R. W. (1989) 'Assessing Trustworthiness in Naturalistic Consumer Research', in E. C. Hirschman (ed.), *Interpretive Consumer Research* (Provo, UT: Association for Consumer Research), p. 69.

Wigzell, J. (1989) 'It's not just what you say; it's also the way you present it', in S. Robson and A. Foster (eds), *Qualitative Research in Action* (London: Edward Arnold), pp. 100–13.

Zaltman, G. and Higie, R. A. (1993) *Seeing the Voice of the Customer: The Zaltman Metaphor Elicitation Technique*, Report no. 93–144 (Cambridge, Mass: Marketing Science Institute).

5
Exploring Buying Decisions in Hypermarkets by Means of Thinking Aloud Protocols

Astrid Spranz

Introduction

Austria's two leading hypermarket chains are fighting a hard battle to win customers' favour. Therefore product ranges are constantly expanding and in-store presentations are becoming more and more sophisticated. A good example of product development is wine. With an average annual per capita consumption of 35 litres, Austrians are dedicated wine lovers (ÖWM, 2000, p. 86). Imported wine accounts for about 20 per cent of total consumption, about half which comes from the neighbouring country of Italy (ÖWM, 2000, p. 88). The two main hypermarkets, which together account for more than 60 per cent of all hypermarket sales, have spent huge sums on promoting their wine ranges. Both have equipped their stores with wooden wine shelves and vineyard-style decorations. In March 2002 they offered about 170 varieties, with slight differences in their respective product mixes. The average size of the Italian wine section was about six metres long and five shelves high (containing about 80 per cent of red wines and 20 per cent of white and rosé). However neither chain offered much point of sale information and there was hardly any information on the products' characteristics on the bottles themselves. On what factors, then, did customers base their choice of Italian red wines?

The study reported here was aimed at providing marketing managers with insights into their customers' shopping decisions. The research design included thinking aloud protocols, qualitative interviews and covert observation. The goals were to gain access to (1) customers' thoughts on the decision-making process via concurrent verbalisation,

(2) customers' self-reflection on their buying behaviour, and (3) additional information on customers' satisfaction, complaints and suggestions via unstructured interviews. The study was carried out in a Viennese hypermarket during closing hours. The task given to the research participants was to think of an event when Italian red wine would be needed. Then, when choosing the wine for the chosen event the individuals were asked to 'think aloud'. Their verbalised thoughts were recorded and they were also filmed by two hidden video cameras. When the task had been completed the participants were interviewed about their experiences during the experiment. Analysis of the verbal data obtained by the protocols and interviews was assisted by the software NVivo. The findings show that the qualitative techniques used in the study can produce a huge quantity of information that is usually not revealed by quantitative methods. The thinking aloud protocol, which is a rather neglected method in European marketing research, proved very fruitful and can be highly recommended for consumer behaviour research.

The study and its goals

In addition to the main research topic (the basis of customers' choice of Italian red wines), several other points of interest arose during the study's evolution. When it was decided to follow a qualitative approach, further areas of investigation were suggested, such as getting feedback from the interviewees about their convenience with the methods used. In addition, a qualitative research is characterised by a conscious interaction and cooperation between the researcher and the subject (Solomon *et al.*, 1999, pp. 24 f.), and as we shall see below, the relaxed, teamwork-like approach worked quite well. The test shoppers would also be encouraged to talk freely about the product group in question, the experimental situation, their personal opinions and their prior experiences (both negative and positive).

To summarise, the experimental setting was designed to focus on the following points:

- Gaining insights into individual buying decisions and revealing aspects of the choice heuristics or rules of thumb used by customers (Bettman, 1979, p. 18).
- Self-reflection by the research participants (the test shoppers) on their buying decision.
- Exploration of the participants' personal wants and needs.

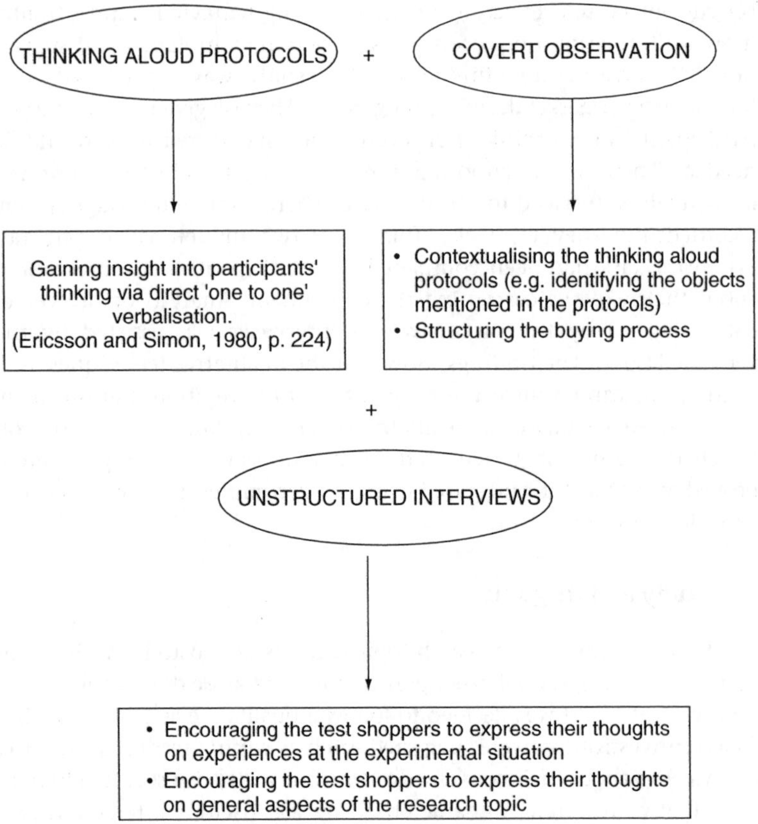

THINKING ALOUD PROTOCOLS   +   COVERT OBSERVATION

Gaining insight into participants'
thinking via direct 'one to one'
verbalisation.
(Ericsson and Simon, 1980, p. 224)

- Contextualising the thinking aloud
  protocols (e.g. identifying the objects
  mentioned in the protocols)
- Structuring the buying process

+

UNSTRUCTURED INTERVIEWS

- Encouraging the test shoppers to express their thoughts
  on experiences at the experimental situation
- Encouraging the test shoppers to express their thoughts
  on general aspects of the research topic

Figure 5.1   The combination of methods selected for the study

Methodology

A qualitative approach seemed most suitable for the study as it offered
techniques to 'get inside the consumer's head' (Green *et al.*, 2000, p. 17).
The chosen methods are shown in Figure 5.1.

In the late 1970s and early 1980s, thinking aloud protocols were used
quite frequently in the United States and were often discussed in the
literature (Bettman, 1970, 1979; Bettman and Park, 1980; Ericsson and
Simon, 1980; Biehal and Chakravarti, 1982). However in the German-
speaking scientific community this method never gained a foothold – it

was hardly mentioned in the literature on methodological theory (Kepper, 1994; Flick, 1998) and rarely implemented (Kaas and Hofacker, 1983; Meyer *et al.*, 1996).

Bettman (1970, 1979) grounded his well-known theory on information processing on a very extensive study using thinking aloud protocols. He defines a thinking aloud protocol as instructing the subject to think aloud when performing the task in question, such as shopping or choosing among alternatives (Bettman, 1979, p. 195). In contrast to retrospective reports (that is, verbalising cognitive processes that have occurred in the past), thinking aloud protocols involve concurrent verbalisation of cognitive processes. 'With this procedure, the heeded information may be verbalised either through direct articulation or by verbal encoding of information that was originally stored in a nonverbal code. With the instruction to verbalise, a direct trace is obtained of the heeded information, and hence, an indirect one of the internal stages of the cognitive process' (Ericsson and Simon, 1980, p. 220).

Covert observation, on the other hand, is a classical technique in consumer behaviour research. The observation can be conducted directly by a researcher who is unknown to the subjects or indirectly by means of a camera. It can take place in either natural or contrived environments. It is argued that in natural environments the subjects tend to be more relaxed and thus provide a truer picture of the phenomenon in question (Boote and Mathews, 1999, p. 19). Boote and Mathews (ibid., p. 20) point out that 'by using observation, market researchers can record what consumers actually do, not what they claim to have done.' However this ignores interpretation on the part of the observer. It is important to stress this point because it was of crucial importance in the study discussed in this chapter. Different observers will interpret the same phenomenon differently and overlook some aspects – there are numerous ways of looking at visual data and interpreting it. Some qualitative researchers have criticised the use of covert observation not only for ethical reasons but also for 'the systematic restraint on disclosing the interior perspective of the field and of the observed persons' (Flick, 1998, p. 141; see also Kepper, 1994, p. 118). Both views are widely discussed in the literature and agreed with in this chapter. Therefore the use of covert observation was very limited in our study. Nonetheless it was indispensable as it provided the contextual data needed to make the thinking aloud protocols comprehensible, as had been revealed in the pretest.

Unstructured interviews are very commonly used in qualitative research and therefore require no detailed description here. In our case their inclusion in the methodological mix was very important as the test shoppers' retrospective descriptions of their experiences during the experiment and their views on anything else that came into their minds in respect of the research topic added richness to the data.

The setting

When thinking about a setting that would suit the complexity of the research topic, several basic problems had to be taken into consideration.

First, in a natural setting such as a busy hypermarket, thinking aloud by the test shoppers would be inhibited by the presence of other shoppers and staff. Therefore a situation in which the test shoppers would feel comfortable had to be created. An empty hypermarket during closing hours was regarded as a suitable compromise.

Second, the possibility of a researcher accompanying the test shoppers during the shopping exercise was considered as this would allow the researcher to ask questions about the participants' cognitive processes while this method had been used in some important research projects,[1] we decided to adopt a non-participatory approach and leave the test shoppers alone.[2]

Third, investigation of a particular product group – in our case, Italian red wines – ideally required a task that would involve those products alone. On the other hand the participants should feel free to choose. Therefore the wording of the task had to involve both freedom of choice and focus on the product category.

Finally, the experimental situation should not differ too much from what would happen in everyday life, so the task of buying Italian red wine had to be embedded in a broader context that would enable the participants to feel familiar with the process.

Based on the above considerations the following procedure evolved. Outside opening hours the participants were led to the hypermarket entrance and given the following instructions: 'Please think of an event for which you would need Italian red wine. The event will take place tomorrow. Take your time to think about it, then briefly describe the event. (At this point the participants' were given time to write down their descriptions.) Now, please take a trolley and buy all the things you need for your chosen event. While doing so, please say out loud everything that comes into your mind. Verbalise your thoughts loudly and clearly, and have fun!' They were then handed a small microphone and taperecorder and reminded to think aloud. In the Italian wine section they were filmed by two hidden cameras so that the direction of their glances and the bottles they touched and/or examined in more detail could be recorded.[3] After they had finished the task they went to the cashier, where they received a receipt.

The interviews were conducted immediately afterwards in the store's cafeteria. This location was chosen because it would enable us to create a casual atmosphere and ensure that the participants' impressions were fresh. The interviews were casual dialogues with no specific structure, lacking even an interview guide. If an interesting point emerged it was examined in depth. Considerable room was left for narratives and flexibility on the part of both interviewer and the interviewees. The latter were free to say as much or as little as they liked and were not pressed to continue if they felt they had said all that they could.

In total (excluding the pretests), 10 individuals aged 22–62 took part in the experiment. The sample was balanced in terms of age range and gender (five women, five men). As the experiment would be rather time-consuming and confined to certain hours, willingness to participate had been the main criterion when drawing the sample.

Data analysis

In qualitative research data analysis is a continuous, creative, interpretative and open-ended process. Several coding schemes have been developed to facilitate connections between certain theories and the data collected (such as information processing theory – Bettman and Park, 1980). In our study the focus of the coding and categorisation process was the usefulness of the results for practitioners rather than adherence to the rigid framework of theoretical perfection. The software NVivo was used to facilitate verbal data management – that is, the storage, indexing and retrieval of the data (Maclaran and Catterall, 2002, p. 30).

NVivo offers a couple of features that help the researcher to link and recontextualise the data at any point during the data analysis process: the importation and integration of multimedia files can easily be effected, and coding and categorising is not bound to a certain sequence. This means that the researcher is free to choose any coding, categorisation and linking process she or he desires, and according to the time available and complexity required (Richards, 2000, pp. 14 f.).

The data obtained from the exercise described above consisted of eight thinking aloud protocols and ten relatively brief interviews, plus nine videos.[4] The verbal protocols and interviews were transcribed and the resulting text was imported into NVivo.[5] As the research topic was restricted to Italian red wine, only text on wine was incorporated. The data was coded according to the topics mentioned and commented upon in order to reveal interesting items on point of sale, preferred wines, brands and so on (free nodes).

After several attempts to bundle and structure the free nodes into tree nodes, a coding scheme emerged out of the data. The tree nodes were named according to their basic topics, such as 'product', 'store and company', 'situation', 'perceived risks of acquisition', and so on. Then the thinking aloud protocol documents were examined for hierarchies of importance, for example (1) brand, (2) type of wine, (3) price and so on. Obvious strategies and verbalised (and therefore conscious) rules of thumb were noted such as 'I always take that one' or 'I always take the most expensive one, so I am sure that it will be okay.' Next the participants' video-recorded movements in the wine section were written down to complete the picture of their areas of interest.

The final step was to summarize the results in such a way as to make them presentable to the managers. To this end the report was split into two main parts: a general part containing interesting general statements (for example about the store and the company) in the form of quotations and descriptions of observed behaviour at the point of sale; and a summary of the main aspects of the individual behaviour of the 10 test shoppers – their strategies, attitudes, physical movements when choosing wine, thoughts and ideas on the point of sale and the product line, and so on. The latter was designed to give marketers an impression of the very personal character of their customers and the qualitative approach of the study.

The results

The results contained a couple of surprises. With regard to the methodology, all the test shoppers were motivated and entertained by the task and the experimental situation in general. The fact that they had been left alone to do the task turned out to be a crucial factor in their sense of case. Some had been disturbed by staff and reported that these encounters had made them feel 'stupid' or 'crazy'. On the other hand the experience of being alone in a supermarket and feeling free to talk aloud were positively evaluated ('It reminded me of shopping in the USA last summer. I was alone in the supermarket at 4 a.m. great!') The tape recordings indicated that some participants had forgotten they were in an experimental situation, while others directed jokes at the microphone or made comments such as 'Uhm, actually I'm not thinking at all, I'm just looking.' During the decision-making process, however, they all seemed to concentrate on the task, as indicated by changes in intonation, unfinished sentences, unusual slang expressions and so on.

When asked about their perceived differences between the experimental situation and everyday life, most of the participants stated that the option of choosing their own event (for example a candlelit dinner for two with pasta and Chianti) had made the situation so natural that the task could be easily fulfilled.

With regard to results of interest for marketing managers, the following examples illustrate the – sometimes stunning – benefits of exploratory mixed-method research.

First, reading the information on bottles or shelves is problematic for long-sighted people. Older people are a very important target group for wine sales and it is they who are most likely to have a problem with eyesight. The test shoppers aged 50 or more found it difficult to read the price tags and wine labels, so their purchases were limited to familiar products or proved to be an adventure because they could not figure out what they were buying or at what price (a big surprise at the checkout!) This problem was also evident in the video-recorded data, which showed typical means of attempting to read small type, such as holding the bottle at arm's-length.

Second, lack of proper organisation is a common phenomenon in hypermarket wine shelves, with products either being missing or placed behind the wrong shelf labels and price cards. This is unacceptable to customers and can lead to stress and anger. The only way to check on a price is to carry the bottle to the cashier, who can find out the price on the scanner.

Finally, some interesting personal strategies were revealed in the study. For example one male test shopper in his early forties looked for and bought the highest priced wine because he considered himself a poor wine expert. According to his thinking aloud protocol and unstructured interview, the only way he could be confident about his choice was to pay a high price. This strategy was the only one in which price came first. The other individuals put more emphasis on aesthetic appearance, type of wine, brand, alcohol content and so on, the ranking of each of these depending on the individual.

In summary, there is no 'most important' product characteristic in wine marketing – every consumer has his or her personal selection criteria, which vary considerably with situational and personal circumstances. It is vital for marketing managers to pay more attention to display and to provide as much legible information as possible about the products. At the moment customers are faced by a jungle of bottles, upon which little or no information is available.

Methodological conclusions

The use of thinking aloud protocols has been criticised in the literature in terms of possible self-sensorship or inability to express thoughts. In this respect, thinking aloud protocols may not reflect what the participants are actually thinking (Bettman, 1979, p. 195). Moreover actions that have been repeated so often that they have become automatic might not be reported, or at least not fully reported. In addition, with very difficult tasks or other actions for which complex cognitive processes are required, participants may cease to verbalise in order to concentrate on cognition (Ericsson and Simon, 1980, pp. 248 f.) One criticism levelled even by researchers who are in favour of the method is the trade-off between speedy execution of the task and concurrent verbalisation. This has been noted in several studies and must be taken into consideration when adopting the method (Ericsson and Simon, 1980, p. 230).

During our interviews some of the participants mentioned that the act of thinking aloud had made them more aware of their own cognitive processes. Some also reported a new awareness of particular stimuli (such as labels bearing symbols of the sun), and of reacting to these more than to others. In this exploratory study, feedback on the individuals' state of mind was welcome and sometimes surprising. Even the participants were surprised at their own behaviour and ways of thinking, evaluating and deciding. It must be stressed that the insights gained by the participants might rebound and their behaviour could change, and that the study concentrated on a single decision at a single point in time. Follow-up studies and a more extensive investigation of customers' behaviour would provide more detailed, more generisable findings.

Another important shortcoming concerns the setting and the task. There is no evidence that the participants normally bought wine in a hypermarket. Some might have preferred other distribution channels or bought directly from Italian producers during their summer holidays. Others might not have bought wines without expert assistance. We simply do not know. Hence the 'natural situation' might actually have been contrived. Also the fact that the participants did not have to buy the selected wines because it was only a game could have caused a strong bias ('There is nothing to lose so let's take the most expensive one.') However the prices of the wines chosen were quite moderate.

Personal conclusions

The project was an exciting experience for all those involved. The thinking aloud protocols proved capable of producing masses of rich data, and in combination with observational material they were a source of very complex information. I am convinced that the data collected during this project could keep an interdisciplinary team occupied for some time. The combination of thinking aloud protocols, covert observation and unstructured interviews can be highly recommended not only in respect of information gathering for marketing purposes, but also for research projects whose main point of interest is to gain insights into customers' shopping experiences. Thinking aloud protocols offer a very comprehensive description of the processes shoppers go through. Moreover, in my experience they can be very helpful in showing interested parties (for example marketing managers) what qualitative research is all about.

Notes

1. For example Ericsson and Simon (1980, pp. 230 f.) and Bettman's major project (Bettman, 1970).
2. Besides the desirability of allowing the participants to make 'natural' decisions, interventions by the researcher could be counter productive in the following way: 'If forced to give reasons for their recognition of a particular stimulus, subjects, lacking direct knowledge of the actual retrieval cues simply speculate and make the same kinds of inferences about the cues that observers would make' (Ericsson and Simon, 1980, p. 252).
3. The existence of the cameras was revealed only after the shopping exercise had been completed.
4. Some of the data fell victim to technical problems and bottles were chosen in areas other than the one filmed.
5. The data recorded on the audio tapes were transcribed word for word with remarks on intonation, pauses so on. The thinking aloud protocols were constantly checked in context with the videos, so that unusual movements and degree of product examination could be taken into account (and referred to as memos or links in the data).

References

Bettman, J. R. (1970) 'Information Processing Models of Consumer Behavior', *Journal of Marketing Research*, vol. 7 (August), pp. 370–6.

Bettman, J. R. (1979) *An Information Processing Theory* (Reading, Mass.: Addison-Wesley).

Bettman, J. R. and Park, C. W. (1980) 'Effects of Prior Knowledge and Experience and Phase of the Choice Process on Consumer Decision Processes: A Protocol Analysis', *Journal of Consumer Research*, vol. 7 (December), pp. 234–48.

Bettman, J. R. and Zins, M. A. (1977) 'Constructive Processes in Consumer Choice', *Journal of Consumer Research*, vol. 4 (September), pp. 75–85.

Biehal, G. and Chakravarti, D. (1982) 'Experiences with the Bettman–Park Verbal-Coding Scheme', *Journal of Consumer Research*, vol. 8 (March), pp. 442–8.

Boote, J. and Mathews, A. (1999) 'Saying is one thing; doing is another: the role of observation in marketing research', *Qualitative Market Research: An International Journal*, vol. 2, no. 1, pp. 15–21.

Ericsson, K. A. and Simon, H. A. (1980) 'Verbal Reports as Data', *Psychological Review*, vol. 87, no. 3, pp. 215–51.

Flick, U. (1998) *An Introduction to Qualitative Research* (London: Sage).

Green, P. E., Wind, Y., Krieger, A. M. and Saatsoglou, P. (2000) 'Applying qualitative data', *Marketing Research*, vol. 12, no. 1, pp. 17–25.

Kaas, K. P. and Hofacker, T. (1983) 'Informationstafeln und Denkprotokolle-Bestandsaufnahme und Entwicklungsmöglichkeiten der Prozessverfolgungstechniken', in Forschungsgruppe Konsum und Verhalten (ed.), *Innovative Marktforschung* (Würzburg and Vienna: Physica), pp. 75–103.

Kepper, G. (1994) *Qualitative Marktforschung* (Wiesbaden: DUV).

Maclaran, P. and Catterall, M. (2002) 'Analysing qualitative data: computer software and the market research practitioner', *Qualitative Market Research: An International Journal*, vol. 5, no. 1, pp. 28–39.

Meyer, M., Buber, R. and Al-Roubaie, A. (1996) 'Cultural Events: Konsumentscheidungsprozesse analysiert mit Protokollen lauten Denkens', *Medienpsychologie*, vol. 8, no. 2, pp. 90–116.

ÖWM (Österreichisches Weinmarketing Service GmbH) (2000) Dokumentation Österreichischer Wein 2001. Wien: ÖWM.

Richards, L. (2000) *Using NVivo in Qualitative Research* (Melbourne: QSR International).

Solomon, M., Bamossy, G. and Askegaard, S. (1999) *Consumer Behaviour – A European Perspective* (London: Prentice-Hall).

6

The Impact of Internet Use on Interfirm Relationships in Australian Service Industries

Sally Rao and Chad Perry

Introduction

The impact of the Internet on business is growing worldwide (Hayes, 1999; *Economist*, 2000). Indeed business-to-business transactions account for over 80 per cent of all Internet transactions (ABS, 2001), totalling more than US$400 billion in 2000 and an estimated US$2 trillion in 2003 (Global Internet Statistics, 2001). While practitioners are realising the potential offered by the Internet to build profitable, long-term relationships with their trading partners (Hamill, 1998, 2000; Seybold, 1999), the topic has received little attention from marketing scholars.

Australia is one of the world's leading countries in Internet use in both business-to-customer (B2C) and business-to-business (B2B) settings. Recently the focus of e-commerce in Australia has shifted from B2C to the effective use of e-commerce tools to make business processes and B2B relationships more efficient (NOIE, 2001). However there appears to have been no investigation of this phenomenon in an organisational context, and in the context of Australian organisations in particular. Given the recency of the phenomenon the usual methods of marketing research, such as surveys or focus groups, cannot be used to investigate it because there are simply not enough respondents available and the foci of the methods are not clear. Hence the study reported in this chapter used the relatively new, qualitative methodology of convergent interviewing to investigate how B2B Internet usage affects interfirm relationships in service industries.

The following sections address research issues in the literature, describe the methodology of convergent interviewing and present the findings of the research, together with a new theoretical framework that integrates the findings.

Research issues

Before the interviews with experts and practitioners began, some preliminary issues in respect of relationship marketing and B2B Internet marketing were identified in the literature (Anderson and Narus, 1984; Sheth and Parvatiyar, 1995; Araujo and Easton, 1996; Hagel and Singer, 1999; Peppers *et al.*, 1999).

Relevantly for this research, the interactivity offered by the Internet allows for personalisation and thus provides unique opportunities for relationship marketing to be practiced at a one-to-one level (Geiger and Martin, 1999; Gillenson *et al.*, 1999; Peppers *et al.*, 1999). Researchers have identified and categorised a number of elements in relationship exchange processes, using terms such as technical and social elements (for example Perry *et al.*, 2002; Rao and Perry, 2002) and structural and social bonds (for example Mattson, 1985; Turnbull and Wilson, 1989; Gordon, 1998; Buttle and Ahmad, 1999). Technical elements include communication and interdependency, while social elements include trust and commitment.

With regard to how the Internet can be used effectively in a B2B context, the Internet can be placed in the technological context of emerging interactive marketing technologies that have a profound effect on the way companies do business (Hoffman and Novak, 1996). In particular, B2B internet marketing is concerned with business-to-business communications and transactions conducted via networked computers. B2B Internet usage includes the use of all three topologies of e-commerce (Internet, Intranet and Extranet) to purchase goods and services, buy information and consulting services, and to submit requests for proposals and receive proposals (Kalakota and Whinston, 1997; Watson *et al.*, 2000). The Internet-based technologies provide effective, efficient and rapid ways for corporate buyers to gather information on available products and services, enable them to evaluate and negotiate with suppliers, facilitate ordering process and access to post-sales services (Wilson and Vlosky, 1998; Vlosky *et al.*, 2000). On the supplier's side, marketing, sales and service information can be readily gathered from customers (Archer and Yuan, 2000).

In brief, the literature suggests that B2B Internet usage emphasises the generation and exploitation of new business opportunities, plus the enhancement and transformation of interorganisational relationships in order to make business more efficient. However there seem to have been no empirical attempts to test the relationship-facilitating aspects of the Internet in a B2B situation. Indeed most of what is known about the potential for Internet-facilitated relationships seems to be anecdotal, experiential, *ad hoc* and descriptive (Peterson *et al.*, 1997). Hence there is a need to construct a comprehensive framework to summarise the relationship-facilitating aspects of the Internet in a B2B context. Based on the survey of the literature and the fact that the Internet is a communication medium, three questions drove the research reported below:

- What effect does Internet usage have on communication in an inter-firm relationship?
- What effect does Internet usage have on the technical and social elements of an interfirm relationship?
- What effect does Internet usage in an interfirm relationship have on business performance?

The qualitative, theory-building methodology of convergent interviewing

Justification for using the convergent interview methodology

Convergent interviewing is an in-depth interview technique with a structured data analysis process. It is used to collect, analyse and interpret qualitative information on a person's knowledge, opinions, experiences, attitudes and beliefs by means of a number of interviews that converge on important issues (Dick, 1990; Nair and Riege, 1995). The process itself is very structured, but the content of each interview only gradually becomes structured as this allows flexible exploration of the subject matter without determining the answers (Nair and Riege, 1995). In this way, more is learned about the issues involved (Dick, 1990).

Essentially, convergent interviewing is a series of in-depth interviews with experts. After each interview, the researcher refines the questions so that the subsequent interviews can converge on the emerging issues in a topic area. In our study, for example, when the first interview was conducted the researcher had only three questions about the research problem. From the analysis of this and succeeding interviews the researcher came up with more and more questions and developed an increasing understanding of the topic area. Probe questions were formulated after each interview so that agreements and disagreements among the interviewees about important information could be analysed. This process is illustrated in Table 6.1. The flexibility of convergent interviewing lies in this continuous refinement of content and process.

Table 6.1   An example matrix of agreements and disagreements about issues raised in five convergent interviews

| | Issue | | | | | | |
Interviewee	1	2	3	4	5	6	7
A	Yes	Yes	–	–	–	–	–
B	Agree	Disagree	Yes	Yes	–	–	–
C	Agree	Disagree	Agree	Agree	Yes	Yes	–
D	Agree	Disagree	Agree	Agree	Agree	–	Yes
E	Agree	Agree	Agree	Disagree	Agree	Agree	Agree

Notes: Interviewee A confirmed one issue (1) suggested in the literature and raised another (2). In the next interview, interviewee B agreed about one of these but disagreed with the other. She then raised issues 3 and 4, which were probed for agreement or disagreement in later interviews. In the interview with D there was no time to discuss issue 6, although a probe question had been formulated for the purpose. D had raised issue 7 early in the interview.
Source: Carson *et al.* (2001), p. 88.

In the early stage of theory building not much is known about the topic area. One or other of the convergent interviews, in-depth interviews or case studies can be used to refine research issues and reduce uncertainty about a research topic (King, 1996).

In-depth interviews versus convergent interviews

To show why convergent interviewing was chosen, this subsection discusses the strengths of convergent interviewing by comparing it with the more often used in-depth interview and case research techniques. The major characteristics of and differences between convergent interviews, in-depth interviews and case studies are shown in Table 6.2 and form the basis of the discussion. Essentially, we argue that convergent interviewing was more appropriate than in-depth interviews and case research because it provided a way of quickly converging on key issues in an emerging area, an efficient mechanism for data analysis after each interview, and a way of deciding when to stop collecting data.

In-depth interviews were not used for this research primarily because convergent interviewing offered a more structured way of processing interviews and analysing data (Table 6.2). That is, convergent interviews were considered more efficient than in-depth interviews for our exploratory research. The advantage that convergent interviewing has over in-depth interviewing is its cyclic nature, which enables the researcher continuously to refine the content and process of the interviews in order to narrow down broad research issues into more focused ones at

Table 6.2 Characteristics of convergent interviews, in-depth interviews and case studies

Characteristics	In-depth interviews	Convergent interviews	Case studies
Main objective	To obtain rich and detailed information	Narrow down research focus	Mainly theory building/ confirmation
Level of prior theory requirement	Low	Low	Medium to high
Process	Flexible – unstructured to structured	Structured process with continuous refinement	Structured standard procedures
Content	Unstructured to structured	Unstructured	Somewhat structured
Strengths	Replication	Cyclic	Replication
Weaknesses	Results may be biased and cannot be used for theory testing	Potential interviewer bias, depends on interviewer's knowledge, not sufficient on its own	Prior theory required

Source: Developed from Yin (1994) and Carson *et al*. (2001).

the end of the research programme (Dick, 1990). A series of 'successive approximations' (ibid., 1990, p. 3) arises from continuous refinement of the process (including the interviewing techniques and sample composition) and content (including research questions and the subject matter of the research) (ibid.; Carson *et al*., 2001). Our research began with a broad field of possible topics and ended with a focused one. In short, convergent interviewing was more suitable than in-depth interviews because it enabled 'the progressive reduction of uncertainty' (Philips and Pugh, 1987, p. 72).

Case research versus convergent interviews

The case research method was not used in our study mainly because there was insufficient prior theory about the integration of Internet and database marketing. While case research can be used to investigate a new research area or a contemporary phenomenon in a dynamically changing, real-life context (Eisenhardt, 1991; Yin, 1994; Carson *et al*., 2001) and is often appropriate for complex situations involving two or more people and/or their organisations, many researchers emphasise the importance of starting case research with a prior theory or 'pre-structure (Miles and Huberman, 1984, p. 17; Yin, 1994). Although some prior theory had been developed, as noted above, it was inadequate for developing questions for an interview guide, which in case research has to be applied consistently in most of the interviews. In a case research project a mix of induction and deduction may be required (Carson *et al.*, 2001). This is often achieved by incorporating convergent interviews into the first stage of a project to provide the prior theory for the development of the interview guide in the second stage (Perry, 2001).

Strengths and limitations of the convergent interviewing technique

Convergent interviewing offered three main strengths in respect of our research. First, convergent interviewing is useful for exploring areas that lack an established theoretical base, as was the case in our research. That is, the flexibility inherent in the convergent interviewing method allows for the refinement of research issues throughout the course of the interviews, resulting in consolidation of the existing body of knowledge and a more precisely defined research problem (Dick, 1990). Second, its flexibility means that all issues related to the research problem can be identified and explored. This allows the researcher to use a funnelling process in which he or she controls the flow of the type of information being sought. Third, the inherent subjectivity of qualitative data can be largely overcome if the interviewer examines the answers after each interview to 'disprove the emerging explanation of the data' (ibid., p. 11). That is, the subjective data collected from each interview was refined through the use of convergence and discrepancy emerged in the subsequent interviews. This added objectivity to the refining of subjective data. Thus rigor was added by limiting subjectivity (ibid.).

There are also limitations associated with the convergent interviewing technique (Woodward, 1997). First, interviewer bias may occur (Dick, 1990). To guard against this the interviewer must not only be skilful and experienced, but also have good knowledge of the subject matter and be able to maintain data quality when recording and analysing the data obtained from the interviews (Aaker and Day, 1990). In our study the researcher had received training in research studies, and had reviewed the literature on Internet and database marketing to obtain background knowledge prior to the interviews.

Second, the convergent interviewing method requires the interviewees to be knowledgeable about the subject matter of the research in order to contribute meaningful information to the exploratory research. In our study this requirement was addressed by using the snowballing technique (ibid.) to gain access to experts in Internet and database marketing. By the end of each interview the interviewee had become sufficiently familiar with the aims of the research to refer the researcher to other experts (it is advisable to ask for more than one name in order to reduce the chance of a project being locked into the mindset of one network).

Finally, convergent interviewing may affect the validity of the research because it is not sufficient on its own (Dick, 1990; Gummesson, 2001) to produce results that can be generalised to the wider population (Maykut and Morehouse, 1994; Marshall and Rossman, 1995). However the aim of our study was to build theory rather than to test theory, and the convergent interviews were used in conjunction with the survey method to validate the theory-building exercise.

On balance, then, for us the strengths of convergent interviewing largely outweighed its limitations.

Establishing the validity and reliability of convergent interviewing research

Validity and reliability in qualitative research can be achieved through forms of cross-checking. Such in-built checks and controls can be summarised as four tests of the research design (Table 6.3): construct validity, internal validity, external validity and reliability (Yin, 1994).

Construct validity refers to the formation of suitable operational measures for the concepts being investigated (Emory and Cooper, 1991). In our study, construct validity was achieved by means of three tactics. First, triangulation of the interview questions was established in the design stage by constructing two or more carefully worded questions that looked at Internet/database marketing from different angles. Second, our methodology included an in-built negative case analysis whereby, during and after each interview, the interviewer attempted to disprove explanations that were emerging from the data (Dick, 1990). Third, the flexibility offered by convergent interviewing allowed the interviewer to re-evaluate and redesign both the content and the process of the interview programme, thus establishing content validity.

Internal validity refers to causal relationships and the influence of one variable on other variables (Zikmund, 1984; Sekaran, 1992). In our study internal validity was achieved by purposeful sample selection on the basis of 'information richness' (Patton, 1990, p. 181), as described in some detail below.

Table 6.3   Tests for the validity and reliability of convergent interviewing

Test	Research design	Phase of research
Construct validity	• Data collected from multiple sources (convergent interviews and survey) provide multiple measures of the same phenomenon	Research design and data analysis
	• Triangulation of interview questions	Research design and data analysis
	• In-built negative case analysis	Data analysis
	• Flexibility of the proposed theoretical framework	Research design and data collection
Internal validity	• Sample selected for information richness	Research design
External validity	• Sample selected for theoretical replication	Research design
Reliability	• Interview guide developed for the collection of data	Data collection and analysis
	• Structured process for the administration and interpretation of convergent interviews	Research design, data collection and analysis
	• Use of a steering committee	Data collection

Source: Developed from Yin (1994), Healy and Perry (2000).

External validity concerns the ability to generalise the research findings beyond the immediate study (Emory and Cooper, 1991; Sekaran, 1992). In our study some external validity was achieved by selecting the interviewees from various areas of the Internet/database marketing field to ensure that a cross-section of opinions was obtained, thus achieving theoretical replication.

Reliability refers to how consistently a technique measures the concepts it is supposed to measure, enabling other researchers to repeat the study and obtain similar findings (Emory and Cooper, 1991; Sekaran, 1992). In our study reliability was secured by means of four tactics, the first two of which were structuring the convergent interviews and structuring the process of recording, writing and interpreting the data. The third tactic – the procedure recommended by Dick (1990), in which at least two interviewers conduct the interviews and work individually but in parallel – was adopted when a coresearcher was available. The fourth tactic was to use a steering committee to help with the design and administration of the interview programme (Guba and Lincoln, 1994). If a number of the members of the committee agreed about a phenomenon their collective judgment could be deemed as relatively objective. We also compared our findings with those of other researchers in the literature, so reliability was addressed as best it could be.

Implementing the convergent interviewing technique

Defining the information required

The first step of planning convergent interviews is to define the information required and the nature of the problem that has given rise to the research (Dick, 1990). As we lacked a firm prior theory (Perry, 1998), in our study an 'enfolding' of the literature approach was adopted (Eisenhardt, 1991, p. 25; Wollin, 1995). That is, the literature was reviewed while the field research was being done. In this process the researcher began with a few propositions and then allowed the data and enfolding literature to suggest new ways of shaping the body of knowledge as the interviews proceeded. The researcher started with a review of the literature on the parent disciplines of relationship and Internet marketing to develop background knowledge of the research subject, establish initial probe questions and select an appropriate group of interviewees (Nair and Riege, 1995). Insights gained from the first two interviews led to more focused literature reviews and helped the development of an initial theoretical framework.

Determining the sample size

The optimal sample size for interviews depends on what is being sought and why, how the findings are to be applied and the researcher's available resources (Patton, 1990). Different researchers suggest different sample sizes for the convergent interviewing method. Dick (1990) suggests that a sample should be 1 per cent of a target population of up to 200, with a minimum of 12 people. Others argue that sample size is determined by the point at which stability is reached, that is, when agreement is reached on all issues (Naire and Riege, 1995). They have found that stability can occur after six interviews, while in Woodward's (1997) experience convergence can occur after only five interviews. In our study, stability occurred after ten interviews.

Determining the sampling method

In qualitative research the sampling method is not random – it is purposeful (Patton, 1990). We initially selected a small but diverse sample of knowledgeable people who did not know each other, and after each interview the interviewees were asked to recommend other suitable interviewees. In other words we started with a few cases and used these cases to identify others in the interconnecting networks, thereby enabling the sample to grow in size (Aaker and Day, 1990; Neuman, 1994). This snowball sampling technique is appropriate when a research project involves a small, specialised population of people who are knowledgeable about the topic in question (Aaker and Day, 1990; Patton, 1990; Neuman, 1994). It is important to select the first interviewees carefully as they must be capable of directing the researcher to others who are not only familiar with the topic of the research but also experts in their own field. In our study the identification of key industry figures was done with the assistance of the Australian Direct Marketing Association (ADMA, 1999). Ten interviewees were selected, seven of whom were marketing managers with considerable experience of Internet marketing. The other three were business/marketing consultants who had worked in their field for a long time.

Conducting the interviews

In a qualitative interviewing process the interviewer acts as the instrument. Therefore care must be taken in both planning and managing the interviews. We based our procedure on the steps recommended by Dick (1990, pp. 12–14), as follows.

Step one: contacting the respondents.   Initial contact with potential interviewees was established by e-mail or phone. When the initial contact was by e-mail it was followed up with a phone call. All the contacts were first given an overview of the research and its purpose (academic research) and then asked whether they would participate in the interviews. If they consented a venue and time were arranged (Carson *et al.*, 2001).

Step two: time and setting.   The interviews were terminated only when no further information could be obtained (Dick, 1990). In later interviews more time was needed as the number of probe questions increased. The interviews lasted between 30 minutes and one hour. All the interviews were conducted at the interviewees' place of work. The interview times were fixed during the initial contact and confirmed a few days prior to the interview.

Step three: establishing rapport and neutrality.   A number of preliminary issues were clarified at the start of the interview in order to establish a rapport and enccourage cooperation during the interview (Carson *et al.*,

2001). The researcher introduced herself and gave a brief explanation of the purpose of the research. The interviewees were also given assurance of confidentiality and asked for permission to tape record the interviews.

Step four: the opening question. The opening question needs to be framed in such a manner as to encourage the interviewee to reveal his or her attitudes towards the research topic without placing boundaries on the response (Dick, 1990). That is, the objective of the opening question is to provide a broad starting point to pave the way for more probing questions (Nair and Riege, 1995) and to define the nature of the topic without implying any constraints on the nature of the response (Carson *et al.*, 2001). The opening question in our study was 'Can you tell me a story of your experience of dealing with another business using the Internet?' (Nair and Riege, 1995; Perry, 1998). This question did not put pressure on the interviewees to think about specific issues, that is, they did not have to intellectualise or justify their responses. Rather they shared their experiences with the researcher in a relaxed manner, and this also helped them to organise their thoughts.

Step five: probe questions. Probe questions follow the opening question and are aimed at keeping the interviewees talking and the interview focused. In convergent interviews, probe questions are also the mechanism by which similarities and dissimilarities revealed in the previous interviews are explored (Dick, 1990; Carson *et al.*, 2001). In our study the probe questions were developed before each interview, based on the results of the preceeding interview. For the first interview a list of ten probe questions – covering the three research issues and based on the literature review and the findings of the first stage of the research (focus groups) – was developed. They were printed in an interview guide and given to the interviewee at the start of the interview. In addition questions such as 'Can you give me an example for this?' and 'Can you elaborate a little?' were used during the course of the interviews. This procedure helped to focus the interview and keep it within the time allotted.

Step six: inviting a summary. When it is apparent that little more information will be obtained, the researcher can start to close the interview by inviting the interviewee to pick out the key points from what has been discussed so far, perhaps also indicating their relative priority (Dick, 1990). In our study the questions asked were 'Of all the issues you have mentioned what are the most and least important issues?' and 'Could you please prioritise them in order of importance?'

Step seven: concluding the interview.   When the interviewee could add no further information the interviewer summarised the interview to ensure that all the questions had been properly investigated and to confirm the interviewee's responses. Then the interviewee was thanked for his or her cooperation and a copy of the data analysis was offered. The interviewee was again assured that all information obtained during the interview would remain confidential and anonymous.

Examples of findings from the convergent interviews

The outcome of convergent interviewing is a list of issues or themes. Table 6.4 lists the themes that emerged during our interviews on the three research issues. As can be seen, there is evidence that using the Internet in a B2B setting has a positive effect on interfirm relationships, although it does not change the general nature of a prospective interfirm relationship. As interviewee E commented, 'If I don't have the solution to your problem or you don't have the need, the relationship does not exist'. However most of the interviewees believed that using the Internet had generally enhanced their relationship with another business, and especially with their customers. From the scant literature and the above findings, a theoretical framework was developed and is summarised in Figure 6.1. This framework captures the structural and social bonds in an interfirm relationship when the firms use the Internet in their exchanges.

Conclusions and implications

There has been little research on the impact of Internet usage on interfirm relationships. From the sparse literature on the topic and our empirical findings from convergent interviews, a conceptual framework has been developed. The major contributions of this chapter are its demonstration of the effectiveness of convergent interviews in marketing research and the conceptual framework, which integrates many research streams with its explicit treatment of social and structural bonds. The framework should help further research in this area of academic inquiry. A further contribution is that the study's focus on service industries complements existing theories that are based mostly on US businesses and non-service industries. In short, convergent interviews are a useful qualitative research method to explore new issues connected with emerging marketing phenomena.

Table 6.4 Summary of the issues raised in the convergent interviews

	Interviewees									
	A	B	C	D	E	F	G	H	I	J
Issue 1: Internet usage facilitates interfirm communication:										
The Internet does not replace other forms of communication	✓	✓	✓	X	✓	✓	✓	✓	✓	✓
Use of the Internet increases the quality of interfirm communication	*	*	✓	✓	✓	✓	✓	✓	✓	✓
Use of the Internet facilitates interfirm information sharing	*	*	✓	✓	✓	✓	✓	✓	X	✓
Use of the Internet has a positive effect on participation	*	*	✓	✓	X	✓	✓	✓	✓	✓
Issue 2: Internet usage affects both technical and social elements:										
Use of the Internet has little effect on interdependency between our customers and us	✓	✓	✓	✓	✓	✓	✓	✓	✓	✓
We are still very dependent on strategic customers and suppliers	✓	✓	✓	✓	✓	✓	✓	✓	✓	✓
We are not as dependent on less strategic suppliers	*	X	✓	✓	X	✓	✓	✓	X	✓
Using the Internet places higher barriers against leaving strategic relationships	*	*	✓	X	X	✓	✓	✓	X	X
A business relationship involves mutual benefits, added value and honesty	*	✓	✓	✓	✓	✓	✓	✓	✓	✓
Communication, interpersonal skills and value proposition are important in building a good business relationship	*	✓	✓	✓	✓	✓	✓	✓	✓	✓
Use of the Internet enhances our relationships with our strategic business partners	X	✓	✓	X	✓	✓	✓	✓	✓	✓
There is a need for cautious use of the Internet in relationship management	✓	✓	✓	✓	✓	✓	✓	✓	✓	✓

Table 6.4 (Continued)

				Interviewees						
	A	B	C	D	E	F	G	H	I	J
There is a need to develop long-term, close relationships with customers	√	√	√	√	√	√	√	√	√	√
Use of the Internet has little effect on the development of trust in the relationship	*	*	√	√	√	√	√	√	√	√
Use of the Internet has a positive effect on the maintenance of trust	*	*	√	X	√	X	√	√	√	√
Use of the Internet has a positive effect on satisfaction with the relationship	*	√	√	X	√	√	√	√	√	√
Use of the Internet has a positive effect on coordinating the relationship	*	√	√	√	√	√	√	√	√	√
Use of the Internet has a positive effect on commitment to the relationship	*	√	√	X	X	√	√	√	√	√
Issue 3: Internet usage is perceived to be positively associated with business performance:										
Use of the Internet has a positive effect on sales and market share	*	√	√	√	√	√	√	√	√	√
Use of the Internet has little effect on the short-term profit level	*	*	√	X	√	√	√	X	√	√
Use of the Internet has a positive effect on the long-term profit level	*	*	√	X	√	√	√	√	√	√
Use of the Internet has a positive effect on returns on assets	*	√	√	X	√	X	√	√	√	X

Notes: √ = interviewee agrees with the statement; X = interviewee disagrees with the statement; * = question was not raised.

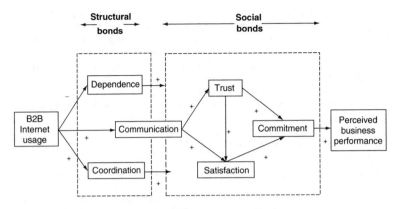

Figure 6.1   Theoretical framework developed from the interview data

The implications for practice are a better understanding of interfirm relationships in an Internet environment. The focus on structural and social bonds in interfirm relationships should help managers to identify new issues to consider in their relationship management. That is, this study should help managers to develop a more complete understanding of the Internet's role in relationship management. The identified technical and social bonds that are affected by the use of the Internet need to be addressed in future theory-testing research. For example structural equation modelling of the survey data could test the statistical generalisability of Figure 6.1.

References

Aaker, D. A. and Day, G. S. (1990) *Marketing Research* (New York: Wiley).

Anderson, J. C. and Narus, J. (1984) 'A model of distributor firm and manufacture firm working partnerships', *Journal of Marketing*, vol. 54, no. 1, pp. 42–58.

Araujo, L. and Easton, G. (1996) 'Network in socioeconomic systems', in D. Iacobucci (ed.), *Networks in Marketing* (London: Sage), pp. 63–107.

Archer, N. and Yuan, Y. (2000) 'Managing business-to-business relationships throughout the e-commerce procurement life cycle', *Internet Research: Electronic Networking Applications and Policy*, vol. 10, no. 5, pp. 385–95.

Australian Bureau of Statistics (ABS) (2001) 'Australians embrace the internet', Australian Government Publishing Service Media Release, http://www.abs. gov.au/Ausstats/.

Australian Direct Marketing Association (ADMA) (1999) *Who is Who in Direct Marketing: Directory of Members of the Australian Direct Marketing Association (ADMA)* (Sydney: ADMA).

Bonoma, T. V. (1985) 'Case research in marketing: opportunities, problems, and a process', *Journal of Marketing Research*, vol. 22, no. 5, pp. 199–208.

Buttle, F. and Ahmad, R. (1999) 'Bonding with customers', in *Proceedings of Academy of Marketing Conference* (Stirling: University of Stirling).

Carson, D., Gilmore, A., Gronhaug, K. and Perry, C. (2001) *Qualitative Research in Marketing* (London: Sage).

Dick, B. (1990) *Convergent Interviewing* (Brisbane: Interchange).

Economist (2000) E-commerce: shopping around the web, *The Economist*, no. 354, pp. S5–S6.

Eisenhardt, K. (1991) 'Better stories and better constructs: the case for rigor and competitive logic', *Academy of Management Review*, vol. 16, no. 4, pp. 620–7.

Emory, C. W. and Cooper, D. R. (1991) *Business Research Methods* (Homewood, Ill. Irwin).

Geiger, S. and Martin, S. (1999) 'The internet as a relationship marketing tool – some evidence from Irish companies', *Irish Marketing Review*, vol. 12, no. 2, pp. 25–36.

Gillenson, M., Sherrell, D. and Chen, L. (1999) 'Information technology as the enabler of one-to-one marketing', *Communications of the Association for Information Systems*, http://cais.isworld.org/articles/2–18/article.htm.

Global Internet Statistics (2001) http://www.glreach.com/globstats/index.php3.

Gordon, I. (1998) *Relationship Marketing: New Strategies, Techniques, and Technologies to Win the Customers You Want and Keep Them Forever* (Toronto: Wiley).

Guba, E. G. and Y. S. Lincoln (1994) 'Competing paradigms in qualitative research', in N. K. Denzin and Y. S. Lincoln, *Handbook of Qualitative Research* (London: Sage), pp. 105–17.

Gummesson, E. (2001) *Qualitative Methods in Management Research* (London: Sage).

Hagel, J. and Singer, M. (1999) *Net Worth: Shaping Markets When Customers Make the Rules* (Boston, Mass.: Harvard Business School Press).

Hamill, J. (1998) *Internet applications: electronic communication and relationship marketing*, http://www.seve.com/sevetopic5.htm.

Hamill, J. (2000) *Internet supported customer relationship management*, http://www.crm-forum.com.

Hayes, F. (1999) 'Amazoned!', *Computerworld*, vol. 33, no. 20 p. 116.

Healy, M. and Perry, C. (2000) 'Comprehensive criteria to judge validity and reliability of qualitative research within the realism paradigm', *Qualitative Market Research – an International Journal*, vol. 3, no. 3, pp. 118–26.

Hoffman, D. and Novak, T. (1996) 'Marketing in hypermedia computer-mediated environments: conceptual foundations', *Journal of Marketing*, vol. 60, no. 3, pp. 50–68.

Kalakota, R. and Whinston, A. B. (1997) *Electronic Commerce: A Manager's Guide* (Reading Mass.: Addison-Wesley).

King, E. (1996) 'The use of self in qualitative research', in J. Richardson, *Handbook of Qualitative Research Methods for Psychology and Social Sciences* (Leicester: BPS Books).

Marshall, C. and Rossman, G. B. (1995) *Designing Qualitative Research* (Newbury Park, CA: Sage).

Mattson, L. G. (1985) 'An application of a network approach to marketing: Defending and changing marketing positions', in N. Dholakia, J. Arndt and

C. Greenwich (eds), *Changing the Course of Marketing Alternative and Paradigms for Widening Marketing Theory* (Greenwich, CT: JAI Press), pp. 263–88.

Maykut, P. and Morehouse, R. (1994) *Beginning Qualitative Research: A Philosophical and Practical Guide* (New York: Burgess Science Press).

Miles, M. B. and Huberman, A. M. (1994) *An Expanded Sourcebook: Qualitative Data Analysis* (Thousand Oaks, CA: Sage).

Nair, G. S. and Riege, A. M. (1995) 'Using convergent interviewing to develop the research problem of a postgraduate thesis', *Proceedings of Marketing Education and Researchers International* (Surfers' Paradise Qld: International Conference of Educators and Researchers).

National Office for the Information Economy (NOIE) (2001) *B2B e-commerce: capturing value online*, http:www.noie.gov.au/publications/NOIE/B2B.

Neuman, W. L. (1994) *Social Research Methods: Qualitative and Quantitative Approaches* (Boston, Mass.: Allyn and Bacon).

Patton, M. Q. (1990) *Qualitative Evaluation and Research Methods* (Newbury Park, CA: Sage).

Peppers, D., Rogers, M. and Dorf, B. (1999) 'Is your company ready for one-to-one marketing?', *Harvard Business Review*, vol. 77, no. 1, pp. 151–60.

Perry, C. (1998) 'A structured approach for presenting theses', *Australasian Marketing Journal*, vol. 6, no. 1, pp. 63–85.

Perry, C. (2001) 'Case research in marketing', *The Marketing Review*, vol. 1, no. 1, pp. 303–23.

Perry, C., Cavaye A. and Coote, L. (2002) 'Technical and social bonds within business-to-business relationships', *Journal of Business and Industrial Marketing*, vol. 17, no. 1, pp. 75–88.

Peterson, R. A., Balasubramanian, S. and Bronnenberg, B. J. (1997) 'Exploring the implications of the Internet for consumer marketing', *Journal of the Academy of Marketing Science*, vol. 25, no. 4, pp. 329–46.

Phillips, E. M. and Pugh D. S. (1987) *How to Get a PhD* (Milton Keynes: Open University Press).

Rao, S. and Perry, C. (2002) 'Thinking about relationship marketing: where are we now?', *Journal of Business and Industrial Marketing*, vol. 17, no. 7, pp. 598–614.

Sekaran, U. (1992) *Research Methods for Business* (Singapore: Wiley).

Seybold, P. B. (1999) *Customers.com: How to Create a Profitable Business Strategy for the Internet and Beyond* (New York: Times Business).

Sheth, J. N. and Parvatiyar, A. (1995) 'The evolution of relationship marketing', *International Business Review*, vol. 4, no. 4, pp. 397–418.

Turnbull, P. W. and Wilson, D. (1989) 'Developing and protecting profitable customer relationships', *Industrial Marketing Management*, vol. 18, no. 2, pp. 233–8.

Vlosky, R. P., Fontenot, R. and Blalock, L. (2000) 'Extranets: impacts on business practice and relationships', *Journal of Business and Industrial Marketing*, vol.15, no. 6, pp. 438–57.

Watson, R. T., Berthon, P., Pitt, L. F. and Zinkhan, G. M. (2000) *Electronic Commerce: The Strategic Perspective* (Fort Worth, Tex.: The Dryden Press).

Wilson, D. T. and Vlosky, R. P. (1998) 'Interorganisational information system technology and buyer–seller relationships', *Journal of Business and Industrial Marketing*, vol. 13, no. 3, pp. 215–34.

Wollin, D. (1995) 'Rigor in theory-building from cases', *Proceedings of the Australia and New Zealand Academy of Management (ANZMAC)* (Wollongong, NSW: ANZMAC).

Woodward, T. (1997) 'Identifying and measuring customer-based brand equity and its elements for a service industry', PhD thesis, School of Marketing and International Business. Queensland University of Technology, Brisbane.

Yin, R. K. (1994) *Case Study Research: Design and Methods* (Beverly Hills, CA: Sage).

Zikmund, W. G. (1984) *Business Research Methods* (Chicago, Ill.: The Dryden Press).

7
Using Focus Groups to Investigate New Ideas: Principles and an Example of Internet-Facilitated Relationships in a Regional Financial Services Institution

Arthur Sweeney and Chad Perry

Introduction

In-depth qualitative research can be used to explore critical issues in a fast-moving field. Specifically, the use of focus groups can uncover how customers perceive new products such as the Internet. Much remains to be understood about electronically facilitated relationships, which are becoming commonplace in financial services and are the focus of this chapter.

The purpose of this chapter is to describe the principles and processes of using focus groups to explore Internet-based relationships between the 'Reward' financial institution in Australia and its customers. Essentially, we argue that focus groups constitute a useful, careful, step-by-step methodology for this type of research.

The research reported here is important because although the financial services industry has a long history of establishing customer relationships because they are central to better business performance (Ennew and Binks, 1996), financial services institutions have not still mastered customer relationships and 'marketers still have much to learn about what it really means to be a relationship partner' (Stewart and Colgate, 1998, p. 276).

This chapter is divided into three main sections: the first defines focus groups and justifies their use in our study; the second describes the steps we followed and the third discusses some outcomes of the study.

The focus group methodology

What is the focus group methodology?

While focus groups are a frequently used tool in qualitative research, a precise definition is difficult to find (Templeton, 1994). One definition is that a focus group is a planned discussion group of about seven to ten people, conducted by a skilled interviewer in a permissive environment in which members of the target market influence each other by responding to comments (Krueger, 1988). This enables the researcher to explore 'the experience of consumers' (Calder, 1977, p. 360). In other words the use of focus groups is an interactive research technique that 'capitalises on the interaction within a group to elicit rich experiential data' (Asbury, 1995, p. 414). We accepted this definition for our study because it differentiates focus groups from discussion groups, nominal and Delphi groups, therapy groups, education groups and decision-making groups (Stewart and Shamdasani, 1990; Frey and Fontana, 1993; Morgan, 1996). Focus groups were considered appropriate for our study as they would enable us to obtain perceptions on Internet and customer relationships that could not be obtained by other methods.

Development of the focus group methodology

Focus groups were adopted in the 1950s to overcome the shortcomings of large sample polling techniques, which provided lots of statistics but little explanatory information (Bellenger *et al.*, 1989, p. 7). The development of focus groups in various applications after World War II culminated in the classic *The Focused Interview* (Merton *et al.*, 1956), which was the first to use the term 'focus group' and initiated some of the processes that are now common practice (Krueger, 1988). Today, focus groups are used in marketing to generate hypotheses, explore opinions, attitudes and attributes, test new product ideas, evaluate advertisements and identify and pretest questionnaire items (Cox *et al.*, 1976; Fern, 1982; Carson *et al.*, 2001).

We considered an alternative to the usual face-to-face format of focus groups. In marketing there is increasing use of Internet chat sessions, which provide real-time results at one fifth to one half of the cost of traditional focus groups (Parks, 1997). At first this method seemed attractive for our purposes because of its use of the Internet. However Internet chats have been criticised for lacking important elements of focus group research, such as group dynamics, the ability to read non-verbal input, the opportunity for client involvement, exposure to external stimuli and effective use of moderator skills (Peebles, 1996; Roller, 1996;

Greenbaum, 1997; Forrest, 1999). Furthermore the usefulness of on-line research is limited by unrepresentative samples, sample self-selection and the difficulties associated with preserving respondent anonymity and confidentiality, as well as problems with layout, presentation and instruction (Palmquist and Stueve, 1996; Comley, 1997). For these reasons we chose to use the conventional focus group methodology.

The psychology of focus group research

As focus groups had their origins in early research on group dynamics, the validity of focus groups as a scientific tool rests on the psychology of small group interaction and the analysis of qualitative data (Stewart and Shamdasani, 1990; Albrecht *et al.*, 1993; Frey and Fontana, 1993). Indeed the main feature of focus groups is collective interaction that produces insights that otherwise would not be possible (Greenbaum, 1988; Morgan, 1988).

That is, focus group psychology recognises that attitudes and percep-tions are developed not in isolation, but in part through interaction with others. People may need to listen to the opinions of others before they can form or solidify their own viewpoints (Krueger, 1988; Patton, 1990; Crabtree *et al.*, 1993), and quality control on data collection is provided by group pressure on false or extreme views (Albrecht *et al.*, 1993). Because the researcher would gain fewer insights into the topic without the interaction, the unit of analysis is the group. In short, focus groups have a chemistry and a dynamic that are greater than the sum of the members (Keown, 1983; Carey, 1994); they offer more excitement and arousal than other techniques (Bristol and Fern, 1996). For the above reasons focus groups were considered an appropriate data collection method for our study.

The key to focus groups achieving the research objectives is cohesion, that is, it is necessary for the members to be cooperative, friendly and supportive of each other's accomplishments (Fuller *et al.*, 1993; Knodel, 1993; Templeton, 1994; Krueger, 1998, 1993). Cohesion can be obtained by mixing genders and ensuring similar personal characteristics and socioeconomic backgrounds, and excluding friends and hostile members because both can impair group formation and interaction (Fern, 1982; Goldman, 1989). Screening may help to eliminate potential problems, but if it does not the moderator needs to affirm that the opinions of all members of the group are valuable (Stewart and Shamdasani, 1990). Importantly the participants must share the common experience that is key to the research problem (Asbury, 1995). We ensured this by recruiting participants who were demographically and financially representative and had similar personal characteristics and socioeconomic back-grounds.

Steps in focus group research

Figure 7.1 shows the main steps in our research, classified into prere-search issues, focus group research issues and post-research issues. The first preresearch task was to prepare a research brief that translated the research problem into research questions and described the type of participants to be included in terms of demographics, product usage or attitudes (Greenbaum, 1988; Tynan and Drayton, 1988; Aaker and Day, 1990; Knodel, 1993; Malhotra, 1993). Accordingly the first author prepared a brief for Market and Communications Research Pty Ltd, the Brisbane research company that conducted the focus groups.

Moderation

The second preresearch task was to select a moderator to focus the group discussion on the subject of interest (Tynan and Drayton, 1988). He or she had to be adequately trained and effective (Rigler, 1987;

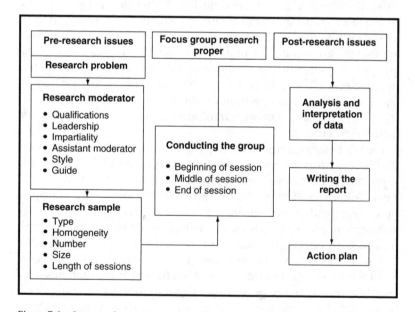

Figure 7.1   Steps in focus group research
Source: Developed from Keown (1983); Greenbaum(1988); Stewart and Shamdasani (1990); Morgan (1993).

Greenbaum, 1988; Morgan, 1993), and have a scientific orientation and sophistication that were consistent with the type of knowledge required from the groups (McDonald, 1993). Because our study only required everyday knowledge, Market and Communications Research provided a professionally trained moderator whose qualifications were suited to the research topic.

As the moderator would be a nominal leader (Stewart and Shamdasani, 1990), he or she also had to be supportive, able to establish a rapport, be comfortable with group dynamics, keep the group on track, maintain enthusiasm and promote free discussion (Krueger, 1988, 1993; Tynan and Drayton, 1988; Bellenger *et al.*, 1989; Albrecht *et al.*, 1993) because too much moderator control would inhibit group interaction (Agar and MacDonald, 1995). The chosen moderator had these leadership qualities.

Moreover the moderator had to recognise that internal or external bias was possible, be sensitive to her own feelings, allow contrary positions and avoid the temptation to please the client (Kennedy, 1989). She also had to be able to suppress dominant participants and encourage passive ones without destroying the group's cohesion (Tynan and Drayton, 1988). It was for these reasons that a professional rather than an in-house moderator was chosen to conduct the focus groups for our research.

In focus group research, decisions have to be made about client attendance at the groups, the number of clients who will attend and any communication between them and the moderator during the group sessions (Greenbaum, 1988). In our study the first author and representatives from Reward watched the groups on video in an adjoining room.

Assistant moderators are not emphasised in the literature, possibly because private researchers find them too expensive and rarely use them. However a moderator and assistant moderator team works well (Krueger, 1988, 1993) because it facilitates the recording of focus group sessions in notes and on tape. In our study the first author performed the assistant's functions, including the taking of comprehensive notes, operating the tapes and video, managing the environment and noting the body language of the participants, thus freeing the moderator to concentrate on directing the discussion.

Because different focus groups have different purposes, moderating styles range from a structured or directive style to a less structured or less directive one (Frey and Fontana, 1993). A directive style allows for greater coverage of topics but at the cost of group synergy and spontaneity, which are desirable if the aim is to generate research hypotheses or diagnose potential problems with a new programme, product or service. A less directive style provides more opportunity for group interaction and discovery and is desirable if the aim is to generate new ideas or encourage creativity. Most focus groups are a mixture of the two styles (Stewart and Shamdasani, 1990). We adopted a tightly structured style because that was the norm for a large research agenda (Morgan, 1992).

The moderator's topic guide sets the agenda for the discussion (Malhotra, 1993; Staddon, 1996). It flows directly from the research questions, should be developed in collaboration with all parties, be designed to proceed from general to specific matters according to their relative importance on the research agenda, and be pretested (Aaker and Day, 1990; Frey and Fontana, 1993; Carey, 1994). In our study the moderator's topic guide was developed by the moderator in collaboration with Reward and the first author, and pretested with Reward staff and customers.

The questions in the guide are designed to stimulate group interaction and extract answers to research problems (Stewart and Shamdasani, 1990). The number of questions depends on the nature of the topic and the participants, and the specific responses requested. Ten to twelve core questions are adequate for a two-hour interview and there may be additional follow-up questions (Krueger, 1993). In the main part of our study the moderator asked some 40 questions about the Internet, and although the discussion was sometimes superficial, strong and clear insights were obtained. With regard to the wording of questions, we included only two 'why' questions to avoid the possibility of participants becoming defensive or rationalising their answers (Krueger, 1988). Most of the other questions began with words such as which, what, how, could and would.

The venue for focus group discussions should be informal as interaction is more intense and consumers share their views more meaningfully in real-life settings (Karger, 1989). The moderator has to organise appropriate seating, refreshments and recording equipment, and as the participants arrive, to greet them and offer them refreshments (Staddon, 1996). It is common for focus groups to be observed and recorded, and while there is no evidence that this radically alters responses, the participants should be briefed about the research client and assured that their responses will be kept confidential (Krueger, 1993; Stewart and Shamdasani, 1990). The overriding considerations for the physical location are that it is comfortable for and accessible by the participants (Asbury, 1995).

In our study the group sessions were conducted away from Reward's premises to ensure that the respondents would not feel under pressure. The sessions were conducted in the evening as that was the time when people seemed most able to engage in and enjoy stimulating group discussions (Tuckel *et al.*, 1993). The sessions were observed and recorded, refreshments were offered as the participants arrived, and before departing they were briefed about the client and assured of confidentiality.

The research sample

The third preresearch task was to decide on the sample. Because the aim of focus groups is to understand rather than to infer, convenience samples are appropriate as random samples (Axelrod, 1975; Krueger, 1988). Hence we used a convenience sample that was representative of Reward's customers. In such research two groups are the minimum as one group may be dangerously atypical and misleading (Staddon, 1996). Additional groups should be conducted until the moderator can anticipate what will be said, which usually happens after three or four groups have been conducted on the same subject (Aaker and Day, 1990; Calder, 1977; Knodel, 1993; Malhotra, 1993; Morgan, 1988). We conducted two groups whose members had access to the Internet and two whose members had no access to the Internet. It became clear after four groups that additional information was unlikely to emerge, so no further groups were conducted.

The size of focus groups is becoming smaller (six to eight participants rather than eight to twelve) because smaller groups tend to be more productive (Aaker and Day, 1990; Shea, 1995), but very small groups limit the range of experiences that can be accessed and the number of new ideas generated (Staddon, 1996). While groups of eight members generate more ideas than groups of four, idea production decreases as group size increases beyond eight (Fern, 1982). However, it can be the case that two mini groups of four people each generate more ideas than one group of eight (Shea, 1995). Overall, the key distinction between small and large groups lies in the group dynamics, which in smaller groups tends to be intense while in larger groups it is more superficial (Morgan, 1992). For our study, groups of six to ten respondents were chosen because in-depth appreciation of the issues was the objective rather than the generation of new ideas.

Establishing a rapport with the participants and adequately exploring the issues usually takes one to three hours, although one and a half to two hours is typical (Malhotra, 1993). Each of the four sessions in our study lasted about two hours (as recommended by Morgan, 1988).

Conducting the groups

The physical arrangement of the group is crucial to the success of the discussion. The participants should be seated in such a way as to be able to make eye contact with the moderator and each other (Stewart and Shamdasani, 1990). Offering a presession snack can help to break the ice, facilitate conversation and help the moderator to assess the participants' characteristics in order to make the optimal seating arrangement (Carey, 1994). Accordingly our sessions began with food and drink.

The beginning of the interview sets the tone for the whole session, and to achieve a rapport, create trust and encourage openness the moderator may use self-disclosure to put the participants at ease and encourage them to reveal sensitive information (Zeller, 1993). The moderator should reassure the participants about the anonymity of their responses and the value of each of their opinions. To facilitate cohesion the participants can be encouraged to introduce themselves, unless such information might bias the group or influence the level of interaction in an unwanted way (Krueger, 1988; Morgan, 1988; Stewart and Shamdasani, 1990; Fuller *et al.*, 1993; O'Brien, 1993; Tuckel *et al.*, 1993).

Our sessions began with the moderator introducing herself, warmly welcoming the participants and giving them an overview of the topic and the rules of participation. They were then invited to introduce themselves. This was designed to establish a rapport, promote cohesion and create a climate that would be conducive to self-disclosure. The participants were assured that their responses would be kept anonymous, that there were no right or wrong answers, that everybody had a contribution to make and that the session would be recorded.

After the introductions, one way of quickly engaging the interest of participants is to raise the topic for discussion and ask for their opinions and feelings or personal anecdotes relating to it (Stewart and Shamdasani, 1990; Staddon, 1996). If further information is to be extracted, probes or follow-up questions ask for more information without suggesting specific answers or making the respondents defensive (Stewart and Shamdasani, 1990). In our study the moderator introduced the topic in a general way and quickly engaged the participants by asking for their personal attitudes towards it. So strong were the feelings among the participants that encouraging conversation was no difficulty. When the moderator needed further information she probed by means of requests for elaboration and clarification (Mariampolski, 1989).

Because participants have been recruited for a specific time, and this should be honoured, an important skill on the part of the moderator is time management (Stewart and Shamdasani, 1990). In our study, because the agenda was lengthy the moderator was under pressure of time, so no summary could be made at the end and no further information could be sought in the conclusion phase.

The analysis and interpretation of data

The three post-research issues can now be considered. When all the focus groups have been held, either the moderator or an analyst analyses the data (Malhotra, 1993). Although this is the most challenging part of focus group research, little has been written about how to do it (Knodel, 1993). To enhance interpretative accuracy, if possible the moderator or assistant should do the analysis as they have heard the discussions and witnessed the participants' body language (Krueger, 1988). The analysis requires a great deal of judgment and care as much of the scepticism about focus groups is due to the perception that the data so obtained is subjective and difficult to interpret. However it can be as rigorous as any other method. The degree of analysis and level of detail and rigour depend on the purpose of the research (Stewart and Shamdasani, 1990).

Data analysis ranges from simple impressions gained from observing and listening, to a more thorough examination of the transcripts, which for a typical two-hour session can yield 40–50 pages of text (Krueger, 1993). Analysis of the transcripts is conducted in two steps: organising the data into meaningful categories or themes, or similar features or concepts (Aaker and Day, 1990; Albrecht *et al.*, 1993; Neuman, 1994; Flores and Alonso, 1995), then looking for patterns within and between the categories (Knodel, 1993). The most useful reports on focus groups capture the full range of impressions on the topic (Flores and Alonso, 1995). One way of facilitating interpretation is to construct an overview grid with topic headings on one axis and focus group session identifiers on the other; the cells contain brief summaries of the discussion for each group (Bertrand *et al.*, 1992; Knodel, 1993). The extent to which consensus within and between the groups is evident on the grids can indicate the reliability of the information collected. In our study the first author attended the sessions and prepared an overview grid of the impressions gained. The moderator's summary of the transcripts, based on the original moderator's guide, was compared with the grid for accuracy.

More sophisticated analytic procedures involve content analysis, which is any data analysis technique that makes replicable and valid inferences from data to their context (Stewart and Shamdasani, 1990). Content analysis can be performed manually or with computer program by attaching labels to chunks of data. A chunk can be a word, a phrase, a sentence or a paragraph (Miles and Huberman, 1994; Neuman, 1994). In our study the moderator analysed the data by content analysis supported by ethnographic statements or direct quotations from the groups (Morgan, 1988).

Writing the report and taking action

The writer of the report has to organise disparate information, analyse the key points, report negative findings and in some circumstances report the findings quickly (Henderson, 1995). Written reports may consist solely of raw data or be descriptive or interpretive, depending on the research objectives (Krueger, 1988). In our study an interpretive report was prepared. This included a summary of the results, illustrative quotes and notes on the meaning of the data. The full report contained some commercially sensitive material that cannot be discussed here, but its content was taken into account when preparing the overview grid.

When the report has been written some form of action might be taken, ranging from immediate action to further research (Keown, 1983). The action in our case was further research, with Reward testing the model of Internet-facilitated relationships in a quantitative survey of its customers.

Limitations of focus group research

The appropriateness and strengths of using focus groups to investigate our research problem have already been discussed. However, as with all research methods, focus groups have limitations. First, the validity of focus group findings can be questioned. The results may be biased by participants who are 'more extroverted, outgoing, and sociable than the "average" individual' (Byers and Wilcox, 1991, p. 67), or by respondents who make little investment in the research process (Tuckel and Wood, 2001). The steps we took in respect of research design, moderation and data analysis, as described above, were aimed at ensuring that there would be some validity in the data collected. Moreover the research was about customers' perceptions of the Internet and there was no reason for the participants to be misleading. Perhaps if the focus groups had consisted of suppliers instead of customers, commercial secrecy may have led to biased discussions. But our focus groups comprised only customers of the one firm and all were interested in improving its service. Nevertheless, because problems in interpretation might exist, the exploratory findings were treated as a preliminary part of a larger study. Quantitative research methods were used at a later stage to test the findings.

Another limitation of focus groups is the possibility of undue influence. The advantage of a group situation is that it encourages interaction and exchanges of view among the participants, but its disadvantage is that someone in the group may influence the other participants' opinions, for example one participant may be more dominant than the others.

On the other hand a group of participants may agree with one another about an issue because disagreement could bring tension and unpleasantness to the meeting. In our study the trained moderator took steps to minimise these possibilities.

Example outcomes

This section briefly discusses the types of finding of our research; further details are available from the first author. The focus group sessions began with a broad question about whether the participants held accounts with more than one financial institution, and then proceeded to discuss their commitment to those institutions. The customers of Reward did not confine their banking to one financial institution but used a number of institutions depending on the range of services offered, the fees charged for such services and the interest rates. The main reason for their divided commitment seemed to be value, that is, what they received in exchange for what they gave, as expressed in phrases such as 'cheaper options', 'greedy fees', 'more services for the same fee' and 'better interest rates'. Significantly, they had a similar view of all financial institutions, whether they were building societies, banks or credit unions.

With regard to their attitudes towards Internet banking (Table 7.1), participants with no access to the Internet were generally negative about Internet banking. While they acknowledged that it might be a good source of banking information and was suitable for people living in remote areas, they were negative about security issues, set-up costs, mistakes and the unsuitability of Internet banking for small businesses. Conversely participants with Internet access were favourably disposed towards Internet banking. Indeed they regarded it as the ultimate banking convenience and superior to existing banking methods, particularly in terms of time savings for travellers and those who banked from a distance. Some of these participants were high-tech, hands-on individuals who liked both technology and people, and thought that Internet banking could simplify and strengthen customers' relations with financial institutions.

The next step in theory-building research is to develop a framework that aids general understanding of the phenomenon in question. The framework we developed is summarised in Figure 7.2. The horizontal axis represents Internet technology (tech). The vertical axis represents 'touch', which refers to the customisation and personalisation of banking

Table 7.1 Internet banking and customer relations – participants' views

	Participants with no Internet access	Participants with Internet access
Service aspects	Existing services should be improved first	Net banking is the ultimate in banking convenience and superior to existing banking, but will not replace other forms of banking
	Great for general banking information but is an incomplete banking service	Net used widely for e-mail, games, chatting, information gathering, entertainment and obtaining general bank information
	Not suitable for small businesses that require paper records	Time savings for travellers and people who bank from a distance
	Security, mistakes and set-up costs are major concerns	Internet banking is cheaper so fees should not apply, but they probably will
	Suitable for remote areas	
Relationship aspects	Increases customer isolation	Customers better informed and in control
	Interactive capability not important	Internet banking is great for 'visual' people and technology buffs
	Internet is impersonal while building societies and based on personal service	Simplifies the relationship with a financial institution
	Less customer control	Strengthens the relationship with a financial institution, especially if fees do not increase
	Loss of personal touch	

services. Box A represents high-tech, high-touch customers with Internet access who liked both high-technology and personal banking. Box B represents low-tech, high-touch customers with no Internet access who preferred personal banking to high-technology banking. Box C represents high-tech, low-touch customers with Internet access who liked high-technology banking but not personal banking. Finally, Box D represents low-tech, low-touch customers with no Internet accesses who liked neither personal banking nor high-technology banking.

Among the participants, the high-tech, high-touch group (Box A) were favourably disposed towards Internet banking, preferring a high-tech,

High

B *High touch, low tech*	A *High tech, high touch*
Customers with no Internet access who prefer personal banking to high-technology banking. Their views on Internet banking are:	**Customers with Internet access who like people and technology banking. Their views on Internet banking are:**
• Great for general banking information but is an incomplete banking service • Not suitable for small businesses that require paper records • Security, mistakes and set-up costs are major concerns • Suitable for remote areas • Increases customer isolation, that is, there is a loss of personal touch • Interactive capability not important • Internet is impersonal while financial services institutions are based on personal service • Less customer control	• It is the ultimate in banking convenience and superior to existing banking but will not replace other forms of banking • It results in time savings for travellers and people who bank from a distance • It is cheaper so fees should not apply, but they probably will • Customers are informed and in control of their financial affairs • Internet banking is great for 'visual' people and technology buffs • Simplifies and strengthens the relationship with a financial institution, especially if fees do not increase
D *Low touch, low tech*	C *High tech, low touch*
Customers with no Internet access who like neither personal banking nor high-technology banking	**Customers with Internet access who like high-technology banking but not personal banking. Their view on Internet banking is:** • It is preferable to have low-touch Internet banking in which the service is not customised or personalised

TOUCH

Low

Figure 7.2 Internet banking and customer relationships

high-touch customised and personalised service. In the view of these 'technically and socially savvy' types, the provision of Internet banking would strengthen their commitment to their banking relationship. In contrast the high-touch, low-tech group (Box B) were generally negative about Internet banking. For these 'socially savvy' types, Internet banking was likely to dilute their commitment to their banking relationship. The high-tech, low-touch participants (Box C) had an affinity with technology but not with people, and would prefer an Internet banking service that would allow them to take advantage of the best aspects of the technology without engaging in social interaction.

Implications for management

Focus group data is only a part of the information needed by managers. While a focus group can explain why things happen, a survey can reveal what is happening. Management needs both. The implications for Reward's managers of the focus group findings described above and a later survey were clear. To ensure that Reward would remain competitive with other institutions that offered Internet banking services, an Internet banking service could be launched as a complement to non-Internet banking services. Indeed the Internet was mainly being used by banks for transaction services such as account and interest rate information, fund transfers and the payment of bills, and not for relationship-enhancing banking that blended financial services with strong social relationship factors.

An example of user-friendly Internet banking would be a Web page that mimicked a banking hall, with an information desk, tellers' windows and security guards, thus making the on-line banking experience similar to face-to-face banking. A banking Web page could also include a chat group facility, providing customers with the opportunity to engage in social experiences such as chatting with bank staff and other customers, getting information, tips and ideas, and sharing experiences. Moreover important social needs such as helping others, sharing with others and being considerate and fair to others could be satisfied by an Internet banking club in which more experienced members could assist newer members to familiarise themselves with Internet banking. In short, a financial services institution should promote Internet banking as a social experience to be enjoyed, and not a technological experience to be feared or endured.

Conclusion

The research reported in this chapter demonstrates the ability of carefully planned focus groups efficiently to investigate emerging issues of major concern to marketing managers. The framework illustrated in Figure 7.1 provides a comprehensive guide to planning and conducting focus groups, and to analysing the data. Our research has revealed that different types of people want to take advantage of Internet banking in different ways – that is, there is no 'one size fits all'. Moreover our findings contradict the consensus in the Australian financial services industry that customers would prefer to conduct their business digitally rather than personally.

In conclusion, focus groups are an effective and efficient tool for tapping into the motivations of customers if they are planned, conducted and analysed in the way discussed above.

References

Aaker, D. A. and Day, G. S. (1990) *Marketing Research* (New York: Wiley).

Agar, M. and MacDonald, J. (1995) 'Focus groups and ethnography', *Human Organisation*, vol. 54, no. 1, pp. 78–85.

Albrecht, T. L, Johnson, G. M. and Walther, J. B. (1993) 'Understanding communication processes in focus groups', in D. L. Morgan (ed.), *Successful Focus Groups: Advancing the State of the Art* (Thousand Oaks, CA: Sage), pp. 51–64.

Asbury, J. (1995) 'Overview of focus group research', *Qualitative Health Research*, vol. 5, no. 4, pp. 414–20.

Axelrod, M. D. (1975) 'Ten essentials for good qualitative research', *Marketing News*, vol. 8, pp. 10–11.

Beck, R. (1994) *Development of a Marketing Focus within a Government Agency* (Brisbane, Qld: University of Technology).

Bellenger, D. N., Kenneth, L., Bernhardt, J. L. and Goldtucker, J. L. (1989) 'Qualitative research techniques: Focus group interviews', in T. J. Hayes and C. B. Tathum (eds), *Focus Group Interviews: A Reader* (Chicago, Ill.: AMA), pp. 10–25.

Bertrand, J. T., Brown, L. F. and Ward, V. M. (1992) 'Techniques for analyzing focus group data', *Evaluation Review*, vol. 16, no. 2, pp. 198–209.

Bristol, T. and Fern, E. F. (1996) 'Exploring the atmosphere created by focus group interviews: Comparing consumers' feelings across qualitative techniques', *Journal of the Market Research Society*, vol. 38, no. 2, pp. 185–95.

Byers, Y. B. and Wilcox, J. R. (1991) 'Focus groups: A qualitative opportunity for researchers', *Journal of Business Communication*, vol. 28, no. 1, pp. 63–78.

Calder, B. J. (1977) 'Focus groups and the nature of qualitative marketing research', *Journal of Marketing Research*, vol. 14 (August), pp. 353–64.

Carey, M. A. (1994) 'The group effect in focus groups: Planning, implementing and interpreting focus group research', in J. M. Morse (ed.), *Critical Issues in Qualitative Research Methods* (Thousand Oaks, CA: Sage), pp. 225–41.

Carson, D., Gilmore, A., Gronhaug, K. and Perry, C. (2001) *Qualitative Research in Marketing* (London: Sage).

Comley, P. (1997) 'The use of the Internet as a data collection method', http://www.sga.co.uk/esomar.html.

Cox, K. K., Higginbotham, J. B. and Burton, J. (1976) 'Application of focus group interviews in marketing', *Journal of Marketing*, vol. 40 (January), pp. 77–80.

Crabtree, B. F., Yanoshik, M. K., Miller, W. L. and O'Connor, P. J. (1993) 'Selecting individual or group interviews', in D. L. Morgan (ed.), *Successful Focus Groups: Advancing the State of the Art* (Thousand Oaks, CA: Sage), pp. 137–49.

Ennew, C. T. and Binks, M. R. (1996) 'The impact of service quality and service characteristics on customer retention: Small businesses and their banks in the UK', *British Journal of Management*, vol. 7, no. 3, pp. 219–30.

Fern, E. F. (1982) 'The use of focus groups for idea generation: The effects of group size, acquaintanceship, and moderator on response quantity and quality', *Journal of Marketing Research*, vol. 19 (February), pp. 1–13.

Flores, J. G. and Alonso, C. G. (1995) 'Using focus groups in educational research: Exploring teachers' perspectives on educational change', *Evaluation Review*, vol. 19, no. 1, pp. 84–101.

Forrest, E. (1999) *Internet Marketing Research: Resources and Techniques* (Sydney, NSW: McGraw-Hill).

Frey, J. H. and Fontana, A. (1993) 'The group interview in social research', in D. L. Morgan (ed.), *Successful Focus Groups: Advancing the State of the Art* (Thousand Oaks, CA: Sage), pp. 20–34.

Fuller, T. D., Edwards, J. N., Vorakitphokatorn, S. and Sermsri, S. (1993) 'Using focus groups to adapt survey instruments to new populations: experience from a developing country', in D. L. Morgan (ed.), *Successful Focus Groups: Advancing the State of the Art* (Thousand Oaks, CA: Sage), pp. 89–104.

Goldman, A. E. (1989) 'The Group Depth Interview', in T. J. Hayes and C. B. Tathum (eds), *Focus Group Interviews: A Reader* (Chicago, Ill.: AMA), pp. 2–9.

Greenbaum, T. L. (1997) 'Internet focus group: An oxymoron', *Marketing News*, vol. 31, no. 5, pp. 35–6.

Greenbaum, T. L. (1988) *The Practical Handbook and Guide to Focus Group Research* (Canada: D. C. Heath).

Henderson, N. R. (1995) 'A practical approach to analyzing and reporting focus group studies: Lessons from qualitative market research', *Qualitative Health Research*, vol. 5, no. 4, pp. 463–86.

Karger, T. (1989) 'Focus groups are for focusing, and for little else', in T. J. Hayes and C. B. Tathum (eds), *Focus Group Interviews: A Reader* (Chicago, Ill.: AMA), pp. 104–7.

Kennedy, F. (1989) 'The focused group interview and moderator bias', in T. J. Hayes and C. B. Tathum (eds), *Focus Group Interviews: A Reader* (Chicago, Ill.: AMA), pp. 56–9.

Keown, C. (1983) 'Focus group research: Tool for the retailer', *Journal of Small Business Management*, vol. 21, no. 2, pp. 59–65.

Knodel, J. (1993) 'The design and analysis of focus group studies: a practical approach', in D. L. Morgan (eds), *Successful Focus Groups: Advancing the State of the Art* (Thousand Oaks, CA: Sage), pp. 35–50.

Krueger, R. A. (1988) *Focus Groups: A Practical Guide for Applied Research* (Newbury Park, CA: Sage).

Krueger, R. A. (1993) 'Quality control in focus group research', in D. L. Morgan (ed.), *Successful Focus Groups: Advancing the State of the Art* (Thousand Oaks, CA: Sage), pp. 65–85.

Malhotra, N. K. (1993) *Marketing Research: An Applied Orientation* (London: Prentice-Hall).

Mariampolski, H. (1989) 'Probing correctly uncovers truth behind answers in focus group', in T. J. Hayes and C. B. Tathum (eds), *Focus Group Interviews: A Reader* (Chicago, Ill.: AMA), pp. 61–2.

McDonald, W. J. (1993) 'Focus group research dynamics and reporting: An examination of research objectives and moderator influences', *Journal of the Academy of Marketing Science*, vol. 21, no. 2, pp. 161–8.

Merton, R. K., Fiske, M. and Kendall, P. L. (1956) *The Focused Interview* (Glencoe, Ill.: Free Press).

Miles, M. B. and Huberman, A. M. (1994) *Qualitative Data Analysis* (Thousand Oaks, CA: Sage).

Morgan, D. L. (1988) *Focus Groups As Qualitative Research* (Newbury Park, CA: Sage).

Morgan, D. L. (1992) 'Designing focus group research', in M. Stewart, F. Tudiver, M. J. Bass, E. V. Dunn and P. G. Norton (eds), *Tools For Primary Care Research* (Newbury Park, CA: Sage), pp. 205–30.

Morgan, D. L. (1993) *Successful Focus Groups: Advancing the State of the Art* (Newbury Park, CA: Sage).

Morgan, D. L. (1996) 'Focus groups', *Annual Review of Sociology*, vol. 22, pp. 129–52.

Neuman, W. L. (1994) *Social Research Methods: Qualitative and Quantitative Approaches* (Boston, Mass.: Allyn and Bacon).

O'Brien, K. (1993) 'Improving survey questionnaires through focus groups', in D. L. Morgan (ed.), *Successful Focus Groups: Advancing the State of the Art* (Thousand Oaks, CA: Sage), pp. 105–17.

Palmquist, J. and Stueve, A. (1996) 'Stay plugged in to new opportunities', *Marketing Research: A Magazine of Management and Applications*, vol. 8, no. 1, pp. 13–15.

Parks, A. (1997) 'On-line focus groups reshape market research industry', *Marketing News*, vol. 3, no. 10, p. 28.

Patton, M. Q. (1990) *Qualitative Evaluation and Research Methods* (Newbury Park, CA: Sage).

Peebles, J. (1996) 'On-line technology creates research tools', *Marketing News*, vol. 30, no. 6, p. 5.

Rigler, E. (1987) 'Focus on focus groups', *ABA Banking Journal*, vol. 97, no. 4, pp. 96–100.

Roller, M. R. (1996) 'Virtual research exists, but how real is it?', *Marketing News*, vol. 30, no. 12, pp. H32–33.

Shea, C. Z. (1995) 'Thinking about focus groups? Think small for big results', *Marketing News*, vol. 29, no. 18, p.19.

Staddon, V. (1996) *Lecture Notes On Qualitative Research Prepared for USQ Marketing Students* (Brisbane, Qld: Staddon Consulting Services).

Stewart, K. and Colgate, M. (1998) 'Marketing relationships and personal banking', *Proceedings of the 27th EMAC Conference* (Stockholm: EMAC), pp. 261–78.

Stewart, D. W. and Shamdasani, P. M. (1990) *Focus Groups: Theory and Practice* (Newbury Park, CA: Sage).

Templeton, J. F. (1994) *The Focus Group: A Strategic Guide to Organizing, Conducting and Analyzing the Focus Group Interview* (Chicago, Ill.: Irwin).

Tuckel, P. and Wood, M. (2001) 'Respondent cooperation in focus groups: A field study using moderator settings', *International Journal of Market Research*, vol. 43, no. 4, pp. 391–407.

Tuckel, P., Leppo, E. and Kaplan, B. (1993) 'A view from the other side of the mirror', *Marketing Research: a Magazine of Management and Applications*, vol. 5, no. 4, pp. 24–7.

Tynan, A. C. and Drayton, J. L. (1988) 'Conducting focus groups – a guide for first-time users', *Marketing Intelligence and Planning in Action*, vol. 6, no. 1, pp. 5–9.

Zeller, R. A. (1993) 'Focus group research on sensitive topics: setting the agenda without setting the agenda', in D. L. Morgan (ed.), *Successful Focus Groups: Advancing the State of the Art* (Thousand Oaks, CA: Sage), pp. 167–83.

8
Coding: A Challenge for Researchers

Doris Ohnesorge

Introduction

Before a researcher starts working, he or she has to answer the following question: What method should I use in order best to achieve the research objectives? In addition to quantitative approaches, several qualitative research methods and software tools have been developed for the specific purpose of helping researchers to process verbal data. However the researcher him- or herself decides which statements belong together, which keywords are coded and how the results are interpreted and prepared for further courses of action. It is a central task of the coding procedure to find out what is essential from the interviewees' point of view. Nevertheless coding is highly vulnerable to mistakes, misperceptions and misinterpretations, and therefore needs special consideration. This chapter discusses the shortcomings of coding and possible ways of dealing with them when analysing unstructured verbal data in an inter-cultural context.

Coding in qualitative research is a central and sometimes complex task, especially when research is conducted not only within or across disciplines, but across cultures. Knowledge of the meaning of culturally biased concepts (terms, statements, ideas) is important throughout the research process, from the research design to the interpretation of results. In all stages, awareness of 'cultural concepts' is fundamental to researchers' understanding of the data.[1]

Thus qualitative researchers are confronted with the problem of understanding people's meanings when they express certain thoughts or ideas. Overcoming complex and difficult obstacles when conducting and interpreting research data in both one's own and other languages requires a great deal of reflection and discussion throughout the research process. A concept in one culture might have a completely different meaning in another culture, not only because a different language is involved but also because 'the background linguistic system (in other words, the grammar) of each language is not merely a reproducing instrument for voicing ideas but rather is itself the shaper of ideas, the program and guide for people's mental activity, for their analysis of impressions, for their synthesis of their mental stock in trade' (Whorf, 1998, p. 89). However in order to gain access to the knowledge of culturally biased concepts, the researcher has to take into account the languages of the interviewer and the interviewee. 'Language is a labyrinth of paths. You approach from *one* side and know your way about; you approach the same place from another side and no longer know your way about' (Wittgenstein, 2001, p. 69).

Coding is not only the foundation of data analysis, it also involves complex connections of meanings in and between interviewee' statements. This chapter illustrates the coding process using the GABEK method.

Research on Austro-Thai business relations

Because Austrians' and Thais' perceptions of business and management practices and communication styles are dissimilar, nuances in statements or opinions can lead to misunderstandings, misinterpretations and possibly even the breakdown of business relation between the parties involved (Ohnesorge, 2002a, p. 112). For the research reported in this chapter, I chose the intercultural approach, which 'is centred on the study of interaction between business people, organisations, buyers and sellers, employees and managers, who have different national/cultural backgrounds' (Usunier, 1998, p. 9).[2] Knapp (2003, pp. 111 f.) states that the way in which an interaction is interpreted is induced through cues from the persons involved and deduced through the ongoing prospective and retrospective context of action. These cues initiate cognitive maps, which are used to interpret the past contents of communication and to orient future actions. Knapp also argues that cognitive maps have an important function in intercultural interpersonal communication: the redress of expectations in standard communication situations and the assumption of shared knowledge make those involved feel more secure when interpreting and acting, especially when communicating with people from different cultural backgrounds.

The following study explored the specific intercultural management requirements for successful communication during the initiation phase of establishing a business relationship in Thailand. Eighteen Austrian and 20 Thai executives working for companies in different industries and located throughout Thailand were interviewed. Each interview took approximately 45 minutes. In order to avoid cultural and language misunderstandings I interviewed the Austrian executives in German and Thai interviewers spoke with the Thai executives in their own language. I also wanted to eliminate the possibility of an interviewee avoiding a topic because of limitations in his or her language skills (Knapp, 2003, p. 122). The German and Thai interviews were subsequently transcribed and translated into English. The aim of the analysis of the unstructured verbal data is to illustrate the Austrian and Thai executives' perceptions of the meeting of cultures in a business environment.[3]

The coding

Seidel and Kelle (1995, p. 52) state that 'although codes represent the decisive link between the original "raw data", that is, the textual material such as interview transcripts or field notes on the one hand and the researcher's theoretical concepts on the other, most of the methodological literature does not concentrate much on coding but rather on how to work with codes and coded material'. Text analysis goes far beyond mere concerns about coding. Nevertheless coding forms the basis of all later work that has to be done (the retrieval of text units, text search possibilities, the building of networks, mind structures, memos, interpretation and so on). The concept of coding has several meanings, and the connotation and function of the concept differ according to the method or software application in question.[4] 'Coding... is actually about going beyond the data, thinking creatively with the data, asking the data questions, and generating theories and frameworks. Coding... is a mixture of data reduction and data complication' (Coffey and Atkinson, 1996, p. 30). It can help to eliminate redundant information and reduce the complexity of the text, thus making it more accessible to the researcher. It also renders this multifaceted procedure structured, transparent and comprehensible; 'it can be used to expand, transform, and reconceptualise data, opening up more diverse analytical possibilities' (ibid., p. 29). Seidel and Kelle (1995, p. 52) identify two modes of coding: '(1) A code can *denote a text passage* containing specific information in order to allow its retrieval. This mode of coding is analogous to the construction of a book index.... (2) A code can also serve to *denote a fact*.' They point out that 'although one can drop the reference of a code to a certain text segment, a code can never lose its referential function'.

One of the strengths of the GABEK[5] method is that every code, every representation of the results is linked and supported by the original text. GABEK is a qualitative research method 'based on natural language processing of individual statements' that 'allows for the transparent organization of knowledge' (Zelger, 2000b, p. 205). Its software application, WinRelan,[6] was developed to facilitate text analysis. Every step of the analysis is strictly rule-based and can be reconstructed and reproduced intersubjectively (Zelger, 2000b, p. 206). There are two main coding methods: (1) object-linguistic coding, which means that lexically relevant terms (keywords) are identified, and (2) metalinguistic coding, through which text- or person-related criteria (age, sex and so on) can be added (Zelger and Oberprantacher, 2002, p. 28). Verbal expressions in text format are accessible for research and the gathering of new knowledge. 'Coding must be done on the language level of the respondents, ... the respondents' evaluations and articulated causal relations must be identified and integrated in the analysis' (Buber and Kraler, 2000, p. 117). A GABEK analysis allows for five coding options (Table 8.1).

Step 1: identifying keywords

The standard procedure in a GABEK WinRelan study is to start by transcribing the interviews and dividing the full text into meaningful text units (sense units) that are transferred to index cards. Figure 8.1 depicts an index card scheme. For each text unit, keywords (key concepts, key terms) are coded by the researcher (object linguistic coding), which results in an index system of all keywords. A keyword (key concept) is 'relevant if one cannot eliminate it without changing the central topic (in the cognitive sense) of the statement' (Zelger and Oberprantacher, 2002, p. 17).

Having divided the text into meaningful units, the actual coding process starts by identifying keywords to represent the text. Every keyword is coded by the researcher him- or herself.[7] The 'coding-rule' of GABEK

Table 8.1   The five coding options in GABEK

Step	Coding	Representation
1	Keywords	List of keywords
2	Criteria	Demographic and selection data
3	Evaluations	List of evaluations
4	Causal relations	List of causal relations
5	Basic values, primary goals, subgoals, measures, constraints	List of basic values, primary goals, subgoals, measures, constraints

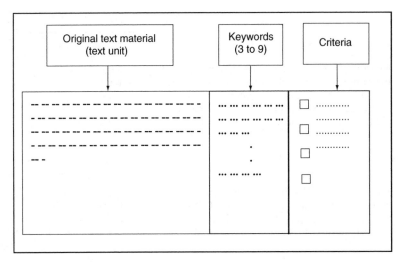

Figure 8.1 An index card scheme

is that one index card should have a minimum of three and a maximum of nine keywords. This rule is based on the limited ability of humans to gather and process information (Zimbardo, 1999, p. 370). Table 8.2 shows the keywords for text units transcribed from the answer given by a Thai executive to the question 'If you think about establishing a business relationship with Austrians, what comes to mind?'

Table 8.2 Keywords derived from a Thai executive's views on Austro–Thai business relations

Text Unit	Keywords
[Formation of business] The common characteristics of Austrians are similar to those of other Europeans. Austrians are rather direct, but at the same time they are shy [index card 1]	Business_formation Characteristics Austrian Similarity European Direct Shy
Sometimes Thai people are too polite to tell the truth [index card 2]	Thai Polite Truth
Europeans are open. Some Europeans are too open and they become aggressive in the Asian view. Their aggressiveness can lead to cultural conflict [index card 3]	European Open Aggressive Asian Problem_culture

Table 8.2   (*Continued*)

Text Unit	Keywords
For example, when negotiating Westerners express their ideas in such an aggressive way that some Thai people become angry. Sometimes Thai people do not talk because this can be seen as politeness [index card 4]	Negotiation Westerners Expression Idea Aggressive Thai Angry Polite Communication
For example the Thai party wants some free products in order to compete in the Thai market. The Austrians turn down that proposal because they do not understand the Thai market [index card 5]	Partner_Thai Product Competition Market_Thai Proposal Understanding Austrian
On the other hand the Thai party does not explain the situation and simply accepts the Austrians' refusal. I think this is a cultural problem [index card 6]	Partner_Thai Explain Situation Accept Refusal Austrian Problem_culture

Data collection

The following thoughts go beyond the mere problems of German–English and Thai–English translations. Although I could speak Thai fairly well, how could I, a native speaker of German, analyse the text in English. Not only would I be analysing the data in a language that neither I nor the Thai interviewees spoke as a mother tongue, but I would also be analysing and interpreting data about a culture into which I had not been social-ised. Intercultural researchers, managers and all other people involved in interactions with people from different cultural backgrounds have to develop a special sensitivity to and consideration for communication. According to Knapp (2003, pp. 122 ff.), 'lingua-franca communication' is not unproblematic. He argues that having to communicate in English is a source of intercultural communication conflicts because the parties concerned might differ broadly in their proficiency in English and their words might contain interferences from their native language. In his example of misunderstandings that occurred during the last minutes before a plane crash, Hinnenkamp (1998, pp. 28 ff.) shows that fatal errors can result from incorrect translations, inappropriate politeness and so on.

Assumptions

The Austro–Thai study included several basic assumptions. First, the concept of culture would apply to national boundaries (even though many subcultures may exist within a particular country; this distinction posed additional problems in that people are increasingly mobile, travel more, have Internet access and so on). Second, it was assumed that management, communication styles and business practices do not follow a universal pattern but are influenced by the complexities of culture (Usunier, 1998, pp. 2 ff.) Third, it was assumed that differences in perceptions in terms of culture, business behaviour, negotiation and communication practices and so on existed between the two parties. Fourth, it was assumed that some of the problems encountered would be to do with the researcher and not the method or software – he or she had to decide which text passage or keywords would be coded, analysed and interpreted. The final assumption was that the research topic was very complex and comprised different perspectives, disciplines and cultures. Hence the research analysis could not claim to be complete.

Language issues

The above comments on language had to be carefully considered during the coding process as well. Almost every Austrian and Thai manager used metaphors to describe some phenomena.[8] Furthermore some of their words derived from Austrian or Thai dialect, which made translation difficult. Also, the use of proverbs, images and non-verbal cues caused translation and coding problems. The following questions arose. Should contextual links such as 'ah', 'hmm', laughter and so on be transcribed? If so, how could they be interpreted properly? Would they provide a better understanding of the data? Were they important at all?[9]

Table 8.2 shows the coding of the chosen text passage. To illustrate potential problems, we shall consider the first text unit in the table and the keyword 'direct'. If Thais say that Europeans are 'direct', what do they mean by that? Does it mean that Europeans speak frankly and express their thoughts aloud? From my experience of working in Thailand I know that Thais also say things to one's face. However does the way they do it differ from that of Europeans? In addition, if Thais use the terms 'Austrians' and 'Europeans' interchangeably, are they really referring to the same concepts? In the fourth text unit in the table the

Thai manager indicates that in trying to be 'polite' Thai people sometimes say nothing at all. We might ask what kind of politeness he means. To the Austrian way of thinking, not saying anything (in this kind of situation) would be considered impolite. Furthermore what adequate and viable conclusions could we draw for negotiations?

Step 2: identifying criteria

The coding of criteria is referred to as 'metalinguistic coding'; criteria or categories do not have to occur in the text (Zelger and Oberprantacher, 2002, p. 28). The appropriate criteria vary from project to project, depending on the kind of information needed. Zelger and Oberprantacher (ibid.) distinguish three criteria: text-related criteria (categories to which the contents of a text unit are attributed), names of individuals (persons who formulated the text unit) and criteria related to individuals, for example age, educational level and so on. 'Meta-linguistic coding of all text units permits a direct analysis of the frequencies for all pairs of criteria or for any combinations of criteria, either in absolute values or in percent' (ibid., 2002, p. 31). Criteria have to be chosen at the very beginning of the coding process. The difficulty at this stage is to identify what kind of information or criteria would be useful for analysing and presenting the research results.

Step 3: identifying evaluated keywords

Positively and negatively evaluated keywords, as well as important statements and/or explicit/implicit wishes, are coded in each index card and reflect the interviewees' point of view. 'We thus obtain those topics which appear most important and urgent to those affected at the time of the interview' (Zelger, 2000b, p. 209). Table 8.3 shows the (in this case only negatively) evaluated keywords on index card 5.

Table 8.3　Evaluation of keywords on index card 5

Keywords	+	0	−
Partner_Thai			
Product			
Competition			
Market_Thai			
Proposal			x
Understanding			x
Austrian			

As Knapp (2003, p. 125) points out, the interpretation of cues is based on understanding of the standard communication processes of the learned foreign language, on its culture orientation and on stereotypical knowledge about the 'normal' behaviour of the foreign party in terms of his or her native language and culture. Not only might the interviewee and researcher have preconceived ideas about each other's cultures, but their knowledge of cultural differences could also lead to a distorted picture of the current situation, as social and cultural changes over time might not be taken into account. According to Hinnenkamp (1998, p. 61), functioning communication means that the parties interpret and draw conclusions about what each other says, does or signals, and if such cues are interpreted incorrectly, this could give rise to misunderstandings. In the Austro–Thai study the Thai manager did not explicitly say that he considered it negative that Austrians did not understand the Thai market (Table 8.2, index card 5). However, based on his tone of voice it was assumed that (in this particular situation) Austrians' lack of understanding of the Thai market was perceived negatively, so the keyword 'understanding' was coded as negative. Another problem was that I did not conduct the Thai interviews myself. This could be seen as a disadvantage because I did not experience the situation first hand and therefore had difficulty judging whether or not the interviewee expressed certain statements in a negative way, but on the plus side the fact that I was distanced from the situation meant that I was not influenced by sympathy for or preconceived ideas about the interviewee.

When coding the evaluations I listened to the tapes and concentrated on the voice. Did it rise or get louder? Was the statement expressed in a rough way? Did a raised voice necessarily mean that the interviewee was getting angry about a certain point? Could I rightly conclude that because a statement was expressed in a rough way the situation in question should be evaluated as negative from the interviewee's point of view? Another factor that was considered was the kind of vocabulary used. Did the interviewee use harsh and/or soft terms, and in what combination? Also, what should be done with keywords that already had a negative connotation (angry, aggressive and so on)? Should they all be coded as negative?

Special consideration should be given to the fact that all these measures involved cues that required interpretation by the researcher. Furthermore the interviews were translated into English after transcription. The important point here was the actual meaning of a thought or idea expressed in a statement so culturally based concepts that could not be translated were left in the original language. Nevertheless the answers to the following questions had strong implications for coding. Did the same cue always mean the same (or at least a similar) thing? Was it possible that the interviewee had used the term 'anger' in a positive way?

One possible way of avoiding these sorts of pitfall would be for a person other than the researcher to do the coding. This could result in a more neutral investigation that was not swayed by a preconceived view of the situation and persons involved. On the other hand personal assessments of the researcher would be lost. Another approach would be to code only explicitly mentioned negative or positive statements. However this could result in failure to capture the whole situation.

Step 4: identifying causal relations

In this step explicit and implicit causal relations between keywords in an interviewee's statements are identified. Causal assumptions 'are opinions on cause–effect relations based on empirical experiences over time or discussions with other people' (Zelger and Oberprantacher, 2002, p. 46). The entire text is coded again in a new way and placed in a square matrix. The coding of causal relations is rule-based. The following question is posed: 'Does the author of the text believe that the growth of the variable A^{10} leads to the increase or decrease of the variable B?' (ibid., p. 47). Opinions expressed by interviewees include variations on coding possibilities.[11] After coding implicit and explicit causal relations the researcher can automatically generate a causal network for each key concept he or she is interested in (Gadner and Zelger, 2000). This makes it possible to explain and understand facts, connections and concepts. Figure 8.2 shows an index card (5) with coded causal relations in the statement 'the Thai party wants some free products in order to compete in the Thai market. The Austrians turn down that proposal because they do not understand the Thai market.'

Keywords		A	B	C	D	E	F	G
Partner_Thai	A							
Product	B							
Competition	C							
Market_Thai	D							
Proposal	E							
Understanding	F							
Austrian	G				–		–	

Figure 8.2   An index card (5) with coded causal relations

This coding means that the more Austrians become involved, the less they know about the Thai market, and the more Austrian they are, the less they understand the Thai market. More generally, a plus would mean an increase in the influenced variable while a minus would mean a decrease. Influences on variables can also be seen as favourable or unfavourable. The latter was identified in index card 5.

At the beginning of the causal relation coding it was difficult to identify 'quasi' causal relations: which variable influenced or was influenced by another variable. Furthermore the interviewees' opinions, assumptions or intentions were not always clearly expressed.

Step 5: identifying basic values, aims, measures and constraints

Assumed basic values, primary goals, subgoals, measures and constraints (Figure 8.3) can be identified in the automatically generated causal relation list. 'Usually, basic values are connected to each other and all sorts of goals in causal connections' (Gadner and Zelger, 2000, p. 239). Basic values function as the basis for and validation of goals. Primary goals depend on the fulfilment of basic values. Subgoals can be used to support the implementation of certain measures. Measures can affect expressed goals and basic values (Maier and Zelger, 1999, pp. 169 ff.)

Coding possibilities	Symbol
Basic value Influenced by many other variables Has little or no influence on other variables	
Primary goals Influenced by many other variables	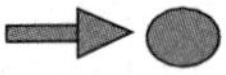
Subgoals Influence or are influenced by other variables	
Measures/consequences Influence other variables	
Constraints Have a lot of influence on other variables For a certain period it is not possible to manipulate them	

Figure 8.3 Causal coding

Table 8.4 Thais' perception of Austrians' (index card 1)

Keywords	Coded assumptions
Business_formation	Primary goal
Austrian	Constraint
Characteristics	Constraint
Similarity	Primary goal
European	Constraint
Direct	Measure/consequence
Shy	Constraint

The coded assumptions for the statement 'The common characteristics of Austrians are similar to those of other Europeans. Austrians are rather direct, but at the same time they are shy' are shown in Table 8.4.

Because it is not possible to code assumptions about basic values, primary goals and so on on the basis of just one index card, the assumptions allotted to the keywords in Table 8.4 extend to all the index cards in the project. The GABEK method provides indications of the meaning of a basic value, primary goal or measure, but the researcher has to assign them. With regard to Usunier's statement that 'The prevailing values in a particular society and the extent to which they are respected in the everyday behaviour of individuals, are important because they may impinge on the willingness to take risks, on leadership styles, and on the relationships between superiors and subordinates' (Usunier, 1998, p. 19), difficulties arose when coding the Thai managers' perspective. How did they define basic values, primary goals, subgoals or measures? Not only might the Austrians and Thais have had different basic values or goals, but they might also have understood the concepts in completely different ways.

The above discussion of the various coding issues shows that coding can be difficult, contradictory and problematic. However it does provide insights into the data. It uncovers the structure of the text and therefore aids the researcher's understanding of central themes and interviewees' concerns. The further development of qualitative methods and software tools could assist the researcher in this important task. With regard to the GABEK method, the software WinRelan offers the following advantages (Buber and Kraler, 2000, pp. 128 ff.):

- Intersubjective comprehensibility: every step in the analysis can be linked and supported by text, which means that an observer can follow all of the researcher's work.
- Modelling and theory development: it is possible to develop hypotheses and concepts. GABEK can also be used as a methodology for theory development.
- Proximity to data: throughout the coding process the researcher works with the original text. The hermeneutical approach during the analysis process also allows close work with the original data.
- User friendliness: the original data is accessible with one mouse click. Furthermore the programme can process multiple languages and offers a well-structured arrangement for navigating through the various features.
- Presentation tool: it is possible to present the results directly from the software. If the audience has any questions, a text passage connected with a presented result can be shown. It also can be used to give direct feedback to the interviewees themselves.

Conclusion

GABEK can help to reveal the proper meanings of concepts and thereby enhance (intercultural) understanding and communication. The research process involves constant decision making by the researcher about further steps to take in conditions of uncertainty. Intercultural research offers many peripheral rewards for the researcher: wonderful and often surprising experiences, in-depth insights, perceptions, a touch of the exotic and the chance to broaden one's horizon.

The researcher can approach the text from many different perspectives and disciplines. 'Intercultural' coding using the GABEK method is a way of establishing central themes in a topic, systematising the analysing procedure and accessing the thoughts of people from various cultures. Coding helps the researcher to become more sensitive to important themes and more aware of the problems involved from the interviewees' point of view. In intercultural research it is important to make the method of approaching the text transparent, open up the perspective on essential issues and make the researcher's thoughts comprehensible. Questioning the data helps to broaden its complexity and thus opens the way to different topics that could examine both strong and weak signals for topics. Coding makes the researcher more sensitive to the basic values and primary goals of other cultures, which can in turn lead to discussions with other researchers. Finally, the research results can help to improve communication between people of different cultures and enhance intercultural understanding, as well as offering possible solutions to intercultural conflicts.

In any reading or interpretation of the research discussed above, the inevitable existence of an Austrian cultural bias has to be taken into account.

Notes

1. The following illustrations are drawn from my study on perceptions between Austrian and Thai executives during an initiation process of establishing a business relationship in Thailand. Although I lived in Thailand for some time and speak Thai fairly well, fully understanding the ideas expressed in certain statements was very difficult. I found it very useful to discuss several concepts and their meanings with both Thais and Austrians.
2. There is a distinction between the terms cross-cultural and intercultural in English. However the German word for both terms is *interkulturell*, that is intercultural. Therefore the usage of this term can be misleading in the sense that some authors use *interkulturell* or intercultural when they actually mean cross-cultural. This is not necessarily because they are not aware of the different definitions, but simply because they come from a different cultural or language background. An attempt to classify and refine the definition of concepts used in international business research has been made by Usunier (1998, pp. 2–24). Another difficulty with intercultural research is that researchers come from a variety of cultural backgrounds and deal with problems from different perspectives and disciplines. This raises questions about predefined culturally biased concepts used by the researcher.
3. For details of the study see Ohnesorge (2002b).
4. For an overview of the various applications of and approaches to qualitative research see Denzin (2000) and Bauer and Gaskell (2000).
5. GAnzheitliche BEwältigung von Komplexität, Holistic Processing of Complexity, © Zelger, 1990–2003. For details of the method see Zelger (1999, 2000a).
6. Windows Relational Analysis, © Zelger, 1990–2003.
7. QSR N6 offers automated coding. For controversial opinions on and a discussion of automated coding see Buber and Kraler (2000, p. 133).
8. Coffey and Attkinson (1996, pp. 85–9) discuss the implications of and possible problems with the use of metaphorical statements in qualitative research.
9. Hinnenkamp (1998, pp. 73 ff.) emphasises that although we might not be able to identify or even be aware of such cues, we unconsciously perceive and interpret them. He illustrates the problem with an example of communicating on the phone. If the person we are speaking to does not respond to something we have said, we immediately ask 'Do you understand?' Or we interpret the lack of response as a sign that he or she is tired or is not paying attention. Hinnenkamp argues that if we had not perceived the missing cue, we would not have reacted at all.

10. 'Expressions, which are linked by causal relations, are called causal variables or simply variables, since they refer to situations that are experienced as changeable' (Zelger and Oberprantacher, 2002, p. 47).

11. For an overview of various coding possibilities see Ohnesorge (2002b, p. 55).

References

Bauer, M. W. and Gaskell, G. (eds), (2000) *Qualitative Researching with Text, Image and Sound. A Practical Handbook* (Thousand Oaks, CA: Sage).

Buber, R. and Kraler, C. (2000) 'How GABEK and *WinRelan* support qualitative research', in R. Buber and J. Zelger (eds), *GABEK II: Zur Qualitativen Forschung–On Qualitative Research* (Innsbruck, Vienna and Munich: StudienVerlag), pp. 111–37.

Coffey, A. and Atkinson, P. (1996) *Making Sense of Qualitative Data. Complementary Research Strategies* (Thousand Oaks, CA: Sage).

Denzin, N. K. (ed.) (2000) *Handbook of Qualitative Research* (Thousand Oaks, CA: Sage).

Gadner, J. and Zelger J. (2000) 'Organizational Development by GABEK', in R. Buber and J. Zelger (eds), *GABEK II: Zur Qualitativen Forschung – On Qualitative Research* (Innsbruck, Vienna and Munich: StudienVerlag), pp. 233–58.

Hinnenkamp, V. (1998) *Mißverständnisse in Gesprächen: Eine empirische Untersuchung im Rahmen der interpretativen Soziolinguistik* (Opladen and Wiesbaden: Westdeutscher Verlag).

Knapp, K. (2003) 'Interpersonale und interkulturelle Kommunikation', in N. Bergemann and A. L. J. Sourisseaux, *Interkulturelles Management* (Berlin and Heidelberg: Springer,), pp. 109–35.

Maier, M. and Zelger, J. (1999) 'Schulentwicklung an berufsbildenden mittleren und höheren Schulen in Tirol', in J. Zelger and M. Maier (eds), *GABEK: Wissensverarbeitung und Wissensdarstellung* (Innsbruck and Vienna: StudienVerlag), pp. 159–81.

Ohnesorge, D. A. (2002a) 'Auf der Suche nach Vorbildern: Was können wir von der thailändischen Dienstleistungskultur lernen?', in H. H. Hinterhuber and H. K. Stahl (eds), *Erfolg durch Dienen? Beiträge zur wertsteigernden Führung von Dienstleistungsunternehmen*, Innsbrucker Kolleg für Unternehmensführung, Band 4 (Renningen: Expert), pp. 112–130.

Ohnesorge, D. A., (2002b) 'Inter-Cultural Management: Interactions and Transactions between Austrian and Thai Companies' (unpublished diploma study, University of Innsbruck).

Seidel, J. and Kelle, U. (1995) 'Different Functions of Coding in the Analysis of Textual Data', in U. Kelle (ed.), *Computer-Aided Qualitative Data Analysis. Theory, Methods and Practice* (London: Sage), pp. 52–61.

Usunier, J. C. (1998) *International and Cross-Cultural Management Research* (London: Sage).

Whorf, B. L. (1998) 'Science and Linguistics', in M. J. Bennett (ed.), *Basic Concepts of Intercultural Communication* (Yarmouth and Maine: Intercultural Press), pp. 85–95.

Wittgenstein, L. (2001) *Philosophische Untersuchungen; Philosophical Investigations*, trans. G. E. M. Anscombe (Oxford: Blackwell).

Zelger, J. (1999) 'Wissensorganisation durch sprachliche Gestaltbildung im Verfahren GABEK', in J. Zelger and M. Maier (eds), *GABEK: Wissensverarbeitung und Wissensdarstellung* (Innsbruck and Vienna: StudienVerlag), pp. 41–87.

Zelger, J. (2000a) 'Parallele und serielle Wissensverarbeitung: Die Simulation von Gesprächen durch GABEK', in R. Buber and J. Zelger (eds), *GABEK II: Zur Qualitativen Forschung – On Qualitative Research* (Innsbruck, Vienna and Munich: StudienVerlag), pp. 60–5.

Zelger, J. (200b) 'Twelve Steps of GABEK*WinRelan*: A Procedure for Qualitative Opinion Research, Knowledge Organization and Systems Development', in R. Buber and J. Zelger (eds), *GABEK II: Zur Qualitativen Forschung – On Qualitative Research* (Innsbruck, Vienna and Munich: StudienVerlag), pp. 205–20.

Zelger, J. and Oberprantacher, A. (2002) 'Processing of Verbal Data and Knowledge Representation by GABEK-WinRelan [97 paragraphs]', *Forum Qualitative Sozialforschung/Forum: Qualitative Social Research* (on-line journal), vol. 3, no. 2, http://www.qualitative-research.net.

Zimbardo, Ph.G. (1999) *Psychologie* (Berlin, Heidelberg and New York: Springer).

Part III

Methods and Analysis

9
Issues in Mixing Qualitative and Quantitative Approaches to Research

Pat Bazeley

Introduction

After a period in the paradigmatic wilderness, mixed-method research has regained not just acceptability but also popularity, with a significant number of studies arguing its virtues in terms of greater understanding and/or the validation of results. But all is not plain sailing – working with mixed methods raises a range of issues above and beyond those encountered with a particular methodology. Not the least of these is that there is no single mixed-method methodology and the term can be applied to widely divergent approaches to research.

Defining mixed methods

Tashakkori and Teddlie (1998) argue that the term 'mixed model' is more appropriate than 'mixed method' for research in which different approaches are applied during any or all of a number of stages of the research, their point being that mixing often extends beyond just the methods used in the research. Indeed the mixing of methodologies within a broad quantitative or qualitative approach can raise almost as many issues as when working across approaches (Barbour, 1998). Mixing can also occur across different disciplinary traditions, for example in social history or when scientists engage in social research to evaluate the impact of their work. It is therefore necessary to clarify just what is being mixed and how it is being mixed. The 'mixing' may be nothing more than side-by-side or sequential use of different methods, or it may be that different methods are fully integrated in a single analysis (Caracelli and Greene, 1997).

Defining qualitative and quantitative

Most social scientists think of mixed methods in terms of some combination of qualitative and quantitative approaches to research, and such combinations will be the focus of this chapter. Here too there are definitional problems – problems that relate to paradigmatic and other issues that are typically associated with mixing methods. Qualitative and quantitative approaches have been distinguished (and thereby defined) on the basis of the type of data used (textual or numeric, structured or unstructured), the logic employed (inductive or deductive), the type of investigation (exploratory or confirmatory), the method of analysis (interpretive or statistical), the approach to explanation (variance theory or process theory) and the presumed underlying paradigm (positivist or interpretive/critical, rationalistic or naturalistic). Perhaps our inability to specify clearly what all of us have a general sense of is indicative of the lack of a clear distinction – that what we are talking about is a continuum, with a number of independent dimensions upon which any particular research can be placed. If one uses numbers, interpretation is still involved. If one's data are texts, counting may still be appropriate. Variables do not necessarily have clear-cut meanings; processes can be revealed through numeric analysis as well as through narrative, and so on. This inability definitively to distinguish one approach from another has implications for the acceptability of mixing methods in that 'lines of conflict' cannot be clearly drawn.

Because there is no necessary congruence between the various dimensions of the quantitative–qualitative distinction, the terms themselves are most useful either for providing a sense of overall direction in a study (hence my use of the term 'approaches'), or simply as descriptors of the type of data being used (textual or numeric). Even the latter is problematic (suggesting that approach and data type are necessarily linked), but it at least avoids the problems associated with suggesting there are such things as quantitative or qualitative paradigms or methodologies.

Paradigms

Approaches to defining 'qualitative' and 'quantitative' have long been associated with different paradigmatic approaches to research – different assumptions about the nature of knowledge (ontology) and the means of generating it (epistemology). The idea that one's paradigmatic view of the world might be related to the way one has gone about researching the world was prompted by Kuhn (1963), while Lincoln and Guba's (1985) work on naturalistic inquiry contributed significantly to the 'paradigm wars' of the 1980s. Their concern about the paradigmatic assumptions that underlay research was taken up by many of those who were writing about approaches to social research and social research methodology in that period. Much of this concern was a reaction to the earlier dominance of the 'positivist' world view, which privileged objective observation and precise measurement over the interpretation of subjective experiences and constructed social realities. Researchers who believed that there were strong associations between paradigm, methodology and methods consequently considered that different methodologies and methods were philosophically incompatible, making their combination logically impossible. During this period, therefore, mixed-method research was strongly attacked and it fell from favour among methodologists.

The positivist approach to social and behavioural science, adopted at the urging of John Stuart Mill and others in order to build respectability among scientists (Guba and Lincoln, 1994), has, Howe and Eisenhardt (1990) suggest, not only served social science badly but has also been largely ignored as a basis for natural science. They argue that all scientific observation, analysis and theorising involves acts of interpretation, and that all investigation is theory laden. It may be too simplistic to suggest, however, that if all research is interpretive there is no problem. Based on their review of 56 mixed-method studies, Greene *et al.* (1989, p. 271) conclude that 'the notion of mixing paradigms is problematic for designs with triangulation or complementary purposes, acceptable but still problematic for designs with a development or expansion intent, and actively encouraged for designs with an initiation intent'.

It could be said that the paradigmatic issues raised by mixed-method research remain unresolved. Indeed one cannot research or prove paradigms, and paradigmatic debates can never be resolved. The early 1990s saw a series of rejoinders to those who had given paradigms so much attention (particularly evident in the *Educational Researcher*), plus a shift in emphasis to the more tractable issues of design and methods (Krantz, 1995) and features of the knowledge claims that could be generated (Greene and Caracelli, 1997). Pragmatism increasingly overruled purity (Rossman and Wilson, 1985) as the perceived benefits of mixing methods in 'getting research done' came to be seen as outweighing the importance of the philosophical difficulties of their use (Miles and Huberman, 1994). Thus according to Miles and Huberman (ibid., p. 41), 'The question, then, is not whether the two sorts of data and associated methods can be linked during study design, but whether it should be done, how it will be done, and for what purposes.'

Purpose and design

Often the purpose for choosing a mixed-method design is not made clear by the researcher (Greene *et al.*, 1989), potentially leading to confusion in the design phase of the study. Some studies may be considered as not employing mixed methods at all insofar as they do not give recognition to the full contribution of each method (Patton, 1988). The reasons for needing mixed methods include corroboration, expansion and initiation (Rossman and Wilson, 1985). Initiation, in the form of an iterative, nested, holistic or transformative design (Caracelli and Greene, 1997), requires the integration of methods, in contrast to the simpler component designs that are typically used for corroboration or expansion. When the purpose of the research is made clear and is theory-driven (that is, presented through a logical chain of evidence), then that substantive focus becomes a superordinate goal that limits the tensions involved in mixing methods (Chen, 1997).

Many of the works on mixed-method designs (Morse, 1991; Creswell, 1994; Morgan, 1998) focus on the use of component (parallel or sequential) designs in which the different elements are kept separate, thus allowing each element to be true to its own paradigmatic and design requirements (but raising the question of whether such cases really do constitute a mixed-method study or are two separate studies that happen to be about the same topic). Likewise most reports on mixed-method studies report either parallel or sequential component designs. Few studies report truly integrated designs (Greene *et al.*, 1989), perhaps because the technology for managing integrated analyses is still in development (Bazeley, 2002).

Triangulation is a term that has been greatly misused in relation to purpose and design since Denzin's (1970, 1978) popularisation of it. It was initially conceived as the conduct of parallel (or otherwise duplicated) studies using different methods to achieve the same purpose, with a view to providing corroborating evidence for the conclusions drawn, that is, as a validation technique (drawn from the concept of triangulation in surveying). In more recent years it has, often been used loosely as a synonym for mixed methods without regard to either of the conditions inherent in the original concept, and as a consequence it has lost its original meaning. It has been argued that, in any case, triangulation does not assist validation as each source must be understood on its own terms (Fielding and Fielding, 1986; Flick, 1992). The original model of triangulation assumes a single reality and ignores the symbolic interactionist foundation of much qualitative work that proposes that different methods (or researchers or participants) will necessarily view or construe the object of the research in different ways. And as researchers use different methods, they play different roles and have different relationships with the researched – the latter, for example, being variously labelled as respondents, subjects, participants or informants (Barbour, 1998).

Alternative methods may also 'tap different domains of knowing' (Mathison, 1988, p. 14) or encourage or allow expression of different facets of knowledge or experience. For example people who respond to interview questions or open-ended questions will often raise quite different issues from those provided for in a structured questionnaire that asks essentially the same question. Interviews and focus groups generate different information, reflecting public versus private views (Morgan, 1993) and a preparedness to deal with more sensitive issues in interviews (Kaplowitz, 2000). Therefore while the use of parallel methods may not provide corroborative evidence, it may well add depth or breadth to a study and perhaps even hold the key to understanding the processes that are occurring (Jick, 1979; Mark *et al.*, 1997). In the third edition of his book, Denzin (1989) himself abandons the idea of triangulation as a validation tool, suggesting instead that it overcomes personal biases arising from single methodologies. 'The goal of multiple triangulation is a fully grounded interpretive research approach. Objective reality will never be captured. In-depth understanding, not validity, is sought in any interpretive study' (ibid., p. 246). (This statement implies that objective reality and validity are the same thing, and that each is unrelated to in-depth understanding. It seems that it is difficult not to tie oneself in knots, whichever way one turns!)

Despite it being one of the more commonly stated reasons for engaging in a mixed-method study, it would appear that the corroboration of findings is not only a dubious intention but also one that is almost doomed to failure.

Methods

Although paradigms may be implied, when it comes to reporting studies they are rarely mentioned (Riggin, 1997). The focus is much more on the methods used and the results obtained. Despite the tendency for some to write about quantitative and qualitative paradigms, or to assume that someone working with numbers and statistics has a positivist perspective, it is generally recognised that there are no direct or exclusive correspondences between paradigms, methodology and methods. Indeed 'research methodologies are merely tools, instruments to be used to facilitate understanding' (Morse, 1991, p. 122). With the debate on the value of quantitative versus qualitative methods moderating to a recognition that both have a place, the 'real issues', according to Patton (1989, p. 181), have become 'methodological flexibility and appropriateness'.

When methods are mixed without careful consideration of the precise assumptions or rules and expectations regarding their conduct, corruption of the methods can occur, such that results obtained by them become subject to question. Assumptions about sampling, which will be discussed in the next section, provide the most blatant but not the only example of this problem. Mixed-method studies in which just a few observations or interviews are conducted to supplement quantitative data collection 'cheapen' qualitative methods in a way that Patton (1988) likens to the difference between loving intimacy and a one-night stand. The corruption may be out of ignorance, or because those using multiple strategies for investigation take shortcuts in order to cope with the greater time commitment required (Bryman, 1988). The term 'Blitzkrieg ethnography' (Rist, quoted in Bryman, 1988), for example, has been applied to work conducted in a number of multisite, multi-method studies that claim an ethnographic component, where there has not been proper immersion in the site. 'Ethnography is a methodological approach with specific procedures, techniques, and methods of analysis' (Fetterman, 1984, p. 23), and for the method to be valid one needs to adopt its values as well as its techniques. Conflicts of this type might also be interpreted as disciplinary purists being precious about the traditional approaches to research in their discipline, or at least about the labelling of those approaches. A balance needs to be struck, then, between adherence to the total package of techniques, perspectives and values associated with a traditional method, and the ability to extract useful strategies from those traditions – recognising the ways in which they have been modified and the implications of doing so (Smith and Robbins, 1982).

Mixed methods often combine nomothetic and idiographic approaches in an attempt to serve the dual purposes of generalisation and in-depth understanding – to gain an overview of social regularities from a larger sample while understanding the other through detailed study of a smaller sample. Full integration of these approaches is difficult, hence the predominance of component studies. Case-oriented quantification (Kuckartz, 1995) has been proposed as a way of bringing these together by providing understanding of the individual while also supporting typification. Kuckartz's software program winMAX was specifically written to support such a goal. Similarly Ragin's (1987, 1995) method of qualitative comparative analysis (QCA), also translated into software, is an attempt to develop typologies and related understandings while retaining the richness of the qualitative case.

In my own work I have set up a model for the analysis of a database in which qualitative coding is converted into quantitative variables that can be fed into a predictive regression model. I have also used correspondence analysis to help to reveal dimensions derived from the coding of descriptive data. In each case a qualitative database is necessary to provide an understanding of the meanings of the concepts and variables used, and of how the statistically derived models work out for 'real people', but the statistical analysis also provides access to patterns, trends and underlying dimensions in the data that are not readily evident in the detail of the qualitative analyses. Methods such as these, in which the same data are treated both hermeneutically and statistically, along with those proposed by Kuckartz (1995) and Ragin (1987, 1995), provide integrated (holistic) techniques for viewing data both nomothetically and ideographically.

In the final analysis, methodology must be judged more by how well it informs research purposes than by how well it matches a set of conventions (Howe and Eisenhardt, 1990). What counts for good research will not necessarily match what counts as orthodox methodology. The standards that Howe and Eisenhardt (1990) suggest should be applied include the following:

- Do the chosen methods provide data that can answer the question?
- Are the background assumptions coherent?
- Are the methods applied well enough for the results to be credible?

Sampling

Typically one expects quantitative research to rely on a large, randomly drawn sample, while qualitative studies are associated with smaller, purposive (non-random) samples. But there are no statistics for generalising from small purposive samples and it is not possible to do fine hermeneutic analysis on data from large random sample. Cases for detailed study can be identified within larger samples (Nickel *et al.*, 1995), while computerisation can facilitate testing – across a larger selection of texts – of the generality of ideas developed through fine-grained interpretive analysis of a subset of those texts (Bazeley, 2002).

With computerisation of qualitative analysis and the increasing use of qualitative analysis software by those trained only in quantitative approaches to research, there is a tendency for researchers to include much larger volumes of unstructured data than have traditionally been used in qualitative approaches. Stratified random sampling or quota sampling replaces purposive sampling to meet expectations for the generalisation of results, as understood in statistical terms, and the inappropriate application of rules of one method distorts, and potentially invalidates, the assumptions of another.

When qualitative programs are able to provide statistical summaries there is a temptation to overinterpret numbers (frequency or cross-tabulated data) generated by coding texts from a small, purposively drawn sample. When the sample comprises fewer than 20 it is inappropriate to report percentages, and few inferential statistical procedures can be applied to such small samples. The chi-square statistic cannot be validly used to test a relationship between variables when there are small expected frequencies (nor can it when categories are not mutually exclusive), and samples in the range of 10 to 20 cases per variable are required for multivariate analyses. At the same time there is nothing to be gained from substituting vague terms (more, most) for actual numbers when those numbers are available.

The researcher's view of the generic and specific properties of a single case provides a basis for sampling decisions. The opportunity to conduct a detailed study while maintaining balance and variety may be more important than satisfying selection criteria based on a sampling of attributes (Stake, 1994). Symbolic interactionists argue that every case is a sample of its broader population and that the similarities across a population are greater than the differences between populations, and therefore it is appropriate to treat each case as being, in general terms, representative of their population. Such approaches are unacceptable, however, to statisticians.

However it is with integrated methods that apply both hermeneutic and statistical analyses to the same data that difficulties are most likely to arise, generating a need to trade off between the intensiveness of detailed hermeneutic analysis and the extensiveness of statistical inference to larger populations (Prein and Kuckartz, 1995). Sampling issues must be resolved with respect to the purpose of the research, and in particular how the results are to be generalised to a population beyond the sample. For example it matters whether it is descriptive information or understanding of a process that is to be learned and generalised from the sample.

Analysis

Without computerisation the researcher's capacity to integrate different data types in an analysis has been limited. Typically, statistical data have been analysed using a computer and in-depth text data have been analysed without. Recent developments in computer software for qualitative data analysis (QDA) have brought about a revolution in textual analysis. Even more recent developments in QDA software – specifically the ability to export coding information in tabular form – herald a revolution for integrated mixed-method analysis. It is in the conversion of qualitative data to quantitative code for statistical analysis (often referred to as the quantitising of qualitative data) that most problems arise.

The use of codes

Coding or the categorisation of data is undertaken to facilitate understanding and retrieval of information in almost all approaches to analysis. Whether they are called variables, themes, concepts, categories or values, responses are coded. And codes are the means by which data are transferred from one format into another, or between QDA and statistical software. The kinds of things codes can stand for are similar in the various softwares, but the way they are generated and used are often quite different, making for potential interpretation complications when they are read in a different context.

While the categories developed through a qualitative analysis may be defined *a priori*, QDA software allows for the generation of new codes as the analysis progresses, for the rearrangement of codes without loss of data and, for some software, for coding on from existing codes into new categories. Researchers who use a statistical program, in contrast, have to define their variables before coding, and changing them involves recategorising already coded data. This can be a problem if a researcher is determined to have a common coding system across data types in order to obtain comparability of conclusions from the different data sources.

Both statistical and QDA programs use codes for demographic and project related information as well as to capture topic themes and concepts. Representational/descriptive categories (for example 'does research'), instrumental/interpretive categories (for example 'being stimulated by or passionate about research') and analytic concepts ('identification as a researcher', 'addiction to research') can all be represented by codes or scores in the various softwares. But it is here that the similarity ends. A code in a statistical data set has to represent fully the category or concept for which it stands. Unlike a qualitative data set, there can be no recourse to the original source to check what was meant by it or review different interpretations of it.

Because codes are the only medium for communicating information in a quantitative data set, they are necessarily precise in what they are conveying; they are unidimensional (Sivesind, 1999) and directional. With qualitative data the text that supports a code is always available for review, and dimensions within it (which initially may not have been apparent to the coder) may become obvious during that review, or be revealed through pattern or comparative analysis. Thus qualitative coding has singularity rather than unidimensionality, in that all the text on a particular issue, idea or experience can be assigned the same code, regardless of the way it is expressed. Often such coding is also multidirectional, for example when all the text on competence is coded together, simply because it is about that concept and regardless of whether it is about high or low degrees of competence. (It is possible that analysis will reveal additional dimensions or types of competence as well as its quantity.)

When a qualitative theme code is quantitised its meaning becomes fixed and unidimensional. When directionality has not been embodied in the qualitative coding, statistical analysis involving variables must be carefully interpreted. The exported variable may simply have been a record of whether an issue was raised or a feeling discussed, without indication of how it was dealt with or perceived. If direction is needed for interpretation in the statistical analysis, it is necessary to code on the qualitative data to provide that directionality before exporting the coding information. This is perhaps the most crucial issue in the interpretation of quantitised data.

The counting of codes

The way in which (qualitative) texts are segmented in QDA software, whether data are being exported for each coded segment or whole documents, the way in which overlapping codes are dealt with and the method of scaling all have implications for the generation, processing and interpretation of numeric data from the coding of qualitative text.

Depending on the program used, the researcher may have a choice of exporting dichotomous (0/1) codes that indicate the presence or absence of a concept, counts that give the frequency of mentions, or a measure that indicates the relative volume of text coded in a particular way in a document. Counts (other than 0/1) are influenced by the way in which data are segmented as a basis for counting, and frequency counts are affected by the overall length of the source documents. Counts and proportions are also problematic in that they assume a level of (ratio) scaling that ignores the meaning of missing data (scored as 0) in a qualitative data set and the potential disjuncture between 0 and 1 in a continuous scale derived from such data.

In practical terms QDA software packages differ in whether information relating to each coded segment is the basis for exported data or whether data for each document or the case as a whole are being exported. This has implications for data handling (for example the need to aggregate data in order to obtain patterns for respondents) and for the recognition of intersections in coding. Researchers who use exported coding information therefore need to try out and become familiar with the transfer syntax used in their selected software.

Issues for statistical analysis

Inferential statistics are based on the assumption of random or representative selection of cases, and error rates in derived estimates of population characteristics are proportional to sample size. Sample selection and sample size therefore limit the kind of statistical procedures that can legitimately be used and the ability to generalise to a larger population.

Each statistical technique carries particular assumptions that must be met for appropriate use of that technique. For data derived from qualitative coding, most measures (including scaled measures) will be nominal or ordinal rather than interval, distributions may be unknown and normality cannot be assumed. For descriptive reporting, medians are likely to be more appropriate than means. Lack of independence in observations for some types of data can create a problem of multi-collinearity (Roberts, 2000). Similarly chi-square analysis carries the assumption that categories on the same axis are mutually exclusive. While classic multivariate techniques based on the general linear model are strict in their assumptions, exploratory multivariate techniques such as cluster and correspondence analysis can generally be applied to quantitised data when conditions of normality and randomness are not necessary met – although even these techniques are not appropriate if all the variables are not equally relevant to all cases (Prein and Kuckartz, 1995).

Different approaches to data analysis treat variations and exceptions differently. Statisticians often simply dismiss 'outliers' from their analysis and rely on probability estimates to deal with variation across the sample. Variation is an 'error' when the goal is to describe the typical. In a qualitative approach the researcher uses variation to illuminate developing theories and modifies theory to take account of exceptions (Miles and Huberman, 1994; Barbour, 1998).

A pragmatist's approach to analysis

When the evidence from different sources conflicts it is necessary to determine how to weight the various components or, preferably, to seek reasons for the discrepancy. Ultimately, mixed-method analysis (like almost any other) is a process of piecing together bits of a puzzle to find answers to questions (Jick, 1979). Numbers should be used when they can help to answer questions, and verbal comments should never be ignored.

> From data in the form of numbers, one makes inferences in the same way as with data in the form of words, not by virtue of probabilistic algorithms. Statistics are not privileged. Inference is not mechanised. With this way of viewing knowledge, 'mixed' methods may even be a misnomer, as both surveys and participant observation yield equivalent data. Inferences are based on the inquirer's coordinating multiple lines of evidence to gain an overall understanding of the phenomenon ... Yet, because the inquirer is the instrument, all information flows through a single perspective. (Smith, 1997, p. 77)

In my experience, and as hinted at earlier, rules are often broken: the wise mixed-method researcher knows what assumptions underlie the methods of analysis being used, understands the implications of not fully meeting those assumptions, and takes that into account when drawing and presenting conclusions.

Pragmatics

Quite apart from arguments about paradigms, methods and analysis, there are a number of practical issues that affect mixed-method research. Most obviously, the use of multiple methods increases the time required to complete a study and the cost of conducting the study, particularly if a component design is used.

A more critical practical problem relates to the researcher's skills and knowledge. Good mixed-method research requires a good working knowledge of the methods used, their assumptions, and analysis procedures and tools, as well as an ability to understand and interpret results derived from the various methods. While they might be able to adapt to and learn new methods, researchers brought up in the traditions of

a particular discipline often do not have knowledge of other methodologies, particularly the tacit knowledge that comes from years of immersion
in the literature and research associated with those methodologies.
Moreover years of disciplinary training can lead to methodological
prejudice (Reichardt and Cook, 1979; Patton, 1988), which can result in
a tendency to choose methods because they are within one's area of
expertise rather than because they are the best way of answering the
questions posed (Jick, 1979; Bryman, 1988).

Similarly the level of understanding of the audience, can be a problem.
The mixed-method researcher has to discuss methods that may be unfamiliar to readers from one side or the other (Creswell, 1994). Stakeholders,
granting bodies, thesis examiners, journal editors and readers may all
struggle with particular (but different) elements of a presentation; all have
their own biases and methodological preferences and tend to understand
the terms used from the perspective of their own framework, even when
an alternative framework is spelt out.

Writing up

Writing a mixed-method report is rather like writing a qualitative analysis
report in that it is unlikely to follow a traditional format. When determining how best to present the ideas and evidence generated during
the study, one issue of concern is the degree to which the quantitative
and qualitative components can or should be integrated. While this
may be influenced by the degree to which they were integrated during
the study, it is not necessarily determined by that. All too often the
results and conclusions from one type of data or analysis are presented,
and then the results and conclusions from the other; only afterwards is
an attempt made to draw them together in a general conclusion (if at all).
If the different approaches have been designed to contribute to a
common understanding, then even if they have been used side by side
or in sequence, separating them when reporting and interpreting the
findings is likely to result in a report that is disjointed and possibly
repetitive. It is better progressively to unveil the relevant evidence on
a path towards a common conclusion than to organise on the basis of
the methods used.

Is validity enhanced?

Mixed methods are used to enrich understanding of an experience or issue
through the confirmation of conclusions, the extension of knowledge

or the initiation of new ways of thinking about the subject of the research. Mixed methods are neither more nor less valid than specific approaches to research. As with any research, validity stems more from the appropriateness of the methods, the thoroughness and effectiveness with which they are applied and thoughtful weighing of the evidence than from the application of a particular set of rules or adherence to an established tradition. Critical factors in mixed-method research include:

- Clarity of purpose, basis and focus, giving direction to the study and a logical basis for explanation.
- Awareness of the limitations of traditional methods when they are modified in a mixed-method environment.
- Appropriate use and interpretation of quantitised coding from qualitative data.
- Varied methods of treating 'error' or 'deviance'.
- Appropriate generalisation, given the chosen sample and methods.

References

Barbour, R. S. (1998) 'Mixing qualitative methods: Quality assurance or qualitative quagmire?', *Qualitative Health Research*, vol. 8, no. 3, pp. 352–61.

Bazeley, P. (2002) 'Computerized data analysis for mixed methods research', in A. Tashakkori and C. Teddlie (eds), *Handbook of Mixed Methods for the Social and Behavioural Sciences* (Thousand Oaks, CA: Sage), pp. 385–422.

Bryman, A. (1988) *Quantity and Quality in Social Research* (London and New York: Routledge).

Caracelli, V. J. and Greene, J. C. (1997) 'Crafting mixed-method evaluation designs', in J. C. Greene and V. J. Caracelli (eds), *Advances in Mixed-Method Evaluation: The Challenges and Benefits of Integrating Diverse Paradigms* (San Francisco, CA: Jossey-Bass), pp. 19–32.

Chen, H. (1997) 'Applying mixed methods under the framework of theory-driven evaluations', in J. C. Greene and V. J. Caracelli (eds), *Advances in Mixed-Method Evaluation: The Challenges and Benefits of Integrating Diverse Paradigms* (San Francisco, CA: Jossey-Bass), pp. 61–72.

Creswell, J. W. (1994) *Research design: Qualitative and Quantitative Approaches* (Thousand Oaks, CA: Sage).

Denzin, N. K. (1970) *The Research Act* (Chicago, Ill.: Aldine).

Denzin, N. K. (1978) *The Research Act* (New York: McGraw-Hill).

Denzin, N. K. (1989) *The Research Act* (Englewood Cliffs, NJ: Prentice-Hall).

Fetterman, D. M. (1984) 'Ethnography in educational research: The dynamics of diffusion', in D. M. Fetterman (ed.), *Ethnography in Educational Evaluation* (Newbury Park, CA: Sage), pp. 21–35.

Fielding, N. G. and Fielding, J. L. (1986) *Linking Data: The Articulation of Qualitative and Quantitative Methods in Social Research* (Beverly Hills, CA: Sage).

Flick, U. (1992) 'Triangulation revisited: Strategy of validation or alternative?', *Journal for the Theory of Social Behaviour*, vol. 22, no. 2, pp. 175–97.

Greene, J. C. and Caracelli, V. J. (1997) 'Defining and describing the paradigm issues in mixed-method evaluation', in J. C. Greene and V. J. Caracelli (eds), *Advances in mixed-method evaluation: The challenges and benefits of integrating diverse paradigms* (San Francisco, CA: Jossey-Bass), pp. 5–18.

Greene, J. C., Caracelli, V. J. and Graham, W. F. (1989) 'Toward a conceptual framework for mixed-method evaluation designs,' *Educational Evaluation and Policy Analysis*, vol. 11, no. 3, pp. 255–74.

Guba, E. G. and Lincoln, Y. S. (1994) 'Competing paradigms in qualitative research', in N. K. Denzin and. Y. S. Lincoln (eds), *Handbook of Qualitative Research* (Thousand Oaks, CA: Sage), pp. 105–17.

Howe, K. R. and Eisenhardt, M. (1990) 'Standards for qualitative (and quantitative) research: A prolegomenon', *Educational Researcher*, vol. 19, no. 4, pp. 2–9.

Jick, T. D. (1979) 'Mixing qualitative and quantitative methods: Triangulation in action', *Administrative Science Quarterly*, vol. 24, pp. 602–11.

Kaplowitz, M. D. (2000) 'Statistical analysis of sensitive topics in group and individual interviews', *Quality and Quantity*, vol. 34, pp. 419–31.

Krantz, D. L. (1995) 'Sustaining versus resolving the quantitative–qualitative debate', *Evaluation and Program Planning*, vol. 18, no. 1, pp. 89–96.

Kuckartz, U. (1995) 'Case-oriented quantification', in U. Kelle (ed.), *Computer-Aided Qualitative Data Analysis: Theory, Methods and Practice* (Thousand Oaks, CA: Sage), pp. 158–76.

Kuhn, T. S. (1963) 'The essential tension: tradition and innovation in scientific research', in C. W. Taylor and F. Barron (eds), *Scientific Creativity: Its Recognition and Development* (New York: Wiley), pp. 341–54.

Lincoln, Y. S. and Guba, E. G. (1985) *Naturalistic Enquiry* (Beverly Hills, CA: Sage).

Mark, M. M., Feller, I. and Button, S. B. (1997) 'Integrating qualitative methods in a predominantly quantitative evaluation: A case study and some reflections', in J. C. Greene and V. J. Caracelli (eds), *Advances in Mixed-Method Evaluation: The Challenges and Benefits of Integrating Diverse Paradigms* (San Francisco, CA: Jossey-Bass), pp. 47–60.

Mathison, S. (1988) 'Why triangulate?', *Educational Researcher*, vol. 17, no. 2, pp. 13–17.

Miles, M. B. and Huberman, A. M. (1994) *Qualitative Data Analysis: An Expanded Sourcebook* (Thousand Oaks, CA: Sage).

Morgan, D. L. (ed.) (1993) *Successful Focus Groups* (Newbury Park, CA: Sage).

Morgan, D. L. (1998) 'Practical strategies for combining qualitative and quantitative methods: Applications to health research', *Qualitative Health Research*, vol. 8, no. 3, pp. 362–76.

Morse, J. M. (1991) 'Approaches to qualitative–quantitative methodological triangulation', *Nursing Research*, vol. 40, pp. 120–3.

Nickel, B., Berger, M., Schmidt, P. and Plies, K. (1995) 'Qualitative sampling in a multi-method survey', *Quality and Quantity*, vol. 29, pp. 223–40.

Patton, M. Q. (1988) 'Paradigms and pragmatism', in D. M. Fetterman (ed.), *Qualitative Approaches to Evaluation in Education: The Silent Scientific Revolution* (New York: Praeger), pp. 116–37.

Patton, M. Q. (1989) *Utilisation-Focused Evaluation* (Newbury Park, CA: Sage).

Prein, G. and Kuckartz, U. (1995) 'Computers and triangulation. Introduction: Between quality and quantity', in U. Kelle (ed.), *Computer-Aided Qualitative Data Analysis: Theory, Methods and Practice* (Thousand Oaks, CA: Sage), pp. 152–7.

Ragin, C. C. (1987) *The Comparative Method: Moving Beyond Qualitative and Quantitative Strategies* (Berkeley, CA: University of California Press).

Ragin, C. C. (1995) 'Using qualitative comparative analysis to study configurations', in U. Kelle (ed.), *Computer-Aided Qualitative Data Analysis: Theory, Methods and Practice* (Thousand Oaks, CA: Sage), pp. 177–89.

Reichardt, C. S. and Cook, T. D. (1979) 'Beyond qualitative *versus* quantitative methods', in T. D. Cook and C. S. Reichardt (eds), *Qualitative and Quantitative Methods in Evaluation Research* (Beverly Hills, CA: Sage).

Riggin, L. J. (1997) 'Advances in mixed-method evaluation: A synthesis and comment', in J. C. Greene and V. J. Caracelli (eds), *Advances in Mixed-Method Evaluation: The Challenges and Benefits of Integrating Diverse Paradigms* (San Francisco, CA: Jossey-Bass), pp. 87–94.

Roberts, C. W. (2000) 'A conceptual framework for quantitative text analysis', *Quality and Quantity*, vol. 34, pp. 259–74.

Rossman, G. B. and Wilson, B. L. (1985) 'Numbers and words: Combining quantitative and qualitative methods in a single large-scale evaluation study', *Evaluation Review*, vol. 9, no. 5, pp. 627–43.

Sivesind, K. H. (1999) 'Structured, qualitative comparison: between singularity and single-dimensionality', *Quality and Quantity*, vol. 33, pp. 361–80.

Smith, A. G. and Robbins, A. E. (1982) 'Structured ethnography: The study of parental involvement', *American Behavioural Scientist*, vol. 26, no. 1, pp. 45–61.

Smith, M. L. (1997) 'Mixing and matching: Methods and models', in J. C. Greene and V. J. Caracelli (eds), *Advances in Mixed-Method Evaluation: The Challenges and Benefits of Integrating Diverse Paradigms* (San Francisco, CA: Jossey-Bass), pp. 73–86.

Stake, R. E. (1994) 'Case studies', in N. K. Denzin and Y. S. Lincoln (eds), *Handbook of Qualitative Research* (Thousand Oaks, CA: Sage), pp. 236–47.

Tashakkori, A. and Teddlie, C. (1998) *Mixed Methodology: Combining Qualitative and Quantitative Approaches* (Thousand Oaks, CA: Sage).

10

Consumer Behaviour in Recreational Areas of Shopping Malls: A Mixed-Model Research Design

Renate Buber, Johannes Gadner and Bernhart Ruso

Introduction

This chapter discusses a research design for an empirical study in the field of consumer research using a mixed-model, mixed-method approach.[1] 'Mixed model studies combine qualitative and quantitative approaches across all phases of the research process (such as conceptualisation, data collection, data analysis, and inference)', while mixed-method studies combine qualitative and quantitative approaches to research, for example in the data collection stage (Tashakkori and Teddlie, 1998, pp. ix, 1).

The hypotheses for the study were based on an evolutionary psychological model of key factors that affect individual behaviour – prospect refuge, phytophilia, hydrophilia and zoophilia – and a behavioural psychology-oriented motivation model used in consumer behaviour research. Two different epistemological positions guided the study: the researchers acted as detached observers (positivist) and as part of the research instrument (interpretivist).

The study comprised two phases. The first consisted of a literature review, hypotheses development (set 1), environmental set-up, data collection (video observation of the behaviour of buyers, non-buyers and passers-by, plus interviews with buyers, non-buyers and passers-by) and an interdisciplinary workshop. The second phase consisted of hypotheses development (set 2) based on the workshop results, environmental set-up, data collection (again, video observation of the behaviour of buyers, non-buyers and passers-by) and a final workshop to conceptualise a structural model of consumer behaviour in recreational areas.

The observational data were analysed with special software. The verbal data (interview transcripts) were analysed by means of the GABEK method and its computer application WinRelan. While the quantitative approach produced data on how people reacted to certain environments (recreational areas) in terms of entering the area, interacting and communicating with others, buying or not buying items from a vending machine, the time spent in the area and so on, the qualitative approach was intended to answer the question of why people react to certain environments in specific ways.[2] The use of a mixed-model, mixed-method approach was aimed at gaining a better understanding of the behavioural processes and motivations of consumers in different environmental settings.

Evidence in the literature suggests that recreational areas in shopping malls designed according to human evolutionary needs elicit (buying) behaviour that is associated with well-being (Gates and Rohe, 1987; Kuo *et al.*, 1998; Schäfer *et al.*, 1999) and optimises key parameters of consumer behaviour (Salzberger *et al.*, 1993).[3] Therefore the research design drew on various models from marketing and consumer behaviour, anthropology, and evolutionary and behavioural psychology.[4] Special attention was paid to subjective emotional responses of consumers to the environment.

The following section provides a brief overview of theories and models from evolutionary psychology, behavioural psychology, marketing and consumer behaviour, and the theory-based research process. The subsequent sections consider the hypotheses that guided the research and describe the research process. The methodology is explained in detail.

Theories and models

Evolutionary psychology and the human environment

The ability of humans to assess and adapt to their environment has ensured the evolutionary survival of mankind (Orians and Heerwagen, 1995). We can assume that the mechanisms that trigger and control such behaviour are deeply rooted in our being. In the context of people's perception and evaluation of the shopping environment, an environment that satisfies all their biological needs will evoke feelings of happiness and well-being (Tuan, 1974; Relph, 1976). This will encourage them to seek such locations, stay there for longer periods of time and form an emotional attachment to them (Tuan, 1974; Relph, 1976; Ulrich *et al.*, 1991; Orians and Heerwagen, 1995; Atzwanger *et al.*, 1998). Such reactions first developed among the tribal societies of the Pleistocenic savannahs many thousands of years ago and have not changed since. Therefore they are key to understanding behaviour in today's urban environments. Many of these thoughts and ideas are summed up in habitat theory (Appleton, 1975, 1984) and savannah theory (Orians and Heerwagen, 1995). In the past three decades these theories have prompted a huge number of empirical studies on the preferred features of landscapes and the natural world. The results show that several key factors in evolution still affect individual behaviour, including prospect refuge, phytophilia, hydrophilia and zoophilia, which elicit strong responses in research subjects and are easy to manipulate in experiments (Ruso *et al.*, 2002, pp. 282 f.).

The prospect refuge quality of a location refers to individuals' ability to view the surrounding environment from that location without being seen, which is an important factor in their sense of safety (Ruddell and Hammitt, 1987; Fisher and Nasar, 1992; Atzwanger *et al.*, 1998; Tassinary *et al.*, 1999). Phytophilia is a liking for plants. In evolutionary terms, trees and flowers were signs of water and food. Moreover trees provided shelter, firewood and building material. Nowadays pictures of landscapes featuring plants evoke a more positive response than ones without plants. Plants not only have a positive effect on well-being and health, but also reduce stress and stimulate cognitive activity (Ulrich *et al.*, 1991; Yang and Brown, 1992; Kuo *et al.*, 1998; Oberzaucher, 2000). Hydrophilia is a liking for water (Herzog, 1985; Burmil, Daniel and Hetherington, 1999), which for our forebears was not only a resource in itself but also indicated good hunting grounds and was important for orientation. Today it increases well-being, evokes social communication and interaction and elicits explorative behaviour (Pitt, 1989; Oerter, 1997; Ruso and Atzwanger, 2000). Finally zoophilia, a liking for animals, has its roots in the early struggle for survival (Orians and Heerwagen, 1995).

It is evident that the evaluation of human environments is a highly complex cognitive process which has to be reduced to a number of single features for empirical research. In the field of evolutionary psychology it is commonly agreed that the abovementioned factors (prospect refuge, phytophilia, hydrophilia and zoophilia) are appropriate for the operationalisation of research variables. With regard to our research design, as most landscape preference studies had concentrated on these factors many of the methodological problems with such stimuli had already been addressed and most of the research variables in question were well known and well tested. Another advantage of using these factors to test the effect of the environment on consumer behaviour was that they were relatively easy to manipulate in an experimental setting. For our research a real life setting was chosen to ensure high validity. Many of the problems associated with real life settings, such as sampling and changing environmental factors, were avoided by the setting of the study. A shopping mall offered a constant environment in terms of temperature, humidity and light, but other features were constantly changing so the subjects of the study were not likely to realise that experimenters were manipulating some aspects of the environment. Another advantage was the large number of people to observe (in a preliminary study the behaviour of 30 000 people was analysed). Such a huge sample would ensure homogenous sets of data.

The motivational basis of human behaviour

According to behavioural psychology, behaviour is based on specific cognitively, emotionally and socially structured motivations (Miller *et al.*, 1960; Bowlby, 1969a, pp. 38 ff.; Gottlieb, 1992). It has been suggested that motivations – that is, the motivational systems that facilitate individuals' behaviour – are organised and influenced by several discrete but interrelated systems of different origin (Stern, 1985, pp. 238 f.) This multiple causality of behavioural motivation is filtered, condensed and mediated by the brain and the endocrine system and directed towards a temporary goal that is selected according to the subjective importance of an object and in relation to the degree of arousal/activation (Bloom and Lazerson, 1988). Consequently motivation can be defined as an internal drive or arousal in connection with a specific goal orientation (Bowlby, 1969b, pp. 68 f.).

In other words perceived information about an object or an external stimulus activates a goal-directed behavioural sequence. Therefore behavioural regulation is always a three-step information–organisation–action process (Oeser and Seitelberger, 1995, p. 24):

1. Specific external (or internal) information relating to environmental (or internal) events is perceived.
2. The perceived information is cognitively processed and organised according to social, emotional and cognitive schemes in order to develop behavioural alternatives based on goal-directed cognitive maps (Oeser and Seitelberger, 1995, pp. 69 f., 83 ff.)
3. These cognitive maps serve as guidelines or plans to organise actions and control actual behaviour (Bandura, 1986; Gadner, 1998, 1999).

Our study attempted to analyse this process. Interviews were conducted to investigate (1) how consumers perceived a specific external event, that is, a staged environment in the shopping mall to satisfy people's evolutionary needs (prospect refuge, phytophilia, hydrophilia and zoophilia), (2) the consumers' internal reactions towards this environment, and (3) the behavioural ways in which they responded to it.

Consumer research and environmental psychology

Consumer behaviour is influenced by, and can be described and explained with the help of, a large range of variables. A core variable investigated in consumer behaviour studies is 'attitude': attitudes influence behaviour, behaviour influences attitudes. Even though the three-part model of attitudes – consists of knowledge (convictions), emotions (which are related to convictions and measurable by physiological reactions) and behavioural intentions (Zimbardo, 1999, p. 614) – is heuristic it is widely accepted in consumer behaviour research (see Kroeber-Riel and Weinberg, 2003, pp. 170 f.). In such research, motivation is defined as a hypothetical construct to explain the causes of behaviour and thus answer the question of why individuals behave in certain ways (see Beckmann, 1996).

Referring to cognitive theory, Kroeber-Riel and Weinberg (2003, pp. 141–68) define motivation as consisting of primary drives (emotions) and cognitive processes (goal orientation, behavioural programmes). The discussion on the theoretical basis of the construct of motivation is summarised by Kroeber-Riel and Weinberg (ibid., pp. 145 f.) as follows:[5] as it is defined in cognitive theory, motivation largely corresponds to attitudes. As the actual consumer's research paradigm can be characterised by a cognitive orientation, the constructs of motivation and attitudes are similarly operationalised. The measurement of attitudes replaces the measurement of motivation (Wiswede, 1990, p. 421).[6] The cognitive orientation of motivation essentially equals the 'means–end analysis' of attitudes (Rosenberg, 1956; Howard and Sheth, 1969, p. 129). Hence attitudes can be traced back to (1) the perception of whether and to what extent an object can be used to reach a (consumption) goal and (2) the subjective importance of that goal. According to Kroeber-Riel and Weinberg (2003, p. 148), motivation can be structured into (1) the extent of product knowledge the consumer needs for buying motivation, and (2) the process of acquiring product knowledge. Accordingly motivation can be based on rational insight, conditioning, imitation learning and so on.

The analysis of motivation based on product knowledge has been elaborated extensively with the 'laddering concept' (see for example Gengler and Reynolds, 1995; Reynolds and Whitlark, 1995). 'Ladder interviews' mostly contain 'why' questions. For example, 'Why is this product important for you?' Answer: 'It does not make me as tired as alcoholic drinks do.' The next question would be, 'Why is it important for you not to be tired?' (Reynolds and Gutman, 1988; Peter *et al.*, 1999, p. 74). In laddering studies 'the emphasis is on discovering the relationship between product attributes and consumer benefits and values, or means-end chains; the ladder metaphor implies that the researcher is going deeper and deeper, from abstract goals to more specific means of achieving those goals' (Churchill and Iacobucci, 2002, pp. 274 f.)

Even though the definition of motivation differs between the various theories, there is tacit agreement that motivation contains an activation component as well as a cognitive component of goal-oriented behaviour regulation (Stellar, 1994). In consumer behaviour studies motivation and attitudes are mostly investigated by quantitative methods, usually questionnaires with five- or seven-step attitude-scale items. Regardless of the research paradigm and the type of scale used, we suggest that the emotional and the cognitive components be measured separately (see also Bagozzi and Burnkrut, 1979, 1985). Conventional attitude scales and the Fishbein method measure the cognitive component while the semantic differential and directly requested assessments measure emotions. Without dismissing the efficiency of using item batteries, it must be said that for the investigation of why consumers behave in a certain way, unstructured, undisguised interviews are more likely to produce insights in to deeper motivations and attitudes. The information obtained from consumers in their own words through interviews can be extremely rewarding and insightful (Churchill and Iacobucci, 2002, p. 274). Consequently a kind of laddering technique was used in the qualitative part of our study.

As the study investigated behavioural and emotional responses to physical stimuli in the environment, the environmental psychological model of Mehrabian and Russell (1974) was used in the development of the research design. Mehrabian and Russell (ibid., p. 8) suggest that three emotional response variables (pleasure, arousal and dominance) mediate a variety of approach-avoidance behaviours. The environmental psychological model is well supported by numerous empirical studies of marketing and retailing issues. Both the conceptual model and the empirical findings correspond nicely to the theories and empirical data from evolutionary psychology. The realisation that the theories and findings of very different research schools were so interwoven con-firmed our decision to use mixed methods.

The mixed-method approach

Traditional studies of human behaviour mainly use questionnaires and observation. Questionnaires offer the advantages of being flexible and easy to use. Furthermore they have been used for a long time and are therefore well tested and accepted as reliable research tools. Observation gives the researcher the chance to obtain data on real behaviour, unbiased by rationalisation and verbalisation. A non-intrusive method such as the use of a hidden video camera further reduces the possibility of biased data. However, while both methods provide data on how people behave they cannot answer the question of why people behave in the way that they do.

Traditional studies on consumer behaviour have predominantly used structured questionnaires, especially when investigating motivation and attitudes (Kroeber-Riel and Weinberg, 2003, pp. 19 ff.) Item batteries, questionnaires and quantitative models still dominate applied consumer research (for example Fishbein and Ajzen, 1975; Trommsdorff, 1975; see also Kroeber-Riel and Weinberg, 2003, pp. 196 ff.) However, because there has been a general change of values in society it has become more difficult to forecast consumers' behaviour with traditional methodologies. The 'hybrid' consumer behaves unpredictably, for example he or she may drive a very expensive car but buy low-priced food from a discount retailer.[7] 'Why' questions are most suitable for investigating the motivation and attitudes that underlie heterogeneous behaviour. According to Carson *et al.* (2001, p. x), 'Marketers' need for deep and detailed qualitative research becomes more crucial. Its importance lies in the need to understand phenomena and to gain meaningful insights into circumstances and changes. The contribution that qualitative research can make to this understanding and insight is immense.'

The use of qualitative and quantitative methods in our research enabled us to investigate the motivational basis of consumer behaviour in shopping malls and support the findings with numerical data. The aim of the first part of the study was to understand consumer behaviour in general and consumer behaviour in the environmental setting of the study in particular.

The research design

The research design included the research process, the hypotheses, the environments, the experiments and the methods.

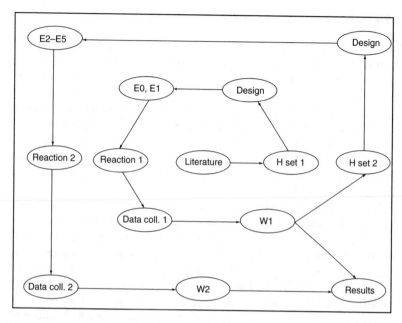

Figure 10.1   The two stages of the research process

Key:

H. set 1	First hypothesis set, based on the literature
E0, E1	Environments in the first stage of the research. E1 based on H. set 1
E0	Reference environment
Reaction 1	Subjects react to E1 and E0
Data coll. 1	Stage 1: data collected by means of observation (video) and interviews
W1	Interdisciplinary workshop at the end of stage 1
H. set 2	Second hypothesis set, based on the results of W1
E2–E5	Environments two to five, redesigned according to H. set 2
Reaction 2	Subjects' react to environments E2–E5
Data coll. 2	Stage 2: observational data collected
W2	Second interdisciplinary workshop

The research process

Figure 10.1 illustrates the two stages of the research process. In the first stage the initial environment (E1) was designed according to our literature-based hypotheses (H. set 1). In experiments Ex0 and Ex1 the subjects and their reactions to the environment (E1) were measured and tested against their reactions to the control environment (E0). Their behaviour was videotaped and their thoughts and motivations were investigated by means of interviews. The findings of the observational data and the interview data were discussed in an interdisciplinary workshop (W1), the purpose of which was to develop a second set of hypotheses (H. set 2).

In stage 2 of the study the environment was redesigned according to the set 2 hypotheses. In experiments 2–5 the subjects' reactions to the new environments (E2–E5) were again videotaped. Finally, the findings of both the observations and the interviews were discussed in the second workshop, the purpose of which was to develop a conceptual model of consumer behaviour in recreational areas of shopping malls.

The hypotheses

As stated above, the research design included two sets of hypotheses, the first based on the literature and the second generated from the findings of the qualitative analysis of the interviews. Based on a consideration of the theoretical models discussed earlier we assumed that recreational areas in shopping malls designed according to evolutionary needs of humans (prospect refuge, phytophilia, hydrophilia and zoophilia) would optimise key parameters of consumer behaviour. This led to the following hypotheses (see also Table 10.1, p. 167):

- If the environment in the recreational area of a shopping mall is designed according to evolutionary needs, people will stay longer than they will in a place that does not satisfy their needs.
- Such an environment will attract more people to come closer to its centre.
- Consumers will explore, interact and buy more in an environment that satisfies their evolutionary needs.

The environments

Based on a study by Ruso and Atzwanger (2001) on the effect of water on well-being in a similar setting, in our study we experimented with six different environments (E0–E5). In a shopping mall a nine square metre recreational area was set up using the ethologically relevant features described above. Figure 10.2 shows the initial environment (E1). In the second stage of the study the recreational area was adapted according to the results of stage 1 (environments E2–E5). The control environment (E0) contained only benches and a vending machine.

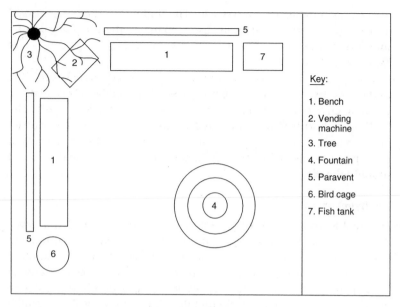

Figure 10.2   Design of recreational environment E1

Observational data

Data collection

Over a period of three months the behaviour of the all individuals (buyers, non-buyers, leisure seekers and passers-by) in environments E0–E5 and the surrounding area was recorded by means of a video camera positioned several metres above the ground. To facilitate accurate analysis of people's movements in the area, the video film was processed digitally. Five images per second with a resolution of 184×140 pixels were recorded. As a preliminary step, an image without passers-by was taken from each 30 minute sequence; this served as a reference image. Then every image from the video sequence was compared with it and pixels that differed from the reference image were marked. Pixel blots of a certain size were defined as targets, and their coordinates and circumference were saved in a data file. Each target corresponded to a person or thing that was visible on the examined image but was absent on the reference image. In the next step a trend calculation measured the movement of each passer-by. The data files included information on the exact position of the person, his or her duration of stay, distance from other persons and

Table 10.1   Operationalisation of the hypotheses

Hypotheses	Measurement parameters	Units (number)
In recreational areas that meet evolutionary needs people are more likely to:		
Stay longer	Duration of stay	Seconds
Be attracted	Frequency of use	Passers-by Leisure seekers Buyers Non-buyers
Be close to the centre	Distance	Metres
Gather information	Rate of exploration	Physical contact with a feature
Interact	Rate of interaction	Physical contact with another person
Buy products	Readiness to consume	Purchases

whether or not the person stopped in the area, explored features in the area and interacted with others.

Data analysis

As shown in Table 10.1, several behavioural parameters were used to measure the effect of the recreational area on visitors to the shopping mall. Duration of stay and rates of interaction were chosen as relevant parameters for well-being because both tend to increase when a place is experienced positively (Mehrabian and Russell, 1974; Zajonc, 1980; Zimbardo and Weber, 1994).

These parameters have also been applied in other contexts (Gates and Rohe, 1987; Schiefenhövel and Grammer, 1988; Atzwanger *et al.*, 1998; Schäfer *et al.*, 1999). In the evaluation of housing complexes for instance, duration of stay is relevant because people tend to avoid places they find unpleasant and stay longer in places that provide them with a sense of security and well-being (Gates and Rohe, 1987; Schäfer *et al.*, 1999). Weisfeld (1999) has found that interaction rates and explorative behaviour can be attributed to well-being. Pitt (1989) investigated the effect of waterscapes on social behaviour and observed larger group sizes and higher affiliation among river recreationalists than among other outdoor recreationalists. Finally, Kuo *et al.* (1998), conclude that environments with natural features such as trees encourage creativity among children and motivate social games.

Each one of the measurement parameters was used to evaluate the subjects' reactions to the different environments and we were eager to learn which forms of behaviour were affected most, how they were connected and whether the findings were consistent with those from the interviews.

The interviews

Data collection

During the period of observation, 30 consumers[8] (buyers, non-buyers, leisure seekers and passers-by) were asked to take part in open-ended, unstructured interviews. After a talk on the aims of the study they were taken to a near by room to be interviewed. Unstructured, open-ended, in-depth questions were used to collect verbal data on their motivations and the reasons for their actions in the experimental area, plus their perceptions of it. The interviews were tape-recorded and transcribed. The following questions guided the interviews:

- What was it about the environment that motivated you?
- What were your reasons for staying there and for moving closer to the centre of the recreational area?
- Which features of the environment attracted you?
- What motivated you to gather information, communicate with others and buy/not buy goods from the vending machine?
- What emotions and feelings were evoked by the environment?

These questions were aimed at identifying similarities and differences between buyers, non-buyers, leisure seekers and passers-by in respect of their motivations, attitudes, values, drives, desires and needs.

Data analysis

The aim of the qualitative analysis was to identify consumers' motives for using/not using the recreational area, their attitudes towards it, their thoughts on and reactions to the environment in question, and their reasons for buying/not buying items from the vending machine.[9] The analysis was supported by the GABEK method (Zelger, 1999a, 1999b; Zelger *et al.*, 2000; Zelger and Gadner, 2000; Buber and Kraler, 2000, p. 114) and its software application WinRelan (Zelger, 2000). The analysis produced a Gestalten tree, causal networks, and evaluation profiles, as follows.

For the Gestalten tree (Zelger, 1999b), text units were defined according to their specific content and meaning. The text units were coded to identify and mark relevant key concepts. The texts were organised into provisional text groups (clusters of texts) according to their conceptual content, and then processed into a meaningful and consistent network of test-relevant key concepts. Since individual interviewees emphasised different aspects of the situation, their arguments were structured into thematic problem fields and focal points according to the test-relevant key concepts. The final systematisation of the verbal data was the Gestalten tree. The structures and contents of the interviewees' arguments were analysed in order to reveal their motives for entering, attitudes towards and estimations of the recreational area, its effects on individual behaviour and crucial elements of the buying/non-buying decision.

With regard to causal networks, the interviewees' statements on perceived causal relations were represented as a complex network of causes and effects. The value systems of the interviewees were represented in significant core variables.

Finally, with the evaluation profile the interviewees' positive and negative evaluations of the investigated situation were listed.

Conclusion

This chapter has discussed a mixed-model, mixed-method research design for an empirical study in the field of consumer research. The aim of the study was to gain insights into consumers' behaviour in shopping mals. Observations of people in an experimental setting were combined with interviews.

The results of the research are expected to enhance our understanding of environmental influences on consumer behaviour in shopping malls as well as environmentally elicited buying/non-buying decisions. Situation-dependent effects on buying/non-buying behaviour together with patterns in consumers' explanations of their buying/non-buying decisions and behavioural responses to the environment will be identified and organised systematically. Moreover they will serve as the basis for the development of a structural model for environmentally influenced buying/non-buying decisions and marketing planning decisions on, for example atmospherics, outlet design, product positioning, personal selling and so on.

Notes

1. Most marketing and marketing management literature and research adhere to the positivism paradigm and give quantitative answers to research questions. For qualitative approaches in marketing management research see Gummesson (2000) or Laurent (2000) for validity questions. Qualitative approaches to

marketing and marketing management research are still underused. The value of interpretative qualitative research methodologies for marketing is discussed in Carson *et al.* (2001, pp. 64 ff.)

2. For detailed discussions of how to plan qualitative research see Bazeley and Richards (2000), Patton (2000) and Morse and Richards (2002).

3. There is a large number of reasons why people visit shopping malls. See for example Westbrook and Black (1985); Babin *et al.* (1994); Haubl (1996); Roy (1994); Eggert (1998); Falk (1998).

4. For reasons why pragmatism is the most appropriate justification for the use of mixed-method, mixed-model studies in the behavioural and social sciences see Tashakkori and Teddlie (1998, pp. 20 ff.)

5. A brief summary of motivation and attitudes as crucial constructs in consumer behaviour is provided in Sheth *et al.* (1999, pp. 340 ff., 386 ff.)

6. This hypothesis is sometimes criticised (Kroeber-Riel and Weinberg, 2003, p. 145).

7. For more information on trends in buying behaviour see Haller (1999). 'Hybrid' consumer behaviour and its consequences for retail companies is discussed in Schmalen (1994).

8. For choice of sample size in a GABEK WinRelan analysis see Hofer (2000). For more general information on samples see Merkens (2000). Sudman (1980) discusses the issue of how to improve the quality of shopping centre sampling.

9. For an analysis of text gained from thinking aloud protocols using AQUAD see Meyer *et al.* (1996).

References

Appleton, J. (1975) *The Experience of Landscape* (London: Wiley).

Appleton, J. (1984) 'Prospect and refuge re-visited', *Landscape Journal*, vol. 3 (Fall), pp. 91–103.

Atzwanger, K., Schäfer, K., Kruck, K. and Sütterlin, C. (1998) 'Wohlbefinden und Kooperation im öffentlichen Raum', *Report Psychologie*, nos 5–6, pp. 450–5.

Babin, B. J., Darden, W. R. and Griffin, M. (1994) 'Work and/or Fun: Measuring Hedonic and Utilitarian Shopping Value', *Journal of Consumer Research*, vol. 20, no. 4, pp. 644–56.

Bagozzi, R. P. and Burnkraut, R. E. (1979) 'Attitude organization and the attitude–behavior relationship', *Journal of Personality and Social Psychology*, vol. 37, pp. 913–29.

Bagozzi, R. P. and Burnkraut, R. E. (1985) 'Attitude organization and the attitude–behavior relation: A reply to Dillon and Kumar', *Journal of Personality and Social Psychology*, vol. 49, pp. 47–57.

Bandura, A. (1986) *Social Foundations of Thought and Action: A Social Cognitive Theory* (Englewood Cliffs, NJ: Prentice-Hall).

Bazeley, P. and Richards, L. (2000) *Qualitative Project Book* (London, Thousand Oaks and New Delhi: Sage).

Beckmann, J. (1996) 'Aktuelle Perspektiven der Motivationsforschung: Motivation und Volition', in E. H. Witte (ed.), *Sozialpsychologie der Motivation und Emotion* (Vienna and Lengerich: Pabst), pp. 13–33.

Bloom, F. E. and Lazerson, A. (1988) *Brain, Mind and Behavior* (New York: W. H. Freeman).

Bowlby, J. (1969a) 'Instinctive Behaviour: An Alternative Model', in J. Bowlby (ed.), *Attachment and Loss (Volume 1): Attachment* (London: Hogarth Press), pp. 37–57.
Bowlby, J. (1969b) 'Behavioural Systems Mediating Instinctive Behaviour', in J. Bowlby (ed.), *Attachment and Loss (Volume 1): Attachment* (London: Hogarth Press), pp. 65–84.
Buber, R. and Kraler, C. (2000) 'How GABEK and *WinRelan* Support Qualitative Research', in R. Buber and J. Zelger (eds), *GABEK II. Zur Qualitativen Forschung – On Qualitative Research* (Innsbruck, Vienna and Munich StudienVerlag), pp. 111–37.
Burmil, S., Daniel, T. and Hetherington, J. (1999) 'Human values and perceptions of water in arid landscapes', *Landscape and Urban Planning*, vol. 44, pp. 99–109.
Carson, D., Gilmore, D., Perry, C. and Gronhaug, K. (2001) *Qualitative Marketing Research* (London, Thousand Oaks and New Delhi: Sage).
Churchill, G. A. and Iacobucci, D. (2002) *Marketing Research. Methodological Foundations* (Australia, Canada, Mexico, Singapore, Spain, UK and US: South Western Thomson Learning).
Eggert, U. (1998) *Der Handel im 21. Jahrhundert* (Dusseldorf and Regensburg: Metropolitan Verlag).
Falk, B. (1998) *Das große Handbuch Shopping Center* (Landsberg am Lech: moderne industrie).
Fishbein, M. and Ajzen, J. (1975) *Belief, Attitude, Intention and Behavior: An Introduction to Theory and Research* (Reading, Mass.: Addison-Wesley).
Fisher, B. S. and Nasar, J. L. (1992) 'Fear of crime in relation to three exterior site features: prospect, refuge, and escape', *Environment and Behavior*, vol. 24, pp. 35–65.
Gadner, J. (1998) 'Embodying Culture. Anthropological Contributions to Cognitive Science', *Evolution and Cognition*, vol. IV, pp. 70–80.
Gadner, J. (1999) 'Kommunikation und Information: Zur Bedeutung der sozialen, kognitiven und emotionalen Dimension menschlicher Ontogenese und Verhaltensregulation. Eine empirische Untersuchung vom philosophisch-anthropologischen Standpunkt', unpublished dissertation, University of Vienna.
Gates, L. and Rohe, W. (1987) 'Fear and Reaction to Crimes', *Urban Affairs Quarterly*, vol. 22, pp. 425–53.
Gengler, C. E. and Reynolds, T. J. (1995) 'Consumer Understanding and Advertising Strategy: Analysis and Strategic Translation of Laddering Data', *Journal of Advertising Research*, vol. 35, no. 4, pp. 19–33.
Gottlieb, G. (1992) *Individual Development and Evolution. The Genesis of Novel Behaviour* (New York: Oxford University Press).
Gummesson, E. (2000) *Qualitative Methods in Management Research* (Thousand Oaks, London and New Delhi: Sage).
Haller, S. (1999) 'Die Verkaufsförderung im Handel', in W. Pepels (ed.), *Verkaufsförderung* (Munich and Vienna: Oldenbourg), pp. 239–70.
Haubl, R. (1996) 'Welcome to the pleasure dome: Einkaufen als Zeitvertreib', in H. Hartmann (ed.), *Freizeit in der Erlebnisgesellschaft* (Bonn: Westdeutscher Verlag), pp. 199–224.
Herzog, T. R. (1985) 'A Cognitive Analysis of Preference for Waterscapes', *Journal of Environmental Psychology*, vol. 5, pp. 225–41.

Hofer, J. (2000) 'Zur Stichprobengröße bei GABEK-Untersuchungen', in R. Buber and J. Zelger (eds), *GABEK II. Zur Qualitativen Forschung – On Qualitative Research* (Innsbruck, Vienna and Munich: StudienVerlag), pp. 165–84.

Howard, J. A. and Sheth, J. N. (1969) *The Theory of Buyer Behaviour* (New York: Basic Books).

Kroeber-Riel, W. and Weinberg, P. (2003) *Konsumentenverhalten* (Munich: Vahlen).

Kuo, F. E., Bacaicoa, M. and Sullivan, W. S. (1998) 'Transforming inner city landscapes. Trees, Sense of Safety and Preference', *Environment and Behaviour*, vol. 30, pp. 28–59.

Laurent, G. (2000) 'Improving the external validity of marketing models: A plea for more qualitative input', *International Journal of Research in Marketing*, vol. 17, nos 2–3, pp. 177–82.

Lorenz, K. (1973) *Die Rückseite des Spiegels. Versuch einer Naturgeschichte menschlichen Erkennens* (Munich: Piper).

Lorenz, K. (1992) *Die Naturwissenschaft vom Menschen* (Munich: Piper).

Mehrabian, A. and Russel, J. A. (1974) *An Approach to Environmental Psychology* (Cambridge, Mass. MIT Press).

Merkens, H. (2000) 'Auswahlverfahren, Sampling, Fallkonstruktion', in U. Flick, E. von Kardorff and I. Steinke (eds), *Qualitative Forschung. Ein Handbuch* (Reinbek: Rowohlt), pp. 286–99.

Meyer, M., Buber, R. and Al-Roubaie, A. (1996) 'Cultural Events: Konsumentscheidungsprozesse analysiert mit Protokollen lauten Denkens', *Medienpsychologie*, vol. 8, no. 2, pp. 90–116.

Miller, G. A., Galanter, E. and Pribram, K. H. (1960) *Plans and the Structure of Behaviour* (New York: Holt, Rinehart & Winston).

Morse, J. M. and Richards, L. (2002) *Readme First for a User's Guide to Qualitative Methods* (Thousand Oaks, London and New Delhi: Sage).

Oberzaucher, E. (2000) 'Phytophilie oder Die Erhöhung der Gründichte am Arbeitsplatz als Instrument zur Steigerung von kognitiven Leistungen', unpublished diploma manuscript, University of Vienna.

Oerter, R. (1997) *Die Psychologie des Spiels* (Weinheim: Psychologie Verlags-Union).

Oeser, E. and Seitelberger, F. (1995) *Gehirn, Bewusstsein und Erkenntnis* (Darmstadt: Wissenschaftliche Buchgesellschaft).

Orians, G. H. and Heerwagen, J. H. (1995) 'Evolved Responses to Landscapes', in J. H. Barkow, L. Cosmides and J. Tooby (eds), *The Adapted Mind: Evolutionary Psychology and the Generation of Culture* (New York: Oxford University Press), pp. 555–79.

Patton, M. Q. (2000) *Qualitative Evaluation and Research Methods* (Newbury Park, CA: Sage).

Peter, J. P., Olson, J. C. and Grunert, K. G. (1999) *Consumer Behavior – Marketing Strategy Perspectives* (London: McGraw-Hill).

Pitt, D. G. (1989) 'The attractiveness and use of aquatic environments as outdoor recreation places', in I. Altman and E. Zube (eds), *Public Places and Spaces* (New York: Plenum Press), pp. 217–53.

Relph, E. (1976) *Place and Placelessness* (London: Pion).

Reynolds, T. J. and Gutman, J. (1988) 'Laddering Theory, Method, Analysis and Interpretation', *Journal of Advertising Research*, vol. 28, no. 1, pp. 11–31.

Reynolds, T. J. and Whitlark, D. B. (1995) 'Applying Laddering Data to Communications Strategy and Advertising Practice', *Journal of Advertising Research*, vol. 35, no. 4, pp. 9–17.

Rosenberg, M. J. (1956) 'Cognitive Structure and Attitudinal Affect', *Journal of Abnormal and Social Psychology*, vol. 53, pp. 367–72.

Roy, A. (1994) 'Correlates of Mall Visit Frequency', *Journal of Retailing*, vol. 70, pp. 139–61.

Ruddell, E. J. and Hammitt, W. E. (1987) 'Prospect Refuge Theory: A psychological orientation for edge effect in recreation environments', *Journal of Leisure Research*, vol. 14, pp. 249–60.

Ruso, B. and Atzwanger, K. (2000) 'Wasser als Gestaltungselement der Innenarchitektur beeinflusst das menschliche Verhalten', *Homo*, vol. 51 (suppl.), p. 133.

Ruso, B. and Atzwanger, K. (2001) 'Water-Induced Well-Being in Shopping Malls', in M. Schultz, K. Atzwanger, G. Bräuer, K. Christiansen, J. Forster, H. Greil, W. Henke, U. Jaeger, C. Niemitz, C. Scheffler, W. Schievenhövel, I. Schröder and I. Wiechmann (eds), *Homo – Unsere Herkunft und Zukunft* (Göttingen: Cuvillier), pp. 182–6.

Ruso, B., Renninger, L. and Atzwanger, K. (2002) 'Human habitat preferences: a generative territory for evolutionary aesthetics research', in E. Voland and K. Grammer (eds), *Evolutionary Aesthetics* (Heidelberg: Springer), pp. 279–94.

Salzberger, T., Holzmüller, H. and Maier, G. (1993) 'Die Konsumentenzufriedenheit mit innerstädtischen und peripheren Einzelhandelsagglomerationen', working paper, Department of Marketing, Vienna University of Economics and Business Administration.

Schäfer, K., Atzwanger, K., Wallner, B. and Grammer, K. (1999) 'Human evolutionary aspects and urban dwelling features', *Collegium Antropologicum*, vol. 23, no. 2, pp. 369–78.

Schiefenhövel, W. and Grammer, K. (1988) *Sozialverhalten als Maß für Wohlbefinden und Wohnzufriedenheit. Interdisziplinäre Methoden und Vergleichsgrundlagen zur Erfassung der Wohnzufriedenheit* (Vienna: Institut für Stadtforschung).

Schmalen, H. (1994) 'Das hybride Kaufverhalten und seine Konsequenzen für den Handel. Theoretische und empirische Betrachtungen', *Zeitschrift für Betriebswirtschaft*, vol. 64, no. 10, pp. 1221–40.

Sheth, J. N., Mittal, B. and Newman, B. T. (1999) *Customer Behavior. Consumer Behavior and Beyond* (Fort Worth, Tex.: Dryden Press).

Stellar, E. (1994) 'The Physiology of Motivation', *Psychological Review*, vol. 101, no. 2, pp. 301–11.

Stern, D. (1985) *The Interpersonal World of the Infant. A View from Psychoanalysis and Developmental Psychology* (New York: Basic Books).

Sudman, S. (1980) 'Improving the Quality of Shopping Center Sampling', *Journal of Marketing Research*, vol. 17 (November), pp. 423–31.

Tashakkori, A. and Teddlie, C. (1998) *Mixed Methodology. Combining Qualitative and Quantitative Approaches* (Thousand Oaks, London and New Delhi: Sage).

Tassinary, L. G., Johnson, S. P., Lawson, K. and Parsons, R. (1999) 'Experimental Examination of the Prospect-Refuge Theory', *Psychophysiology*, vol. 36, p. 113.

Trommsdorff, V. (1975) *Die Messung von Produktimages für das Marketing* (Cologne: Heymann).

Tuan, Y. (1974) *Topophilia* (Englewood eliffs, NJ: Prentice-Hall).

Ulrich, R. (1986) 'Human Responses to Vegetation and Landscapes', *Landscape and Urban Planning*, vol. 13, pp. 29–44.

Ulrich, R., Simons, R. F., Losito, B. D., Fiotito, E., Miles, M. A. and Zelson, M. (1991) 'Stress recovery during exposure to natural and urban environments', *Journal of Environmental Psychology*, vol. 11, pp. 201–30.

Weisfeld, G. (1999) *Evolutionary principles of human adolescence* (New York: Basic Books).

Westbrook, R. A. and Black, W. C. (1985) 'A Motivation-Based Shopper Typology', *Journal of Retailing*, vol. 61, no. 1, pp. 78–103.

Wiswede, G. (1990) 'Motivation des Kaufverhaltens', in G. C. Hoyos, and W. Kroeber-Riel (eds), *Wirtschaftspsychologie in Grundbegriffen* (Munich: Piper), pp. 420–7.

Yang, B. and Brown, T. J. (1992) 'A Cross-Cultural Comparison of Preferences for Landscape Styles and Landscape Elements', *Environment and Behaviour*, vol. 24, pp. 471–507.

Zajonc, R. B. (1980) 'Feeling and Thinking', *American Psychologist*, vol. 35, pp. 151–75.

Zelger, J. (1999a) 'Wissensorganisation durch sprachliche Gestaltbildung im Verfahren GABEK', in J. Zelger and M. Maier (eds), *GABEK: Wissensverarbeitung und Wissensdarstellung* (Innsbruck and Vienna: StudienVerlag), pp. 41–87.

Zelger, J. (1999b) 'Gestaltenbäume als fraktale linguistische Strukturen', in W. Löffler and E. Runggaldier (eds), *Vielfalt und Konvergenz der Philosophie* (Vienna: Hölder-Pichler-Tempsky), pp. 116–22.

Zelger, J. (2000) 'Twelve Steps of GABEK *WinRelan*: A Procedure for Qualitative Opinion Research, Knowledge Organization and Systems Development', in R. Buber and J. Zelger (eds), *GABEK II: Zur Qualitativen Forschung – On Qualitative Research* (Innsbruck, Vienna and Munich: StudienVerlag), pp. 205–20.

Zelger, J., Buber, R., Gadner, J., Kraler, C. and Oberprantacher, A. (2000) 'GABEK – A Computer Supported Method for Knowledge Organization', in J. Blasius, J. Hox, E. De Leuuw and P. Schmidt (eds), *Social Science Methodology in the New Millennium*, Proceedings of the Fifth International Conference on Logic and Methodology, 3–6 October (Cologne: P04081.pdf CD-Rom).

Zelger, J., Gadner, J. (2000) 'Knowledge Organization by Procedures of Natural Language Processing', in B. Ganter and G. Mineau (eds), *Logical, Linguistic, and Computational Issues* (Aachen: Shaker), pp. 1–15.

Zimbardo, P. G. (1999) *Psychologie* (Berlin, Heidelberg, New York and Tokyo: Springer-Verlag).

Zimbardo, P. and Weber, A. (1994) *Psychology* (New York: HarperCollins).

11
Exploring Managerial Decisions in Export Strategy Formulation: Austrian Managers' Cognitive Maps

Gerhard Wührer

Introduction

Causal mapping is a simple but powerful technique that can help managers to identify routines that are central to their organisation's success, including routines for the development of export strategies. A short review of the literature (Kwak and Kim, 1999; Tyler and Gnyawali, 2002) shows that cognitive maps are used for operational and strategic decisions relating both to local and to global business (Chandra and Newburry, 1997; Markóczy, 2000). However it is likely that most firms instead rely on careful strategic planning, based on consideration of a number of factors, such as foreign market opportunity, the firm's resources, the type of product in question, life cycles and anticipated demand in the domestic market. As the decision to go international may be carefully mapped out in a planning process (Schneider and Müller, 1989; Evangelista, 1996), more emphasis should be given to the causal maps that managers develop whilst making decisions in general (Eden and Ackermann, 1998; van der Heijden and Eden, 1998) and for export and international marketing in particular (Evangelista, 1996). This statement is not particularly surprising when put into the context of a political view of strategy development (Kaplan and Norton, 2000, p. 167).

Huff and Jenkins (2002) consider the topic under the more general heading of strategic management. The key question is, how is knowledge generated and managed in organisations? 'Knowing' that is exemplified in actions is distinguished from more theoretical knowledge and is found to be more important in practice.

This chapter consists of two main sections. The first explains the elicitation of cognitive maps, plus the advantages and drawbacks of different approaches. The second describes a study of export managers' cognitive maps. The sample consisted of managers attending a post-graduate course in international marketing and export. One hundred and sixty two managers from small and medium-sized companies took part in the study. Qualitative and quantitative data were obtained by means of a mixed-method approach. A number of quantitative tests were carried out to analyse the correlation between the parameters of cognitive maps and the managers' demographic variables. In addition a computer investigation of the cognitive maps was conducted with Decision Explorer.

Cognitive maps

Huff and Jenkins (2002, p. 2) describe cognitive maps as action-oriented representations of the world. When discussing business process design, Kwak and Kim (1999, p. 157) use the definition 'cognitive modelling', which is based on causal maps of cause and effect relationships. These facilitate the explanation and prediction of events that are crucial to environmental understanding. With regard to the field of international business Chandra and Newburry (1997, p. 387) define a cognitive map as 'a set of relationships between both tangible and non-tangible ideas and events which guide an individual or group's thought process and actions'. This is a workable definition in respect of content. According to Huff and Jenkins (2002, pp. 2f.), cognitive maps are visual represent-ations. They show concepts with multiple relationships between them and encourage mentally moving among them.

Procedures for eliciting managerial knowledge

The fundamental methodological questions of cognitive maps have been addressed by various scientific disciplines. Neuroscience (O'Keefe and Nadel, 1978), linguistics (Eco, 1989), philosophy (Varela *et al.*, 1991), cognitive psychology (Kelly, 1963) and knowledge management (Carlsson and Walden, 1996; Ambrosini and Bowman, 2002) have all made major contributions to the field of inquiry. Cognitive mapping was developed as an extension to repertory grids (Kelly, 1963). The mapping of cogni-tive structures in general is a growing research field in management science (Portugali, 1996; Iacobucci, 1998; Ambrosini and Bowman, 2002). Its purpose is to capture the 'personal construct system' (Eden and Ackermann, 1998).

Managerial maps, as cognitive constructs, differ from conventional spatial maps not just in their unusual relationship to the territory but also in the conditions of their use. Terms such as 'competitive space', 'patterns of strategic dimensions', 'strategic argument mapping', 'content and structure of cognitive constructive systems', and 'cognitive maps' characterise the discussion (Huff, 1990). The last of these is linked to strategic decision making in that it explicitly deals with environments and different subsets of the concept (Narayanan and Fahey, 1994).

The basic elements of cognitive maps are entities which describe constructs. The constructs have certain qualities, or attributes. As these qualities or attributes differ between constructs they lead to a distinction between them. According to their similarity they define their spatial position on the map.

Table 11.1 summarises the general purposes of cognitive maps in managerial science. They can be seen as inventories of the mental furniture of decision makers. They investigate relationships, either hierarchical or complex, in a given mental frame of managerial thinking. They can also explain system dynamics or current situations in terms of previous events and provide guidance on changes expected in the future. More complex are maps that show the logic behind conclusions and decisions to act. Finally, maps can specify schemes, frameworks and perceptual codes. 'Those who draw this kind of map, however, claim that an underlying framework affects all of the relationships' (Huff, 1990, p. 16). It is essential for researchers to gain a deep understanding of and a high degree of competence in interpreting the structure.

Figure 11.1 is a typical cognitive map. It represents the beliefs, values and expertise of an export manager dealing with the relevant factors in a successful export strategy. Of course it is a very simplified structure and captures only part of the person's construct system. Constructs (nodes) are linked by chains (shown as arrows). These sequences of linked constructs could also mean different steps of action.

A successful export strategy depends on several influences and concepts. It may start with an export intention supported by top management commitment. This leads to a dynamic culture and customer orientation in the company. Customer orientation itself encourages the design of more attractive products, a strategy which is backed by total quality management and so on. The developed concepts contribute directly and indirectly to the firm's success in export markets. The map also provides a good illustration of how concepts can be linked to each other. A more elaborate map with weighted links could show, for example, the

Table 11.1 General purposes of cognitive maps in managerial science

Attention, association and importance of concepts	*Dimensions of categories and cognitive taxonomies*	*Influence, causality and system dynamics*	*Structure of argument and conclusion*	*Specification of schemes, frames and perceptual codes*
Inventorying of 'mental furniture' and its placement, for example searching for frequent use of related concepts as indicators of the strategic emphasis of a particular decision maker or company. Judgements about the complexity of relationships or differences in the use of concepts.	Investigation of more complex relationships among concepts. Drawing of dichotomised concepts and hierarchical relationships among broad concepts and more specific subcategories. Definition of competitive environments. Exploration of range and nature of choices perceived by decision makers in a given setting.	Focus on action and search for causal relationships among cognitive elements. Focus on how current situations are explained in terms of previous events, what changes are expected in the future.	Attempt to show the logic behind conclusions and decisions to act. Guiding background comes from philosophy, rhetoric and speech communication. Interesting facets are chains of reasoning and the cumulative impact of various evidence.	Cognition is guided by mental frameworks that are not accessible to the individual concerned. Requires the greatest leap from text to map of all the approaches. If the map maker wants to understand the link between thought and action, an understanding of this deeper structure is essential.

Source: Adapted from Huff (1990), pp. 14–16.

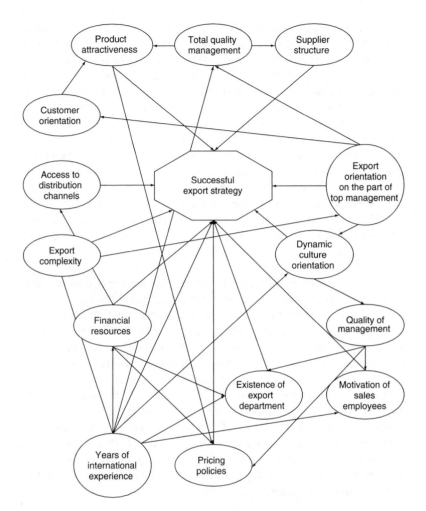

Figure 11.1   Example of a cognitive map of a successful export strategy

influence of 'export orientation on the part of top management' and 'total quality management'.

Cognitive maps can also be presented in the form of a matrix. If weights are added to the arrows the network of concepts becomes a matrix of weighted graphs. A plus sign means a positive and a minus sign a negative influence. The map can be transferred into a matrix. This is done by using the concepts as column and row entries. Where concepts are linked, a matrix cell becomes a 'one' else the entry is 'zero'. Matrices facilitate numerical network analysis (Wasserman and Faust, 1994) and can also be used to construct knowledge systems, for example in strategic management (Carlsson and Walden, 1996). An elaborate procedure to deal with the various qualities of relations is provided by Axelrod (1976). In seminal work on structures in decision making by political elites he examined written documents to develop the cognitive maps.

In this chapter Kelly's (1963) theoretical framework is transformed into a practical tool by representing that part of an individual's construct system which he or she is able and willing to make explicit (Eden and Ackermann, 1998, 2002). It also transcends Kelly's theory as a comprehensive way of understanding sense-making in that there is no explicit causal element in his theory (Jenkins, 1998, p. 236). The model shows the possible actions and outcomes suggested by the mental map an individual uses to explain the world as he or she sees it.

Elicitation of cognitive maps

Research that involves cognitive mapping uses a number of distinct elicitation methods (Table 11.2) based on different methodologies (Jenkins, 1998; for an alternative systematisation see Reger, 1994; Ambrosini and Bowman, 2002). Data gathering can be done by means of interviews or group discussions. While documentary data can be used (Axelrod, 1976), with primary data from interviews and discussions the data closely match the research question. The main elicitation methods are the self-Q technique (developed by Bougon, 1983) and the means–end chain method, which was developed to elicit and analyse consumer cognition rather than managerial cognition. The means–end chain approach evolved from the work of Kelly (1963), as modelled by Hinkle (1965). Laukkanen (1992) offers another approach to cognitive mapping in managerial decision making, while Eden's (1988) mapping approach works as an interactive tool to help clarify strategic problems.

Influences on the formation of cognitive maps

Cross-cultural psychological studies assume that national cultural differences have a strong influence on individual mind sets and world views. According to (Markóczy, 2000, p. 428), individuals' values, norms and general world views are shaped by behaviours that are rewarded or punished from early childhood, as well as by the norms and values that are instilled through socialisation and learning. Social pressure and conformity are major influences on the typical qualities found in cognitive and causal maps. Research findings provide mixed support for these propositions. Besides other considerations, which are not followed further,

Table 11.2 Comparison of elicitation methods

	Self-Q technique (Bougon, 1983)	Means–end chain (Hinkle, 1965)	Laukkanen approach (1992)	Eden approach (1998)
Focus	Elicitation of maps	Elicitation and analysis of maps	Comparisons between maps	Interactive tool for clarifying problems
Process	• Collection of concepts • Verification by feedback to respondent • Identification of causal links • Feedback of map to respondent	• Triadic techniques • Laddering • Matrix construction • Aggregation across respondents	• Programme of three interviews • Coding of interviews, incorporation into maps • Data reduction contained in maps in natural language	• Collection of concepts to be developed from causal links • Feedback to respondents at any time possible by feedback cycles
Critique	• Idiosyncratic elicitation in a relatively unstructured way • Minimises interviewer bias • Optimises reliability • No generation of new concepts possible	• Minimises interviewer influence • Efficient in terms of time, sometimes boring for the interviewee • Overall map of respondents may be atheoretical, therefore of questionable validity	• High content validity • Reliability of coding questionable • Focus of analysis at the level of concepts, not individuals and the context in which they use particular concepts • Software aided	• Well-founded methodology with a highly usable analysis software (Decision Explorer) • Detailed examination of concepts across a population of respondents • Interviewer bias can be supposed when done as personal interviews • Interactive and fast
Time required	• Three to four hours	• 45 minutes to one hour	• Up to nine hours per interviewee	

Sources: Jenkins (1998), pp. 238–40; Ambrosini and Bowman (2002), pp. 19–45.

the question arises as to whether values and world views can be considered as antecedents or influencing factors in respect of strategic issues. Here again the results seem to be inconclusive (ibid.) This might be due to a lack of studies in this area or the neglect of methodological issues, for example the relative impact of cultural in comparison with other factors.

The second set of influences concern organisational situations such as strategic change and managerial cognition. Some general approaches exist to the thinking of and modelling by strategists in situations of organisational stability or change. Strategic change can be described as the interplay of external forces and internal cognitive, cultural and political processes in which individuals with different mindsets and subjective world views interact (Lindel *et al.*, 1998, pp. 76–80).

The third set of influences concerns individuals and the effect that their characteristics have on the formation of causal maps. Individual characteristics include age, education, hierarchical and functional position, personal exposure to international experience, involvement in decision making, functional roles and areas served. Here again the research findings are somewhat inconclusive (Markóczy, 2000, pp. 429, 432), due either to the research approach or to the selection of variables.

The study

Methodology

The sample consisted of 162 managers attending three part-time post graduate courses (in 1998, 1999, and 2000)[1] in export and international marketing at Johannes Kepler University Linz, Austria. A standardised procedure was used for the elicitation of maps. The participants received a large sheet of paper (double letter size) containing neutral instructions on, for example, how to draw concepts and how to link them. They were asked to link the factors positively or negatively, whether they lead to a positive or negative influence on another factor or the final success of the export strategy. Hence the elicitation followed a similar approach to that used by Eden (1988). However there was no discussion between the researcher and the interviewees, so the interactive part was absent.

A standardised questionnaire was handed to the participants shortly after the collection of the maps. It consisted of general questions on the participants' firms, their internationalisation pattern, general success factors in internationalisation strategies and their current implementation, information-gathering procedures and sources, current problems in foreign markets, risk assessment of selected country markets, entry

Table 11.3 General details of the participants (n = 162)

Age	Export experience (years)	Educational qualification (%)	Size of the participants' firms by number of employees (%)
Mean: 29	Mean: 4	Secondary school diploma: 9.5	< 50: 20.2
Mode: 24	Mode: 1	High school without school leaving certificate: 9.5	51–250: 25.3
Minimum: 20	Minimum: 0.5	High school with school leaving certificate: 59.0	251–500: 18.2
Maximum: 45	Maximum: 18	University degree: 21.9	501–1000: 16.2
Std. deviation: 5.7	Std. deviation: 3.3		>1000: 20.2

strategies for Far Eastern markets and success factors in these markets. There were also statistical questions about the participants' firms (number of employees, length of international experience, revenues earned in foreign markets and so on) and questions about the participants themselves (gender, age, experience in international marketing and so on). An identification number for each participant was written on the map and the questionnaire, facilitating combined analysis. The data produced from the questionnaire were comparable to those produced in a study conducted in 1996 (Wührer, 2000). General information on the sample of export managers is shown in Table 11.3. The mean age was 29 years. The participants' export experience ranged from six months to 18 years, thus some had only just commenced their export management activities and some had considerable experience. Their educational qualifications ranged from secondary school diploma to university degree. Most worked in small or medium-sized firms and one fifth worked in larger companies.

Quantitative findings

Structural analysis of each of the cognitive maps was carried out by means of network analysis (Iacobucci, 1998; Wasserman and Faust, 1998). On average the managers elicited about 14 concepts (Table 11.4). The minimum was six and the maximum 32.

Most of the graphs showed directed graphs. A directed graph starts from a construct and points to another one. If it influences the other

Table 11.4   Characteristics of the cognitive maps (n = 146)

	Mean	*Std. dev.*	*Minimum*	*Maximum*
Number of concepts	13.65	4.70	6	32
Density of maps	0.12	0.06	0.0257	0.375

construct in a negative way it has negative weight, the larger it is the more negative influence it exerts on the construct it points at. The weights will be ignored here as only the density of the maps and the number of concepts are of interest at the moment. The density, Δ, of a map or conceptual network is calculated as the sum of all entries in the matrix, divided by the possible number of entries (Wasserman and Faust, 1998, p. 164)

$$\Delta = \frac{\sum\limits_{i=1}^{g} \sum\limits_{j=1}^{h} x_{ij}}{g(g-1)}$$

As each cognitive map contained different number of concepts, applying density measures enabled quantitative comparisons to be made. Figure 11.2 shows the relation between the density of the maps and the number of concepts. As can be seen, there is a non-linear negative relation between the two variables. This means that the density of the maps

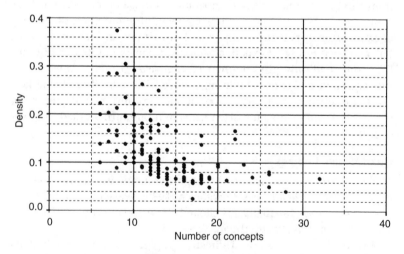

Figure 11.2   Density of the maps and number of concepts

Table 11.5   Non-linear regression summary statistics – dependent variable 'density'

Parameter	Estimate	Asymptotic standard error	Asymptotic 95 confidence interval	
			Lower	Upper
b_0	0.3418	0.0369	0.2688	0.4148
b_1	–0.0800	0.0093	–0.0985	–0.0616
$n = 142$				
$r^2 = 1$				
Residual SS/Corrected SS = 0.37				

decreases with a rise in the number of concepts. It is plausible to suggest that the number of links drawn decreases at an exponential rate. This means that the number of links or relations that can be drawn between concepts has some or other limit or theoretical endpoint. An exploratory analysis of the function describing the curvilinear relation between the concepts elicited and their connection revealed the parameters shown in Table 11.5.

Parameter b_1 shows the decrease in the number of links drawn between concepts in a map describing successful export strategies. The squared correlation between the independent variable 'number of concepts' and the dependent variable 'density' is about 0.37, meaning that about 37 per cent of the variation of density is explained by the number of concepts.

There is no significant correlation between 'number of concepts' or 'density' and 'export experience of managers' (measured in years), 'level of education' or 'age'. Up to a point these results are in conformity with the findings by Markóczy (2000, p. 437), who concludes that in the organisations she investigated neither national culture nor individual characteristics could explain the differences between the maps developed by the participating managers. She also states that planned strategic change in organisations is a major factor in the development of causal maps. This is due to manager's identification with the direction of change and the development of similar beliefs.

Qualitative analysis of the maps

The research approach adopted for the study offered the possibility of combining quantitative and qualitative analyses. Two of the 162 maps have been selected to throw light on managers' thoughts when considering export strategies. Map 1 contained the largest number of concepts (32) and had a density of 0.0685, that is, about 7 per cent of possible links were drawn. Map 2 had the highest density (0.3750) in the sample. It contained eight concepts, some of which were linked. Table 11.6 shows the list of concepts.[2]

Table 11.6 Concepts contained in maps 1 and 2

Map 1	Map 2
1. Successful export strategy (main concept)	1. Successful export strategy (main concept)
2. Employees' qualifications	2. Distribution, logistics
3. International marketing experience	3. Price, calculation
4. Product quality	4. Marketing, sales, advertising
5. Competitive situation	5. Finance, banks, partners, securities
6. Costs	6. Market research
7. Access to raw material	7. Market introduction
8. Human resources	8. Service, product idea
9. Production facilities and machines	
10. Export support offered by government	
11. Product	
12. Market situation, market research	
13. Planning	
14. Distance from target market	
15. Representation in target market	
16. Position in target market	
17. Differentiation	
18. Joint venture	
19. Development of target market	
20. Corporate culture	
21. Entrepreneurship	
22. Enterprise philosophy	
23. Corporate goals	
24. Proprietorship	
25. Market demand	
26. Cultural environment of target market	
27. Patents, licenses, brand copyright	
28. Economic situation in target market	
29. Purchasing power	
30. Currency situation in target market	
31. Stability	
32. International evaluation of market situation	

The author who drew map 1 displayed a differentiated list and configurations of factors about the reasons for a successful export strategy. Using the analytical methods developed by Eden (1988) and Miles and Huberman (1994) several configurations of concepts of maps can be investigated (Banxia, 1997); they can – among others – be named or considered.

Tails

When tails are at the beginning of a chain of arguments they trigger events or actions that have to be carried out. When tails appear higher up (measured by frequency) in a concept map they provide an explanation of other concepts. Tails in maps 1 and 2 answer the question of where successful strategies start, as seen from the participants' point of view.

Co-tails

Looking for co-tails is a more elaborate analysis than searching for tails in a map. An analysis of co-tails reveals concepts that have two or more outcomes. This might be of interest if multiple outcomes form the basis of two or more scenarios about possible future events and strategic alternatives. Co-tails also indicate single actions that enable multiple goals to be achieved.

Heads

Heads have no consequences and are at the top of a chain of argument. 'Successful export strategy...unsuccessful export strategy' is a head concept.

Orphans and domains

Sometimes it is necessary to look in crowded maps for concepts without links and to ask why those concepts are not linked to other domains. A group of concepts which are directly linked are called a domain. This allows the identification of the concepts that are the best elaborated, that are 'busy' or that have a high density of links. Domains can be seen as representing key issues that are worth further examination and/or action.

Clusters

As maps become more complex through the capture of a large number of ideas they can no longer be easily understood. The limit seems to be about 40 concepts. Cluster analysis fosters understanding by breaking down complex maps into more manageable 'chunks'. Key areas or isolated concepts can be identified and might require further links. It should be stated that the analysis takes no account of the concept's text and meaning, as the underlying assumption is that the meaning emerges from the content of the concepts to which it is linked.

Hierarchical sets

The aim of this analysis is to detect hierarchical groups based on specified sets of concepts – concepts that 'seed' the hierarchical sets. Each hierarchical set contains one of the specified sets and all the concepts that explain it. Once the analysis has been done it is possible to determine which specified concepts are well elaborated (that is, create large groups) and which are not by reviewing the size of the groups. This qualitative approach produces 'tear-drop' clusters. Their contents are not mutually exclusive. Each 'tear-drop' represents an integrated body of argument supporting one member of the seed set. Typical examples are means–end chains in which some of the constructs may support different ends or goals (Eden and Ackermann, 1998, pp. 404, 409).

Potency

Potency is a method of analysis that takes its information from the hierarchical sets. It identifies which concepts appear in most of the sets and thus determines their 'potency' in the map.

Loops

Loops are an interesting configuration in maps. They represent a chain of consequences that yield a dynamic outcome by feeding itself, or by controlling itself (negative). They configure a closer linked subsystem in form of loops in the map of concepts. 'Researchers identified the importance of the role of feedback loops within the detection and development of distinctive competencies' (ibid., p. 410).

A check for tails in map 1 identified the following concepts: employee qualification, access to raw material, human resources, production facilities and machines, distance from target market, defined corporate goals, proprietorship, currency situation in target market, stability, and international evaluation of market situation. For the manager who drew the map they were the starting points for a successful export strategy. The co-tails that were found were product, international marketing experience, distance from target market, entrepreneurship, and proprietorship. Identified domains or busy concepts were as follows (in descending order of value):

- Nine links around product.
- Seven links around planning, patents, licenses and brand copyright.
- Six links around economic situation in target market.

- Five links around international marketing experience, situation of competition, and entrepreneurship.
- Four links around market situation and market research, position in target market, and differentiation strategy.
- Three links around product quality, joint venture, development of target market, and proprietorship;
- Two links around costs, export support offered by government, distance from target market, representation in target market, corporate culture, demand, cultural environment of target market, and purchasing power.
- One link around employee qualification, access to raw material, human resources, production facilities and machines, enterprise philosophy, defined corporate goals, currency situation, stability, and international evaluation of market situation.

The co-tail structure illustrates the strategy development process quite distinctly. None of the concepts focuses on the client or customer at the beginning. Therefore strategy development by the company for which the participant worked involved a product-driven ('busy concept') approach to modelling a successful export strategy (the company in question was one of the leading companies in a globally operating industry).

The cluster analysis of map 1 produced no distinct subsets of concepts that could be viewed as clusters. Rather all 32 concepts constituted one cluster. However such a result should be viewed with caution. Cluster analysis is based on structure, not on content. The only characteristic that can be reliably identified is the relative intensity of linkages between concepts. A model that cannot be split into parts has to be analysed as a whole. Well separated small clusters indicate a limited amount of bridging between different parts of the map. Therefore map 1 has to be seen as a holistic view of concepts for a successful export strategy.

With regard to hierarchical sets, a most influencing set of concepts was identified from the loops detected in the map. It consisted of the following concepts: corporate culture, entrepreneurship, enterprise philosophy, defined corporate goals, proprietorship, and employee qualification and skills. This configuration reveals particular strengths or competencies within the organisation. According to Eden and Ackerman (ibid., p. 103) 'competencies often exist regardless of the industry or market. It is their exploitation within a particular market that makes them of particular success.' From a strategic point of view it would be interesting whether these distinctive competencies have characteristics, which are unique, rare among a firm's competition, imperfectly inimitable and valuable. If this is the case these competencies are very unique, as are the links between them and the strategy model developed for export activities (ibid.)

Cognitive map 2 was very different from map 1. A qualitative analysis revealed no tails, no co-tails, no clusters and no domains. From a content point of view, the compiler of map 2 did not take account of environmental factors that should be considered in the development of export strategies (Noonan, 1999). The strategic route chosen revealed a rudimentary marketing-mix understanding of successful export activities. This approach is very questionable, no matter what the actual situation of the company concerned and its environment.

Implications and conclusions

With causal or any other form of cognitive mapping the question 'Are we measuring what we think we are measuring?' (Kerlinger, 1977, p. 457) is rather difficult to answer and can be regarded as a positivistic approach to validity. A more appropriate approach would be to ask the participant whether he or she has been allowed to answer in a way that is salient and meaningful to him or her. In the study reported here the participants had every opportunity to answer in a meaningful way. As for reliability, the same procedure was used for all participants, and no systematic bias could have been caused by the preconceptions of the interviewer, coder or any other individual (Jenkins, 1998, p. 242). The maps were imported into the Decision Explorer software (Banxia Software Limited, 1997) and investigated. Critical issues (Jenkins, 1998, pp. 240–3) that were not addressed in the study were saliency of concept meaning, comparability of maps of individuals, atomistic versus holistic view of maps, and practicability of elicitation method. Ambrosini and Bowman (2002, p. 21) argue that it is important to consider tacit routines in strategic planning. Tacit routines are difficult to elicit because they are deeply embedded in the subconscious mind of organisational members. However they can be elicited through the use of metaphors or storytelling (ibid., p. 29). Future research should consider these and other methodological issues.

Our study was unable to demonstrate that differences in personal characteristics explain variations in the quantitative network structures of maps. This accords with the findings presented by Markóczy (2000, p. 437), who used a different elicitation method. The question is whether the international strategic intentions of the companies where the managers worked contributed to the variations in the maps. Further investigation should concentrate on qualitative analysis of all the causal maps developed by the managers. It should investigate the content of the concepts as well as their patterns (co-tails, clusters and so on). A combined content–pattern analysis would give greater insight into the know-how and process of managerial thinking and argumentation (Cañas *et al.*, 1999). Attention should also be paid to the degree of abstractness of concepts such as 'strategic', 'operational' and so on.

There are also practical issues to consider. Effective organisational knowledge management includes the identification and recording of useful information. A particularly important asset is the knowledge embedded in task experts such as export managers, whose knowledge may be lost with changes in projects or personnel. 'The mapping of concepts provides a framework for making this internal knowledge explicit in a visual form that can easily be examined and shared' (ibid., p. 1). Concept mapping is a useful means of externalising 'internal' expert knowledge, thus allowing the knowledge to be examined, refined and applied. A knowledge base developed by means of cognitive mapping seems to be one of the approaches to build a hyper-knowledge support system (Carlsson and Walden, 1996) in strategic export management. Case and causal reasoning might be a means to enhance and refine expert knowledge in international marketing decision making. Thus it may contribute to mindful learning.

Notes

1. The data set is continuously updated. At the moment about 300 cognitive maps of export managers (years 2001 and 2002) exist and will be investigated in a larger study (Wührer, 2003).
2. The maps are not shown here because map 1 cannot be condensed to a single page without distortions or overlaps.

References

Ambrosini, V. and Bowman, C. (2002) 'Mapping Successful Organizational Routines', in A. S. Huff and M. Jenkins (eds), *Mapping Strategic Knowledge* (London, Thousand Oaks and New Delhi: Sage), pp. 19–45.

Axelrod, R. M. (ed.) (1976) *Structures of Decision: The Cognitive Map of Political Elites* (Princeton, NJ: Princeton University Press).

Banxia Software Limited (ed.) (1997) *Decision Explorer User's Guide Version 3* (Glasgow: Banxia).

Bougon, M. G. (1983) 'Uncovering cognitive maps: the self-Q technique', in G. Morgan (ed.), *Beyond Method: Strategies for Social Research* (Beverly Hills, CA: Sage), pp. 173–8.

Cañas, A. J., Leake, D. B. and David, C. W. (1999) *Managing, Mapping, and Manipulating Conceptual Knowledge*; www.coginst.uwf.edu/projects/caseBasedCapture/AAAICBRCMaps99.htm#_ftn1.

Carlsson, C. and Walden, P. (1996) 'Cognitive Maps and a Hyperknowledge Support System in Strategic Management', *Group Dimensions and Negotiations*, no. 6, pp. 7–36.

Chandra, R. and Newburry, W. (1997) 'A Cognitive Map of the International Business Field', *International Business Review*, no. 6, pp. 387–410.

Eco, U. (1989) *Im Labyrinth der Vernunft. Texte über Kunst und Zeichen* (Leipzig: Reclam).

Eden, C. (1988) 'Cognitive Mapping', *European Journal of Operational Research*, vol. 36, pp. 1–13.

Eden, C. and Ackermann, F. (1998) *Making Strategy. The Journey of Strategic Management* (London: Sage).

Eden, C. and Ackermann, F. (2002) 'A Mapping Framework for Strategy Making' in A. S. Huff and M. Jenkins (eds), *Mapping Strategic Knowledge* (London, Thousand Oaks and New Delhi: Sage), pp. 173–95.

Evangelista, F. (1996) 'Linking Business Relationships to Marketing Strategy and Export Performance. A Proposed Conceptual Framework', in T. K. Madsen (ed.), *Advances in International Marketing*, vol. 8 (Greenwich, CT, and London: JAI Press), pp. 59–83.

Hinkle, D. N. (1965) 'The Change of Personal Constructs from the Viewpoint of a Theory of Construct Implications', unpublished PhD thesis, Ohio State University.

Huff, A. S. (1990) 'Mapping Strategic Thought', in A. S. Huff (ed.), *Mapping Strategic Thought* (Chichester: Wiley), pp. 11–49.

Huff, A. S. and Jenkins, M. (2002) 'Introduction', in A. S. Huff and M. Jenkins (eds), *Mapping Strategic Knowledge* (London, Thousand Oaks and New Delhi: Sage), pp. 1–16.

Iacobucci, D. (1998) 'Cognitive Networks of Services', *Journal of Service Research*, no. 1, pp. 32–46.

Jenkins, M. (1998) 'The Theory and Practice of Comparing Causal Maps', in J. Eden and S. C. Spender (eds), *Managerial and Organizational Cognition* (London, Thousand Oaks and New Delhi: Sage), pp. 231–49.

Kaplan, R. S. and Norton, D. P. (2000) 'Having Trouble with Your Strategy? Then Map it', *Harvard Business Review*, September–October, pp. 167–76.

Kelly, G. (1963) *A Theory of Personality. The Psychology of Personal Constructs* (New York: Norton).

Kerlinger, K. N. (1977) *Foundations of Behavioral Research* (London: Holt, Rinehart & Winston).

Kwak, K. Y. and Kim, Y. G. (1999) 'Supporting business process redesign using cognitive maps', *Decision Support Systems*, no. 25, pp. 155–78.

Laukkanen, M. (1990) 'Describing management cognition: the cause mapping approach', *Scandinavian Journal of Management*, vol. 6, no. 3, pp. 197–216.

Lindel, P., Melin, L., Gahmberg, H. J., Hellquist, A. and Melander, A. (1998) 'Stability and Change in a Strategist's Thinking', in C. Eden and J. C. Spender (eds), *Managerial and Organizational Cognition* (London: Sage), pp. 76–92.

Markóczy, L. (2000) 'National Culture and Strategic Change in Belief Formation', *Journal of International Business Studies*, vol. 31, no. 3, pp. 427–42.

Miles, M. B. and Huberman, M. A. (1994) *Qualitative Data Analysis* (Thousand Oaks, London and New Delhi: Sage).

Narayanan, V. K. and Fahey, L. (1994) 'Evolution of Revealed Causal Maps during Decline: A Case Study of Admiral', in A. S. Huff (ed.), *Mapping Strategic Thought* (Chichester and New York: Wiley), pp. 109–33.

Noonan, C. (1999), *The CIM Handbook of Export Marketing. A Practical Guide to Opening and Expanding Markets Overseas.* 2nd edn (Oxford, Auckland, Boston, Johannesburg, Melbourne and New Delhi: Butterworth – Heinemann).

O'Keefe, J. and Nadel, L. (1978) *The Hippocampus as a Cognitive Map* (Oxford: Oxford Press).

Portugali, J. (1996) 'Inter-representation Networks', in J. Portugali (ed.), *The Construction of Cognitive Maps* (Dordrecht: Kluwer), pp. 11–43.

Reger, R. K. (1994) 'The Repertory Grid Technique for Eliciting the Content and Structure of Cognitive Constructive Systems', in A. S. Huff (ed.), *Mapping Strategic Thought* (Chichester and New York: Wiley), pp. 301–9.

Schneider, D. J. G. and Müller, R. U. (1989) *Datenbankgestützte Marktselektion. Eine methodische Basis für Internationalisierungsstrategien* (Stuttgart: Poeschel).

Tyler, B. B. and Gnyawali, D. (2002) 'Mapping managers' market orientations regarding new product success', *Journal of Product Innovation Management*, no. 19, pp. 259–76.

van der Heijden, K. and Eden, C. (1998) 'The Theory and Praxis of Reflective Learning in Strategy Making', in J. Eden and S. C. Spender (eds), *Managerial and Organizational Cognition* (London Thousand Oaks and New Delhi: Sage), pp. 68–75.

Varela, F., Thompson, E. and Rosch, E. (1991) *The Embodied Mind* (Cambridge, Mass.: MIT Press).

Wasserman, S. and Faust, K. (1994) *Social Network Analysis. Methods and Applications* (Cambridge, New York and Melbourne: Cambridge University Press).

Wührer, G. A. (2000) 'Cognitive Maps of Risky Countries – Eastern and Fareastern Markets', in G. A. Wührer (ed.), *Der Aufbruch ins Dritte Jahrtausend. Die Jahre 1994–1999 aus der Sicht des Instituts für Handel, Absatz und Marketing* (Linz: Trauner), pp. 67–92.

Wührer, G. A. (2003) *Cognitive Maps auf Upper Austria Export Managers – Expertise within a Hyperknowledge Marketing System* (Linz: Trauner).

12

Action Research for Studying Internal Branding

Christine Vallaster

Introduction

In recent decades there has been considerable research interest in the topic of branding (Aaker, 1992; Kapferer, 1997; Keller, 1998; Aaker and Joachimsthaler, 2000). The vast majority of studies analyse brand management processes for products or large companies (Esch and Langner, 1999; de Chernatony *et al.*, 2000; Knox and Maklan, 2001; Hatch and Schultz, 2001). However there is growing interest in 'internal branding' (de Chernatony, 1999; LePla and Parker, 1999), which is seen as a means of creating powerful corporate brands. It involves an organisation aligning its internal processes and culture with those of the brand (Hatch and Schultz, 2001). Yet there is still little understanding of how the process of internal branding should be managed in order to create a unified understanding of a brand among employees. This, we suggest, is because the majority of current marketing research methods and techniques do not allow the capture of dynamic processes. This chapter argues that action research can be considered an appropriate research approach to the study of internal branding.

The chapter is structured as follows. First, some of the most relevant literature on internal branding is reviewed. Then the action research approach is introduced and described.

Theoretical review

In the literature there is a strong focus on how to position a brand in the minds of consumers and how to manage it appropriately (Aaker, 1996; Keller, 1998; Esch, 2001). Brand management considers ways of communicating the brand's identity and attributes to the target audience, ways of measuring the brand's value and reputation, and the impact of changes in societal trends, geographical boundaries and consumer demands. These factors all have an external focus.

However this external focus may irritate consumers if the brand's declared virtues are not reflected in employees' behaviour. As Mitchell (2002, p. 99) puts it: 'You tell customers what makes you great. Do your employees know?' If an organisation's employees do not understand the inherent brand promise they cannot deliver it. For example if a company wants to position itself as an organisation that provides not only a product but also an excellent service it is crucial for employees to know what type of behaviour best conveys this promise. If there is no internal agreement on the core brand values, confusion will reign and building a powerful brand will be impossible (Aaker and Joachimsthaler, 2000). Conversely an understanding of the brand values may encourage employees to find out how they can contribute to the brand's success and hence 'live the brand' (de Chernatony, 2001, p. 34; Tosti and Stotz, 2001, p. 28).

Ensuring that employees share the core values of the brand enables companies to reap the benefits of a common sense of purpose (Mitchell, 2002, p. 99). If this is promoted the employees may start to view themselves as valued members of the organisation. Thus their commitment to the company will increase and they will be motivated to work harder for the success of the brand, and ultimately for the company (LePla and Parker, 1999; de Chernatony, 2001; Mitchell, 2002). However it is unclear how a shared brand understanding is developed amongst employees. It is argued here that there are two reasons for this: the literature on brand management lacks in-depth discussions of the vital part played by leadership and organisational discourse, both of which are crucial to the internal brand management process; and conventional empirical methods are not suitable for analysing the core organisational issues of internal branding. Let us take a closer look at these two issues.

First, only a few authors have recognised the importance of internal brand management. Among these are Thomson *et al.* (1999, p. 820), who have found 'evidence of a new generation of marketing thinking that takes a more balanced perspective, striving to ensure satisfaction amongst both customers and employees'. Indeed a 'growing number of organisations who recognise the need to communicate details of their brands and their strategies to their staff' (ibid.) Keller (1998) suggests that brand mantras can improve internal brand management and de Chernatony (1996) proposes brand taxonomies for integrated brand building. These enable a company to align its employees' values with those of the brand and of the company itself. In essence the goal of internal branding is to turn employees into brand ambassadors who 'live the brand', thereby improving their commitment and development (Boone, 2000).

Internal branding is presented as a means of creating a powerful brand. Managers are told that their companies can enhance brand equity by aligning their employees with the promises that brands make (Tosti and Stotz, 2001). There is some evidence that when employees are committed to their brand, there is likelihood of better performance (de Chernatony, 1999). Moreover a study by Thomson *et al.* (1999, p. 828) suggests that employees' understanding of and commitment to the brand 'lead to greater advocacy, and therefore provide organisations with the much-needed champions'. It is also argued that a greater understanding (intellectual buy-in) and commitment (emotional buy-in) enhance brand equity.

While these studies provide valuable insights into internal brand management, the topics of leadership and organisational discourse have remained untouched.

Leadership and its role in internal branding

Leadership may be vital in providing a context for internal branding. Mitchell (2002, p. 99) has found 'that by applying many of the principles of consumer advertising to internal communications, leaders can guide employees to a better understanding of, and even a passion for, the brand vision'. LePla and Parker (1999) stress that throughout the process of what they call 'integrated branding' it is essential to keep everybody on the same path. They explain that stories are appropriate means of conveying meaning: The '[a]dvantages of stories are that they teach us about behaviour, that they can reinforce employee beliefs and that they create a context. To create a successful corporate story it is necessary to ask employees to tell their versions. Then boil them down to one and finally the synthesised story must be verified by the brand team' (ibid., p. 56). The criteria for a successful story are passion, the values it contains and the vision and reaction of the audience.

In fact leadership has often been likened to conducting a symphony orchestra (Bass and Aviolo, 1994). As the conductor, the leader is the one whose effort, vision and motivation cause the various instrumental parts to become the living whole of music. In each organisation there has to be a pivot, a link that combines objectives with applications in a suitable manner. In the context of internal branding, leadership includes the ability to influence a group towards brand-consistent behaviour. In line with Yukl (1994), it is argued that good leaders are able to design brand-adequate work activities. Yet their role in bringing employees into line with the brand, and thereby facilitating cooperative relationships and teamwork, as well as realising support from outside the group or organisation, has not yet been determined or fully understood.

Organisational discourse

Organisational discourse is a means of creating a shared understanding (Grant *et al.*, 2001) of a brand's core values. The meaning and reality of the core brand values are created through interactions between people. The defined core brand values are communicated to employees, who then formally and informally discuss them. These interactions may eventually provide brand managers with the feedback that is crucial for the alignment of meanings.

Yet during the organisational discourse employees receive and send messages that are translated into subjective meanings, depending on the social or cultural upbringing of the individuals concerned. Both these factors shape people's values, beliefs, feelings and attitudes, and they influence how employees interact with others (Cushner and Brislin, 1996; Griffith and Harvey, 2001). They may even inhibit the development of a common conception of the core brand values, resulting in inconsistent signals being sent to the organisation's audience. A decline in brand equity may be the ultimate consequence.

However there is no clear understanding of how social and cultural elements mediate internal branding via organisational discourse. In order to analyse and understand such complex organisational phenomena as internal brand management it is necessary to adopt a holistic approach to reality. But, this is lacking in contemporary marketing literature as the most commonly used research methods are not suitable for finding answers to the above issues. Marketing research is still dominated by the positivist paradigm, in which our knowledge is derived from 'the world out there' through our sensory or observational experiences combined with logic. Within this paradigm, experimental design and replicable, generalisable findings are emphasised (Preskill and Torres, 1999), so considerable stress is put on things that are easily measured and on technical accomplishment.

However there has been a shift in the methodological approaches applied in marketing research. 'This transition is caused by the limitations experienced in quantitative research and the complacent, taken-for-granted attitude of marketing academics that statistical studies are the key to the truth, the superior approach, the cure of all' (Gummesson, 2002, p. 344). In particular the critical paradigm challenges the teachings of the positivist approach. This derives from the work of Lewin (1946) and emphasises 'praxis', action and reflection. Hence there is more to this paradigm than the mere collection of information on practice or the meanings that people attribute to phenomena and events. Following Gummesson (2002), who argues that there is a need to create more adequate theory in marketing, it is proposed here that action research is an appropriate method of analysing internal branding processes. The focus is on leadership and organisational discourse as the driving forces for aligning employees with the core brand values.

Action research as a tool to analyse internal branding processes

In this section action research and its principal concepts are introduced and then applied to the subject of internal branding. Next an action research model is presented. This involves activities such as planning, acting, observing and reflecting upon what has happened. The data collection methods and analytical process are explained in detail.

Action research: an introduction

'Action research involves the researcher in working with members of an organisation over a matter which is of genuine concern to them and in which there is the intent by the organisation members to take action based on the interventions' (Eden and Huxham, 1996, p. 527). It is based on the concepts of 'change' and 'learning', two outcomes of the effort to understand a complex phenomenon (Rashford and Coghlan, 1994).

Central to understanding change and learning is an appreciation of the learning cycle (as introduced by Kolb and Fry in 1975), in which people learn about the world and themselves by reflecting on past actions. It is the process by which individuals, teams and organisations attend to and understand their experiences, and consequently modify their actions. In general the failure of many efforts is due to the inability to learn from past mistakes. Kolb and Fry's approach to learning consists of four stages (Figure 12.1) and is based on the assumption that the more we reflect on a task, the more we can modify and refine our efforts.

According to Kolb and Fry the learning process can begin at any of the four points as the cycle is continuous. However the learning process often begins with a person carrying out a particular action and then observing the effect of that action. The second step is to understand this effect so that if the same action were taken in the same circumstances in the future it would be possible to anticipate what would follow from

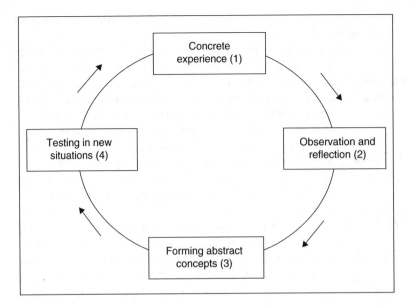

Figure 12.1 The learning cycle
Source: Kolb and Fry (1975). Reproduced with permission.

the action. The third step is to understand the general principle under which the particular circumstance falls. In Coleman's (1976, p. 52) words:

> generalising may involve actions over a range of circumstances to gain experience beyond the particular instance and suggest the general principle. Understanding the general principle does not imply, in this sequence, an ability to express the principle in a symbolic medium, that is, the ability to put it into words. It implies only the ability to see a connection between the actions and effects over a range of circumstances.

Educators who have learnt in this way may well have various rules of thumb or generalisations about what to do in different situations, but they will not be able to verbalise their actions in psychodynamic or sociological terms. Hence there may be difficulty with transfering learning to other settings and situations. However once the general principle is understood the last step, according to Kolb and Fry (1975), is its application through action in a new circumstance within the range of generalisation.

In some representations of learning these steps are depicted as a circular movement, but the process can also be seen as a spiral. Thus 'we will not return to the same place from which we started' (Weinstein, 1999, p. 41). Weinstein further argues that placing 'reflection' at just one location on the spiral would be wrong as it is necessary to engage in reflection at every stage, whether this is to facilitate an immediate action, plan a new one or even just reflect upon what has happened.

Learning involves the detection and correction of error (Argyris and Schön, 1978). When something goes wrong, it is suggested, the first step for most people is to look for another strategy that will address and work in accordance with the governing variables. Argyris and Schön (1974) call this 'single-loop learning'. An alternative response is to question the governing variables themselves, to subject them to critical scrutiny. This they call 'double-loop learning'. Such learning may lead to an alteration in the governing variables, and thus a shift in the way in which strategies and consequences are framed. The two approaches are outlined in Figure 12.2.

Single-loop learning takes place when goals, values, and frameworks are taken for granted. The emphasis is on 'techniques and making techniques more efficient' (Usher and Bryant, 1989, p. 87). Double-loop learning, in contrast, 'involves questioning the role of the framing and learning systems which underlie actual goals and strategies' (ibid.). Here reflection is more fundamental: the basic assumptions behind ideas or policies are confronted, hypotheses are tested and processes are negotiable, not self-seeking (Argyris, 1982). Argyris (1974, 1982) argues that double-loop learning is necessary if practitioners and organisations are to make informed decisions in rapidly changing and often uncertain

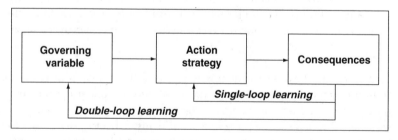

Figure 12.2   Single- and double-loop learning
Sources: Argyris (1992; 1993). Reproduced with permission.

circumstances. This might be of particular relevance in a brand-related context where environmental changes cause a high degree of uncertainty.

Action research applied to internal branding

Employee's brand-related knowledge and belief structures determine the way individuals behave and act towards the organisational environment. By uncovering these structures, it is critically reflected upon the way individuals plan, implement and review their brand-related actions. The focus is on double-loop learning. This means that individuals have to plan, implement and review their brand-related actions, that is, the focus is on double-loop learning.

Following Argyris and Schön (1974), the leader and his or her followers have to uncover the 'theories in use' that govern people's behaviour. These tend to be tacit structures. Their relation to action 'is like the relation of grammar-in-use to speech; they contain assumptions about self, others and environment – these assumptions constitute a microcosm of science in everyday life' (ibid., p. 30). The words employees use to convey what they do in terms of branding or what they would like consumers or other stakeholders to think they do is called espoused theory. This distinction allows us to investigate the extent to which behaviour fits espoused theory and whether inner feelings are expressed in actions.

Argyris (1980) claims that effectiveness results from congruence between theory-in-use and espoused theory. If the gap between the two grows too wide the problem of 'brand misfit' arises. However if the gap is small it creates a dynamic for reflection and for dialogue that provokes brand-adequate and consistent behaviour.

To understand leadership behaviour and learning in a brand-related context, the model (in Figure 12.3) has been developed to guide the analysis of brand-related behaviour by leaders and followers.

The notion of drawing out theory is important for action research. As Eden and Huxham (1996, p. 531) write, action research is 'an approach to theory development which recognises that while the researcher always brings a pre-understanding . . . – a starting theoretical position – to the situation, it is important to defer serious reflection on the role of this until the later stages of the project'. By so doing a holistic and complex body of theory, concepts and experience in respect of managerial practices for internal branding can be generated.

Although the setting may be the same (here we suggest workshops with senior management) each intervention will be different from the last. Each may have a different focus, such as reflection on the current perception of the core brand values, reflection on the current leadership

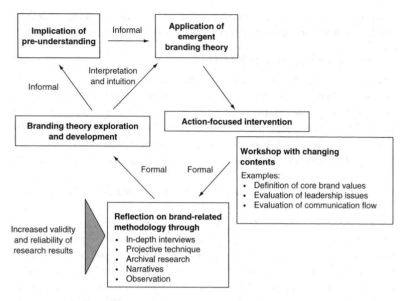

Figure 12.3   The cyclical process of action research in a brand-related context
Source: Based on Eden and Huxham (1996).

style, consideration of sociocultural variables and their impact on organisational discourse, or reconsideration of the current approaches to achieving a shared understanding of the brand's core values. Such workshops may also focus on tools and techniques to develop and apply. Here there is an opportunity to try out a complex theoretical framework for internal branding by analysing its systemic relationship with employees, organisational structures and processes.

In order to increase validity of the results it is recommended to use more than one strategy or source of information for each question (Miles and Huberman, 1994). It is proposed here that a combination of in-depth interviews, projective techniques, archival research, narratives and observation be used to generate data to answer questions on leadership and social/cultural influences during the process of internal branding. Their complementary nature allows to touch upon process drivers such as brand-related knowledge, feelings and beliefs, as well as communicative elements which are highly relevant in general (Vallaster, 2000) and the development of a shared understanding of core brand values in particular. The interviewees could be middle management employees.

Analysis of the data collected from senior and/or middle managers should pay great attention to reliability and validity (Gummesson, 2000), but the process also calls for intuition as it is often impossible to know exactly how to process data and how to arrive at conclusions. While intuition is often called non-scientific and irrational, philosophers define intuition as 'complete knowledge of reality', the 'ability to quickly draw conclusions' and 'the instantaneous perception of logical connections and truths' (Matti, 1999, pp. 5–7). Feedback loops with other research participants' can help to reduce uncertainty about the reliability of the data collected.

Although action research is continuous, once data redundancy or saturation is achieved it is time to finalise the project. It can be assumed that after four to five cycles the value of new data is only marginal and there is no further need to take up the time of the research participants.

Conclusions

Action research can be considered a useful approach to studying the complex process of internal brand management. Contemporary marketing theories still seem to be universally valid and free from specifics of time and place (Clark, 2000) and 'organizational analysis has been adroit at providing an image of dynamics while suppressing processes' (Pettigrew *et al.*, 2001, p. 701). The former (Clark, 2000) suggests that modern social science – and with it marketing theories – seem to be universally valid and free from specifics of time and place, while the latter (Pettigrew, *et al.*, 2001, p. 701) claim that 'organisational analysis has been adroit at providing an image of dynamics while suppressing processes'.

Action research may help to alleviate these criticisms: action research facilitates capturing the dynamic and social elements that influence the process of developing a shared brand understanding as well as the role of the leader who ideally initiates and drives this process. Successful internal branding requires learning at the individual and team levels as employees need to behave in a brand-adequate manner. Although learning can be 'the most powerful, engaging, rewarding and enjoyable aspect of our personal and collective experience' (Honey, 1998, p. 28), it can also be painful if it involves giving up resources and power. Learning may also mean to critically look at and eventually change the way in which employees interact with each other.

To conclude, the holistic action research approach described in this chapter may well prove suitable for understanding managerial phenomena such as internal branding, although the proposed model has yet to be subjected to empirical testing.

References

Aaker, D. A. (1992) 'The Value of Brand Equity', *The Journal of Business Strategy*, vol. 13, no. 4, pp. 27–32.

Aaker, D. A. (1996) *Building Strong Brands* (New York: Free Press).

Aaker, D. A. and Joachimsthaler, E. (2000) *Brand Leadership* (New York: Free Press).

Argyris, C. (1974) *Behind the Front Page* (San Francisco, CA: Jossey-Bass).

Argyris, C. (1980) *Inner Contradictions of Rigorous Research* (New York: Academic Press).

Argyris, C. (1982) *Reasoning, Learning, and Action: Individual and Organizational* (San Francisco, CA: Jossey-Bass).

Argyris, C. (1992) *On Organizational Learning* (Cambridge, Mass.: Blackwell).

Argyris, C. (1993) *Knowledge for Action* (San Francisco, CA: Jossey-Bass).

Argyris, C. and Schön, D. (1974) *Theory in Practice: Increasing Professional Effectiveness* (San Francisco, CA: Jossey-Bass).

Argyris, C. and Schön, D. (1978) *Organizational Learning: A Theory of Action Perspective* (Reading, Mass.: Addison-Wesley).

Bass, B. M. and Aviolo, B. J. (1994) *Improving Organizational Effectiveness through transformational Leadership* (Thousand Oaks, CA: Sage).

Bass, B. M. and Bruce, J. (1994) *Improving Organizational Effectiveness through Transformational Leadership* (Thousand Oaks, CA: Sage).

Boone, M. E. (2000) 'The Importance of Internal Branding', *Sales and Marketing Magazine*, no. 152, pp. 36–8.

Clark, P. (2000) *Organisations in Action: Competition between Contexts* (London: Routledge).

Coleman, J. (1976) 'Differences between experiential learning and classroom learning', in M. Keeton (ed.), *Experiential Learning* (San Francisco, CA: Jossey-Bass), pp. 49–61.

Cushner, K. and Brislin, R. (1996) *Intercultural Interactions: A Practical Guide* (Thousand Oaks, CA: Sage)

Cushner, K. and Richard, B. (1996) *Intercultural Interactions: A Practical Guide* (Thousand Oaks, CA: Sage).

De Chernatony, L. (1996) 'Integrated Brand Building Using Brand Taxonomies', *Marketing Intelligence & Planning*, vol. 14, no. 7, pp. 40–6.

De Chernatony, L. (1999) 'Brand Management Through Narrowing the Gap Between Brand Identity and Brand Reputation', *Journal of Marketing Management*, vol. 15, nos 1–3, pp. 157–79.

De Chernatony, L. (2001) 'A model for strategically building brands', *Journal of Brand Management*, vol. 9, no. 1, pp. 32–44.

De Chernatony, L., Harris, F. and Dall'Olmo Riley, F. (2000) 'Added Value: its Nature, Roles and Sustainability', *European Journal of Marketing*, vol. 34, nos 1–2, pp. 39–56.

Eden, C. and Huxham, C. (1996) 'Action Research for the Study of Organizations', in S. R. Clegg, C. Hardy and W. R. Nord (eds), *Handbook of Organization Studies* (London: Sage), pp. 526–42.

Esch, F.-R. (2001) *Moderne Markenführung. Grundlagen. Innovative Ansätze. Praktische Umsetzungen* (Wiesbaden: Gabler).

Esch, F.-R. and Langner, T. (1999) 'Branding als Grundlage zum Markenaufbau', in F.-R. Esch (ed.), *Moderne Markenführung* (Wiesbaden: Gabler), pp. 407–20.

Grant, D., Keenoy, T. and Oswick, C. (2001) 'Organizational Discourse', *International Studies of Management and Organization*, vol. 31, no. 3, pp. 5–24.

Griffith, D. A. and Harvey, M. G. (2001) 'An Intercultural Communication Model for Use in Global Relationship Networks', *Journal of International Marketing*, vol. 9, no. 3, pp. 87–103.

Gummesson, E. (2000) *Qualitative Methods in Management Research* (Thousand Oaks, CA: Sage).

Gummesson, E. (2002) 'Practical value of adequate marketing management theory', *European Journal of Marketing*, vol. 36, no. 3, pp. 325–49.

Hatch, M. J. and Schultz, M. (2001) 'Are the Strategic Stars Aligned for Your Corporate Brand', *Harvard Business Review*, vol. 4, no. 1, pp.128–35.

Honey, P. (1998) 'The debate starts here', *People Management*, October, vol. 4, issue 19, p. 28.

Kapferer, J.-N. (1997) *Strategic Brand Management: Creating and Sustaining Brand Equity Long Term* (London: Kogan Page).

Keller, K. L. (1998) *Strategic Brand Management* (Englewood Cliffs, NJ: Prentice-Hall).

Knox, S. and Maklan, S. (2001) *Der 360°-Wettbewerb. Vom Marketing zur radikalen Kundenorientierung* (Munich: Financial Times).

Kolb, D. A. and Fry, R. (1975) 'Toward an applied theory of experiential learning', in C. Cooper (ed.), *Theories of Group Process* (London: Wiley), pp. 33–57.

LePla, J. F. and Parker, L. M. (1999) *Integrated Branding: Becoming Brand-Driven through Company-Wide Action* (London: Quorum).

Lewin, K. (1946) 'Action research and minority problems', *Journal of Social Issues*, vol. 2, no. 4, pp. 34–46.

Matti, G. (1999) *Det intuitiva livet* (Uppsala, Sweden: Uppsala University).

Miles, M. B. and Huberman, M. A. (1994) *Qualitative Data Analysis: An Expanded Sourcebook* (Thousand Oaks, CA: Sage).

Mitchell, C. (2002) 'Selling the brand inside', *Harvard Business Review*, vol. 80, no. 1, pp. 99–104.

Pettigrew, A. M., Woodman, R. W. and Cameron, K. S. (2001) 'Studying Organizational Change and Development: Challenges for the Future', *Academy of Management Journal*, vol. 44, no. 4, pp. 697–713.

Preskill, H. and Torres, Rosalie T. (1999) *Evaluative Inquiry for Learning in Organizations* (Thousand Oaks and New York: Sage).

Rashford, N. S. and Coghlan, D. (1994) *The Dynamics of Organizational Levels* (Reading, Mass.: Addison-Wesley).

Thomson, K., de Chernatony, L., Arganbright, L. and Khan, S. (1999) 'The Buy-in Benchmark: How Staff Understanding and Commitment Impact Brand and Business Performance', *Journal of Marketing Management*, vol. 15, no. 8, pp. 819–35.

Tosti, D. T. and Stotz, R. D. (2001) 'Brand: Building Your Brand from the Inside Out', *Marketing Management*, vol. 10, no. 2, pp. 28–33.

Usher, R. and Bryant, I. (1989) *Adult Education as Theory, Practice and Research: The Captive Triangle* (New York: Routledge).

Vallaster, C. (2000) *Strategic Decision Making by Multicultural Workgroups* (Innsbruck: University of Innsbruck).

Weinstein, K. (1999) *Action Learning: A Practical Guide* (Aldershot: Gower).

Yukl, G. A. (1994) *Leadership in Organizations* (Englewood Cliffs, NJ: Prentice-Hall).

13
Developing an Internal Marketing Concept Using Two Methods of Data Analysis

Tine Adler

Conceptual background of the internal marketing approach

In general the real problem of marketing is 'not outside marketing but inside marketing, for example, getting others in the organisation to accept ideas' (Kotler, 1972, p. 48). In theoretical terms this chapter follows the generic concept of marketing (Kotler, 1972), which integrates the general understanding of marketing and Bruhn's (1999) internal marketing concept, focusing on both employees' and customers' interests.[1]

The aim of the study

This chapter is based on a study of internal marketing in a not-for-profit organisation. Not-for-profit organisations do not pay dividends to individuals and shareholders but reinvest their surplus funds in the running of the organisation (Badelt, 2002, p. 9). The study was conducted in a geriatric rehabilitation clinic in Germany. The treatment provided was interdisciplinary and aimed at enabling elderly people to live in their own homes. The clinic had 60 in-patient beds, 15 beds in the day clinic and employed 90 people.

In such organisations, satisfaction of the needs and wants of patients and employees is hard to achieve. Most of the patients are old, ill and unaccustomed to expressing their wishes to staff or family members. The salaries of the employees are lower than in the commercial sector and the work tends to be of low status, which to a certain degree is due to the fact that a high percentage of the staff are volunteers.

There is little literature on management issues in not-for-profit organisations in general and internal marketing issues in particular. Because of this, and because case studies are often the only means of investigating management problems in practice (Buber and Meyer, 1997, p. 5), a case study approach was adopted for the research. Moreover using this approach in the context of internal marketing would support hypothesis generation and model building (Hartley, 1994, pp. 212 ff.; Buber and Meyer, 1997, p. 6).

The research design

In 1999, interviews were conducted at the geriatric clinic with the medical director, the nursing staff manager, the administration manager, the therapeutic staff manager, the chief secretary, the kitchen manager, the electronic data processing manager, one administrative employee and one social worker. The interviews lasted between 30 and 60 minutes. They were tape-recorded and later transcribed.

The first analysis of the verbal data took the form of a qualitative content analysis (Mayring, 1990; Lamnek, 1993; Titscher *et al.*, 1998, pp. 74–92). As the results seemed to be incomplete and not useful for drawing a real picture of the clinic's internal marketing situation, the data were reanalysed using the GABEK method and its computer application WinRelan. Figure 13.1 provides an overview of the research phases.

Phase 1: content analysis

The application of Mayring's (1990) scheme of data analysis[2] to the verbal data produced the following main results:

- The interviewees had no understanding of internal marketing concepts or models.
- There was a strong correlation between the working atmosphere (how the employees worked and how efficient the working-structure was) and internal and external quality (how the employees and customers viewed the quality of the work).
- There were some problems with team-building, communication and motivation, and not enough resources.
- There were no departmental budgets for in-house training because the budget was planned centrally.
- Although a vision statement existed, it was not well-known (the statement was developed by the executives using the Hoshi method[3] and was published in the employees' journal).

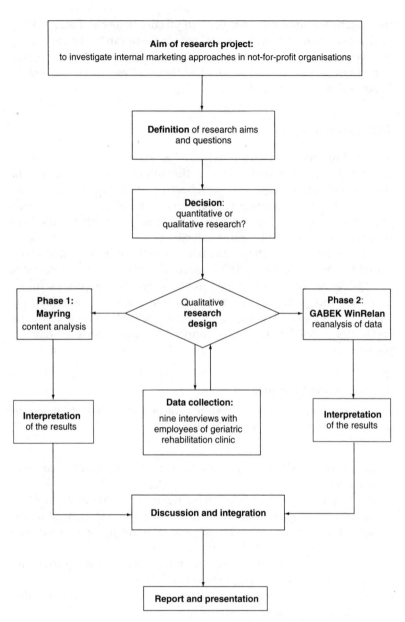

Figure 13.1 The research process

- The workplace was evaluated positively.
- The interviewees came up with many wishes in general and about the flow and style of communication in particular.

In addition to the reported issues, other themes came up after the tape recorder was switched off, including talk of a conflict between the nursing staff manager and the nursing staff. These themes seemed to be important but could not be proved with a content analysis, so another tool was needed. The GABEK method and WinRelan would facilitate the extraction of 'unspoken' material, and hence was chosen for phase 2 of the analysis.

Phase 2: GABEK WinRelan

> GABEK as a concept, a method and a procedure in particular can be characterised as stressing the rational and emotional involvement participation of all people concerned, using their knowledge and their creative capacities, motivating and encouraging personal involvement. (Löckenhoff, 2000, p. 99)

The GABEK method is based on Stumpf's (1939) theory of *Gestaltwahrnehmung* (perceptual gestalten). Zelger has transformed the theory of perceptual gestalten into the concept of linguistic gestalten (Zelger, 1999, pp. 42 ff., 2000, pp. 31ff.). A linguistic gestalt is a 'semantic implication from different statements within a text group' (Zelger, 2000, p. 208f.) GABEK (GAnzheitliche Bewältigung von Komplexität – the holistic processing of complexity) is a qualitative method for analysing qualitative data (such as unstructured text from interviews) and organising, processing and representing knowledge. A rule-based network of data developed by means of GABEK's computer application WinRelan (Windows Relational Analysis) enables the researcher to 'obtain a holistic, integrated view of individual aspects of the particular investigated "situations" (e.g. opinions and attitudes)' (Buber and Kraler, 2000, p. 112).

The reanalysis of the text consisted of the following steps (Zelger, 1999): (a) The definition of text units (542), (b) The coding of keywords (966) and (c) The construction of gestalten, hypergestalten and hyperhypergestalten. This led to a list of keywords and a gestalten tree. Table 13.1 shows the list of keywords and offers a first glimpse of the study's topics.

WinRelan has a cluster analysis capability that facilitates the construction of gestalten. The cluster analysis groups together text units that have a number of keywords in common, but 'not too many' (Zelger, 1996, p. 11). In this study the analysis helped to identify 37 gestalten.

Table 13.1   The list of keywords

Frequency	Keyword
57	Problem
51	Patients
40	Communication, employees
34	Time
29	Medical doctors, nursing staff
27	Professions
26	Further vocational training, therapy
25	Workplace, finance
24	Work, colleagues
23	Administration
22	Personnel

The gestalten tree

The gestalten tree in Figure 13.2 shows 37 gestalten, five hyper-gestalten, two hyperhypergestalten and a summary.[4] A gestalt is defined as a summary of text units that fulfils certain syntactic, semantic and pragmatic rules (Zelger, 1999, pp. 41ff.; Buber and Kraler, 2000, p. 119).

Gestalten.   The 37 gestalten show the main topics in the clinic's internal marketing concept. They have been divided into systematic categories following Bruhn's (1999) integrative approach. According to Bruhn, internal marketing is the systematic optimisation of in-house processes by means of marketing-management and personnel-management instruments. Marketing activities should consequently be addressed to both target groups, customer and employees. Thus marketing should become an organisation's internal philosophy.

The following categories show how internal marketing was seen by the interviewees:

- Internal customers and employee orientation relate to exchanges between the employer and the employees (gestalten 9–13, 16, 17, 19, 21 and 22) and includes problems with communication, goals, personnel policy, working hours, resources and motivation.
- Immediate external customer orientation relates to exchanges between employees and external customers (gestalten 14, 18, 33, 43 and 44).
- Indirect external customer orientation relates to processes between the clinic management and employees and the customers (gestalten 15 and 29).

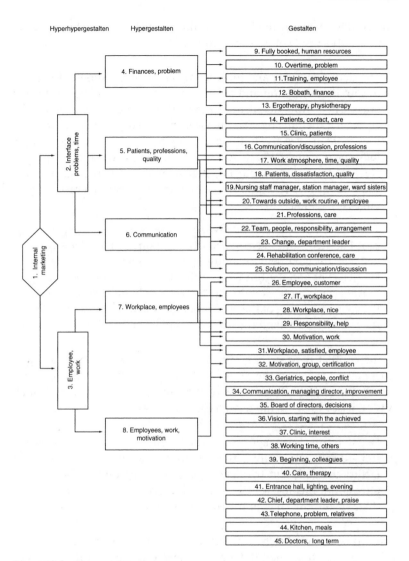

Figure 13.2 The gestalten tree

These results are the basis for the next steps of the analysis (hyper-gestalten and hyperhypergestalten).

The earlier qualitative content analysis produced nearly the same results but there was a remarkable difference in respect of gestalten 19 and 20, which concern problems with the nursing staff manager and conflict between the latter and the nursing staff on the matter of representation and communication:

> The station manager and the nursing staff manager should being able to spot dissatisfaction and talk about it so, that it can be resolved at once. I first think about the nurse and then the nursing staff manager. I tell the nursing staff manager that the department is not o.k., they work incorrectly. In the beginning it was nicer, we had our own full-time nursing staff manager so we could clear up things at once.... Now that we share a nursing staff manager with the other house she's not always here and we are not able to organise everything by ourselves. (gestalt 19)

> The better we work internally, the better the quality expectations can be met and maybe also the working atmosphere will be better...the competence training for employees started with the kitchen staff and continued with the nursing staff manager, they all must become professionals. The employees should be integrated into the course planning of the clinic; there should be transparency, so that they could understand the decisions and what happens. (gestalt 20)

The conflict between the nursing staff manager and the employees became evident when the results of gestalten 19, 20 and 35 were compared. The main problem lay with the clinic's decision making, which was criticised as being top-down rather than bottom-up:

> Decisions must be made – sure. The board of directors – those at the top – decide. Normally if the decisions concern the kitchen or the facility management they ask them. But in the case of therapy it is different, a member of the board of directors is responsible for the therapy, not the chief of the therapists. (gestalt 35)

It can be assumed that all the employees and directors were aware of this dissatisfaction, but it failed to emerge in the content analysis (in phase 1).

For the category 'internal customers and employee orientation' the results clearly matched the internal marketing concept in the literature: the patients were mostly seen as the clinic's customers. For the category 'immediate external customer orientation' the analysis resulted in two gestalten that described the clinic's competition in the external market and customer satisfaction.

Hypergestalten. The five hypergestalten that emerged from the analysis are shown in Table 13.2.

- Finance: the funding of vocational training was seen by the interviewees as problematic. This factor can be considered a starting point for the strategic planning of an internal marketing concept (Bruhn, 1999).
- Internal communication: this theme predominantly involved problems between the nursing staff and the nursing manager, plus a lack of internal customer orientation. It was obvious that a new model of internal communication should be conceptualised and integrated into the clinic's internal marketing concept.
- Workload and working together: these are problems that have to be considered when implementing an internal marketing concept. This hypergestalt deals with competition, and atmosphere, as described by George and Grönroos (1999). Efficient and effective communication between employees is essential to the provision of good patient services and is highly relevant to the goals of internal marketing (Bruhn, 1999, p. 29).

The study's results showed five main themes which should be integrated in a theory-based internal marketing concept for a not-for-profit organisation, namely:

- Workplace atmosphere and conditions.
- Salaries.
- Opportunities for self-realisation (intrinsic motivation).
- Integration.
- Bottom-up and top-down decision making.

Concluding remarks

In this research marketing-relevant and personnel management-relevant themes were discussed in detail. In accordance with Berry (1981) and Stauss and Schulze (1990) interviewees talked about the importance of optimal working atmosphere and workplace design. They also discussed employees' intrinsic motivation, which Bruhn (1999) has defined as being an important goal for the development of an internal marketing concept. Furthermore, interviewees demand for being integrated into the clinic's decision processes. This aspect is intensively recommended by Barnes (1989), Stauss and Schulze (1990), Bruhn (1999) and Buber

Table 13.2 The five hypergestalten and interviewees' comments

Hypergestalt	Comments
Finance	We must have a full house to be economically viable. We have fewer personnel than we need. This is a problem because we have to work overtime. The employees' support is a main aim of internal marketing; employees should get actual training. There are some therapists who are considering work in other fields. At the beginning of the year we ask the employees which training they want to have. We decide about the finances. Training should be in-house. This could better meet the needs of the employees.
Patients (customers), professions and quality	Dissatisfied patients pass on their dissatisfaction to the employees. Dissatisfaction comes from poor quality. Teamwork does not work well. Most problems are among the nurses – with their teamwork and their work with the patients. There are times when the personnel are not very friendly to the patients. This is caused by time pressure. This is a big conflict. At last there should be an overall program optimising the self-confidence and everyday competence of the patients or the avoidance of nursing; every profession has to support this. This needs more time but it is more satisfying for the patients and the nurses. The better it works internally, the better the quality and maybe the working atmosphere is.
Communication	It is necessary that there is an information process and I really hope that my colleagues, the unit leaders inform and talk/discuss – also with new information and changes. The station managers are the speakers, the opinion leaders. They and the nursing department's head should recognise the dissatisfaction and talk about problem solving immediately. They should get together and talk about solutions to the problems. There is some structure in communication – a conference on rehabilitation, discussions about rehabilitation and the morning briefing. It takes up time but it is satisfying.
Workplace and employees	Employees want optimal working conditions and atmosphere, they want to be accepted and to have some freedom for self-determination. They wish to have competencies to decide. If they get enough money they are satisfied. They wish to be integrated in planing processes. Decisions should be made transparent. Employees need time to serve the patients. Otherwise quality will decrease. The better employees perceive the atmosphere, the better they should work and represent the clinic.

Employees, work and motivation	Employees need motivation. I am sure the management has ideas, for example team-building and self-motivation of the group. Employees want their performance to be acknowledged. More time and more employees are needed for the work which has to be done. But even small things are motivating. Everyone is happy when he/she feels that he/she is needed. To work with old people is nice: they are happy when they get a smile. When patients we happy employees are happy as well.

(2000a, 2000b). All in all, the study proves the main issues of the internal marketing concepts presented in the literature. The first elements of an internal marketing concept were revealed by the hypergestalten. The development of a new internal marketing concept at the clinic should be based on these findings and will have to be done very carefully and consequently will take some time. On the other hand the problems revealed by the gestalten could be solved quite quickly.

Notes

1. There are various approaches to internal marketing in the literature. See for example Berry (1981), Barnes (1989), George and Grönroos (1999), Piercy and Morgan (1991) and Stauss and Schulze (1990). For a general overview see Ahmed and Rafiq (2002) and the collection of essays in Varey and Lewis (2000).
2. Mayring's (1990) qualitative content analysis is a rule-based, intersubjective method of analysing text material. It consists of the following steps: (1) summarising, (2) explicating and (3) structuring (Bortz and Döring 2002, p. 332f.).
3. Hoshin Kanri = management by policy = policy development (Bechtell, 1995).
4. The strict rules of GABEK render the hyperhypergestalt and the summary invalid.

References

Ahmed, P. K. and Rafiq, M. (2002) *Internal Marketing. Tools and Concepts for Customer-Focused Management* (Oxford: Butterworth, Heinemann).

Badelt, C. (2002) 'Zielsetzungen und Inhalte des "Handbuchs der Nonprofit Organisation"', in C. Badelt (ed.), *Handbuch der Nonprofit Organisation. Strukturen und Management* (Stuttgart: Schäffer-Poeschel), pp. 3–18.

Barnes, J. (1989) 'The Role of Internal Marketing: If the staff won't buy it, why should the customer?', *Irish Marketing Review*, vol. 4, no. 2, pp. 11–21.

Bechtell, M. L. (1995) *The Management Compass: Steering the Corporation Using Hoshin Planning* (New York: AMA).

Berry, L. L. (1981) 'The Employee as Customer', *Journal of Retail Banking*, vol. 3, no. 1, pp. 33–40.

Bortz, J. and Döring, N. (2002) *Forschungsmethoden und Evaluation* (Berlin, Heidelberg and New York: Springer).

Bruhn, M. (1999) 'Internes Marketing als Forschungsgebiet der Marketingwissenschaft', in M. Bruhn (ed.), *Internes Marketing. Integration der Kunden- und Mitarbeiterorientierung. Grundlagen – Implementierung – Praxisbeispiele* (Wiesbaden: Gabler), pp. 15–44.

Buber, R. (2000a) 'Model Building on Internal Marketing. An Exploratory Study By GABEK', in A. O'Cass (ed.), *Visionary Marketing for the 21st Century: Facing the Challenge* (Proceedings of the Australian and New Zealand Marketing Academy Conference, CD Rom), pp. 143–7.

Buber, R. (2000b) 'Die Einstellung von Führungskräften zum internen Marketing – eine empirische Untersuchung mit GABEK', in R. Buber and J. Zelger (eds), *GABEK II: Zur qualitativen Forschung – On Qualitative Research* (Innsbruck, Vienna and Munich: StudienVerlag), pp. 259–300.

Buber, R. and Kraler, C. (2000) 'How GABEK and *WinRelan* Support Qualitative Research', in R. Buber and J. Zelger (eds), *GABEK II: Zur qualitativen Forschung – On Qualitative Research* (Innsbruck, Vienna and Munich: StudienVerlag), pp. 111–38.

Buber, R. and Meyer, M. (1997) 'Fallstudien – Einsatz in Forschung und Lehre', in R. Buber and M. Meyer (eds), *Fallstudien zum Nonprofit Management* (Stuttgart: Schäffer-Poeschel), pp. 3–15.

George, W. and Grönroos, C. (1999) 'Internes Marketing. Kundenorientierte Mitarbeiter auf allen Unternehmensebenen', in M. Bruhn (ed.), *Internes Marketing. Integration der Kunden- und Mitarbeiterorientierung. Grundlagen – Implementierung – Praxisbeispiele* (Wiesbaden: Gabler), pp. 45–68.

Hartley, J. F. (1994) 'Case studies in organisational research', in C. Cassell and G. Symon (eds), *Qualitative Methods in Organizational Research* (London, Thousand Oaks and New Delhi: Sage), pp. 208–29.

Kotler, P. (1972) 'A Generic Concept of Marketing', *Journal of Marketing*, vol. 36, no. 2, pp. 46–54.

Lamnek, S. (1993) *Qualitative Sozialforschung. Band 2: Methoden und Techniken* (Weinheim: Beltz).

Löckenhoff, H. (2000) 'GABEK in Dialogue, Task, Accomplishment, Conflict resolution. Encouraging and Guiding Social Change', in R. Buber and J. Zelger (eds), *GABEK II: Zur Qualitativen Forschung – On Qualitative Research* (Innsbruck, Vienna and Munich: StudienVerlag), pp. 93–110.

Mayring, P. (1990) *Qualitative Inhaltsanalyse. Grundlagen und Techniken* (Weinheim: Deutscher StudienVerlag).

Piercy, N. and Morgan, N. (1991) 'Internal Marketing – The Missing Half of the Marketing Programme', *Long Range Planning*, vol. 24, no. 2, pp. 82–93.

Stauss, B. and Schulze, H. (1990) *Internes Marketing: Ein Konzept zur innerorganisatorischen Fundierung von Absatzstrategien* (Ingolstadt: Eichstätt).

Stumpf, C. (1939) *Erkenntnislehre* (Leipzig: Barth).

Titscher, S., Wodak, R., Meyer, M. and Vetter, E. (1998) *Methoden der Textanalyse. Leitfaden und überblick* (Opladen and Wiesbaden: Westdeutscher Verlag).

Varey, R. J. and Lewis, B. R. (2000) *Internal Marketing. Directions for Management* (London and New York: Routledge).

Zelger, J. (1996) *Linguistic Knowledge Processing by GABEK. The Selection of Relevant Information from Unordered Verbal Data* (Innsbruck: Institut für Philosophie, preprint 42).

Zelger, J. (1999) 'Wissensorganisation durch sprachliche Gestaltbildung im qualitativen Verfahren GABEK', in J. Zelger and M. Maier (eds), *Verarbeitung und Darstellung von Wissen* (Vienna and Innsbruck: StudienVerlag), pp. 41–87.

Zelger, J. (2000) 'Twelve steps of GABEK *WinRelan*', in R. Buber and J. Zelger (eds), *GABEK II: Zur qualitativen Forschung – On Qualitative Research* (Innsbruck and Vienna: StudienVerlag), pp. 205–20.

Part IV
Results for Marketing Managers

14
Measuring Corporate Globalisation: A Mixed-Method Approach to Scale Development

Petra Kuchinka

Introduction

The aim of this chapter is to develop a scale for measuring firms' level of corporate globalisation. The latter is an important variable in global customer relations and the overall performance of a firm, but while it is often mentioned in the literature (Millman, 1999; Montgomery and Yip, 2000; Wilson *et al.*, 2001) no conceptualisation of it can be found.

As markets globalise, great demands are made on marketing departments, including pressure to make decisions about market entry strategies (Wührer, 1995) and the adaptation of marketing strategies, and to address cultural issues. Corporate globalisation plays a major role not only in classical transaction marketing but also in relationship marketing, and a tool is needed to help companies adapt their strategies to an increasing number of global customers. Global customer management is aimed at retaining customers that go global or are already operating globally. However its implementation is costly and therefore it should only be offered to really global customers that demand it, with different programme strategies that accord with the customer's level of corporate globalisation (LoCG).

The needs of customers and suppliers must be matched because otherwise the supposedly 'global' relationship will end up as merely a global pricing arrangement with no opportunity to enhance firm performance. Hence value will not be created equally on both sides and the partners will not be able to perpetuate a long-term relationship. The assumption of value creation on both sides is based on the principle of relationship marketing.[1] The matching of suppliers' and customers' needs requires effective customer segmentation, which can be conducted by means of quantitative and qualitative selection criteria, one of which is degree of corporate globalisation (Wilson *et al.*, 2002, use the term 'global spread'). That there is positive relationship between the variables 'use of global customer management', 'demand for global customer management by customers' and 'extent of globalisation' has been shown by Montgomery and Yip (1999). It is suggested that customers' degree of corporate globalisation determines the success and effectiveness of a global customer management (GCM) programme, and for this reason customers' LoCG should be calculated to determine whether they are truly operating globally and GCM is needed. Then other qualitative and quantitative criteria are used to select the most profitable and promising customers from among the global ones.

While there is a vast body of literature on strategic and international management, few authors have worked out the properties and dimensions of corporate globalisation from a marketing perspective (That is, a GCM perspective). The importance of key account selection is recognised, but few workable instructions are given. The relationship between the LoCG and GCM is supported by the literature: the degree of corporate globalisation is (1) an important selection criterion for global accounts and (2) relates positively to the demand for GCM by customers and the use of GCM within companies.

However the construct of LoCG has not yet been conceptualised properly or measured adequately. The attempt to measure it dates back to Vernon's multinational enterprise project in the 1960s (Vernon, 1966). However most approaches since that time have been targeted at the degree of internationalisation rather than globalisation and have been limited to geography-based, simple measurements, such as the ratio of foreign employees to total employees in a company (van den Berghe, 2001), the ratio of foreign assets to total assets (Sullivan, 1994) and the proportion of overseas subsidiaries to total subsidiaries (Sullivan 1994; Ietto-Gillies, 1998). Other approaches use indices such as the 'network-spread index' (the number of foreign countries in which the company has foreign subsidiaries divided by the number of countries in which the company potentially could have subsidiaries – UNCTAD, 1998) or the 'transnational activities spread index' (Ietto-Gillies, 1998), but the disadvantages of indices are well known. Moreover most approaches focus on the industry rather than the company level. Because the underlying hypothesis is that each company in an industry has a different LoCG and must adapt its GCM accordingly, industry can be classified as a possible influencing factor but not as a measure. Very few authors have integrated multiple indicators or used multiple dimensions. Most researchers attempt to build theories but rarely reach the measurement stage, although they suggest the measurement.

Therefore the development of a new measurement approach is necessary, and that is the methodological contribution that will be offered in this chapter. The subject of globalisation requires a multidimensional approach to capture its complexity because corporate globalisation cannot be represented by simple geography-based measurements. Corporate globalisation is assumed to have an impact on corporate orientation, processes and strategies. Therefore the scale must include items that describe attitudes, strategies, systems and structures. One of the most important goals of a GCM programme is for the global customer to purchase globally from one's own company. Purchase decisions are made for each value chain activity, which implies that not all value chain activities are globalised at once. The assumption is that companies with different degrees of globalisation will have different packages of globalised value chain activities. No measurement approach that takes this into account can be found. Nor can a measurement that is tied to strategy integration and process coordination, although theory building often moves in this direction.

The development of a new measurement scale is essential (1) to enable companies to use the LoCG as a selection criterion for their GCM target group, (2) to enable companies to design their GCM programmes according to their customers' needs, which are to a certain degree affected by their LoCG, (3) to contribute to the clarification of the dimensions of the construct LoCG, and (4) to extend the existing measurement approaches and present a multidimensional approach that corresponds to the complexity of the construct.

The theoretical framework

Definitions

To identify key characteristics by which corporate globalisation can be measured, it is necessary to examine the literature for definitions that differentiate globalisation/globalised firm from internationalisation/internationalised company, but virtually no operationalised definition of a 'global company' can be found in the literature. Very often the definition of global overlaps the definition of transnational. Moreover, there are divergent opinions on the umbrella term: is it internationalisation or are both terms used synonymously?. And is it a process or a matter of separate categorisation? Globalisation can be defined as process when the term is used generically for companies developing a worldwide orientation. But globalisation can also be defined as a discrete variable when it is used to categorise different strategies to internationalise: international, multinational or global. This leads to different degrees or levels of globalisation. Beamish *et al.* (2000) argue that international strategies have two possible parameter values: multidomestic or global. Other authors, such as Heenan and Perlmutter (1979), Bartlett and Goshal (1989) and Goshal and Bartlett (1998), categorise different types of approach to foreign markets and draw distinct borders. The term globalisation is used loosely in various ways and is often equated with internationalisation. The present author adopts the categorisation approach (Heenan and Perlmutter, 1979; Goshal and Bartlett, 1998; Parvatiyar and Gruen, 2001). Categorisation is required to draw borders between different LoCGs, otherwise no measurement would be possible.

From a marketing point of view, the topic of globalisation is mostly addressed in the field of global marketing and key account management. The literature on global account management is especially relevant for the research questions underlying the present work. Two key issues are coordination and integration. Wilson (1999, p. 31) defines a global customer as a 'multinational customer that has a coordinated procurement and decision making process', and an international customer as an 'account with locations in different parts of the world, but with a decentralised decision making process'. But this represents a strategy that most authors would call multinational/multidomestic or polycentric.

Montgomery and Yip (2000) define a new approach for multinational suppliers to multinational customers who deal globally, which implies global contracts, service quality, prices, products and so on. To meet the demand, suppliers must centralise and integrate globally. Global account management[2] can enhance revenues and profits. A key determinant of success, however, is the stage of corporate globalisation of both the customer and the supplier. A GCM programme can only be implemented successfully if the customer demands global purchasing, service and so on and the supplier responds appropriately (that is, adopts a global strategy). Montgomery and Yip offer a framework for GCM that involves identification of an industry's globalisation drivers (for both customer and supplier, for example global sourcing), a demand for GCM by customers and readiness on the part of suppliers to supply such a service (both depend on organisational heritage and stage of globalisation), and consideration of the performance effect. The drivers and organisational heritage determine a customer's potential as a global account.

Montgomery and Yip (ibid., p. 4) measure this potential by the 'percentage of the [customers'] purchases made on a globally coordinated basis'. For the supplier the measure is *vice versa*: the 'percentage of revenues accounted for by customers buying on a globally centralised basis'. In their study they found that revenues stemming from truly globally coordinated customers add up to about 13 per cent, while international customers account for about 46 per cent and multinational ones 26 per cent. From these percentages one could hypothesise that the start of foreign activity occurs at the international level, followed by a move towards the multinational level and then the global level. This hypothesis could be tested by means of a questionnaire, with respondents being asked when they started their foreign activity. The researcher could then link this variable to their measured degree of foreign activity.

These considerations presented above show that it is almost impossible to unify terminology. Summarizing, the following categories of companies pursuing foreign activities could be identified: international, multinational, global and transnational. The question is, which dimension characterise and differentiate the single categories? Global companies are expected to exhibit interdependence, integration and coordination of value chain activities (that is, of strategies, programmes and processes) as well as a certain degree of centralisation and standardisation. However, national differentiation is also a characteristic of complex global (that is, transnational) companies, which successfully differentiate and integrate at the same time. Reference to the number of processed countries (that is, geography) or the ratios regarding foreign sales to total sales are used to characterise internationally operating companies that also show a degree of centralisation and standardisation (Heenan and Perlmutter, 1979; Martinez and Jarillo, 1989; Goshal and Bartlett, 1998; Parvatiyar and Gruen, 2001). To sum up, various principles (for example centralisation versus decentralisation) can be identified when examining all the definitions of a global company. An overview of the principles that are considered as representative or non-representative of corporate globalisation, as mentioned in literature, is provided in Table 14.1.

The global as well as the transnational category are the interesting ones regarding the application of GCM. Therefore the research described in this chapter will be guided by the following definition of a global company: a global company is an enterprise that is integrated through close coordination of the value chain activities. If it simultaneously strives for local differentiation it will reach the fully globalised stage (also called a 'transnational company').

Table 14.1 Summary of the main principles, based on the theoretical framework

Corporate globalisation	
Representative	*Non-representative*
• Interdependence • Integration • Coordination • Centralisation • Standardisation	• Market-by-market adaptation • National differentiation • Geography

However the classification of the investigated companies will be performed empirically and not by definition: it is difficult to draw definitional demarcation lines between different degrees of corporate globalisation. Therefore an inductive method will be used and the demarcation lines defined by means of empirical data. One hypothesis is that only a very small proportion of fully globalised companies (that is, transnational companies – Bartlett and Goshal, 1989) exist (cf. the empirical test of Bartlett and Ghoshal's organisational typology by Leong and Tan, 1993). But local differentiation and global integration are only two of the constituent dimensions and the subject requires a multi dimensional approach. As the aim is to cluster companies according to their LoCG in the various categories (international, multinational, global, transnational and so on – all the factors that characterise these categories have to be considered: integration, coordination, interdependence, national differentiation, centralisation and standardisation. In addition, value chain activities will be included to test the hypothesis that not all value chain activities are globalised at the same time and same amount.

1. If companies rank high on the dimension local adaptation, they will show low values on all other dimensions.
2. If companies rank high on the dimensions centralisation and standardisation, they will show low values on all other dimensions.
3. Most companies will be characterised by high values on the dimension global integration and low values on local adaptation.
4. Only few companies will rank high on global integration and show certain local adaptation.

5. GCM is mostly used within firms pursuing global integration and localisation in parallel.
6. It is assumed that a typical order exists in which the value chain activities are globalised.

The research methodology

In order to gain a deep understanding of the research area, both qualitative and quantitative approaches are needed. This view is supported by Kaplan (1964, p. 207), who states that 'Quantities are *of* qualities, and a measured quality has just the magnitude expressed in its measure'. Miles and Huberman (1994, pp. 40 ff.) consider that the distinction between qualitative and quantitative is not well-aimed. They prefer to separate analytic approaches aimed at understanding a few controlled variables, and systemic approaches aimed at understanding interactions between variables in a complex environment. However, combining both types of approach is appropriate for the research discussed here because (1) it will enable the connection of literature with managerial practice, and (2) it will provide richer detail and facilitate new lines of thinking (Rossman and Wilson, 1984; Miles and Huberman, 1994, p. 41).

Construct measurement

The aim of applied science is to understand and predict real phenomena. To be able to accomplish this the researcher must choose a theoretical explanatory approach for each problem considered. A characteristic that all approaches have in common is that they specify relationships between abstract concepts or constructs (Sullivan and Feldman, 1979, p. 9). Then a connection can be drawn between theoretical analysis and empirical problem setting through the development and implementation of measuring techniques. These techniques capture observable properties of each unit of analysis (Werani, 1998, p. 78). In turn these properties reflect the characteristics of the abstract constructs in use. The observable properties captured by the measurement are designated as indicators of abstract, unobservable and not directly measurable constructs (Sullivan and Feldman, 1979, p. 9). The measurement process can be defined as the connection of abstract concepts or constructs with empirical, numerically recordable indicators (Carmines and Zeller, 1979, p. 10; Werani, 1998, p. 78). (See also Figure 14.1.) This definition implies that beyond the explicit theories and hypothesis a second theory – the so-called auxiliary theory – may be needed. The auxiliary theory defines the relationships between the theoretical and empirical approaches, and therefore between abstract

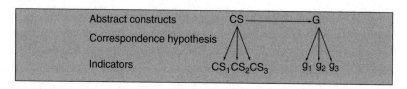

Figure 14.1   Measurement of abstract constructs
Sources: Werani (1998), p. 79; based on Sullivan and Feldman (1979), p. 12.

constructs and observable indicators. These relationships, which are also referred to as the 'correspondence hypothesis' or 'epistemic correlations', operationalise abstract hypothetical constructs (Backhaus *et al.*, 2000).

These reflections so far can be summarised with the help of an example taken from the subject of this research: one abstract concept respectively construct, namely the level of corporate globalisation, builds the theoretical basis. In order to test any hypotheses concerning causal relations of other constructs (for example company size (CS) is causal for the LoCG) with the LoCG, it is necessary to make the abstract construct measurable, that is to operationalise the construct through observable indicators. This is done on the basis of the correspondence hypothesis, which in this case states that the LoCG can be grasped by three indicators (for example g_1–g_3). The empirical values can be gained by questioning a certain number of respondents.

Reliable statements on the relationship between company size and the level of corporate globalisation can only be made if there are significant relationships between (1) the indicators CS_1, CS_2, CS_3 and company size, and (2) the indicators g_1, g_2, g_3 and the level of corporate globalisation. If the relationships between indicators and constructs are weak or specified in a false way, wrong conclusions will be drawn (Werani, 1998, p. 80).

Procedure

The research design is shown in Figure 14.2. Developing a primary understanding of the construct 'global' required a qualitative methodology.[3] Expert interviews were conducted in different industries[4] in order (1) to examine variables representing the degree of foreign activity from the point of view of commercial practice, and (2) to compare the research propositions with the literature. The qualitative research approach was chosen (1) because corporate globalisation is a complex phenomenon enabling different assignments of key characteristics. The aim is to examine the differences between theoretical and practical approaches for further indicator development.

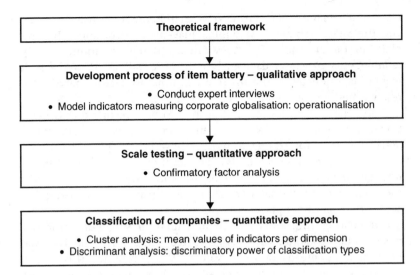

Figure 14.2 Research design

On this basis an interview guide was developed. The guide included the following modules: key characteristics of corporate globalisation, the key account management programmes used (national, international or global account management and how these were defined) and key account selection criteria and procedures. The interviews were transcribed and the software NVivo was used to link the concepts and dimensions of corporate globalisation.

The result of the qualitative stage was a preliminary model of dimensions and indicators to measure the level of corporate globalisation. These were combined with findings in the literature and reported to the interviewees for refinement and development. Reporting was one way of enhancing the 'validity' of the qualitative research;[5] triangulation was another (group discussion, expert interviews and a standardised questionnaire). The development of the measurement scale was based on the results of this qualitative analysis. The definition of dimensions was completed at the end of this stage.

The next step was the final operationalisation of the dimensions in the form of an item battery, which was integrated into a questionnaire. The indicators were already partly developed in the defined dimensions 'geographical and structural centralisation' versus 'decentralisation', 'standardisation versus national adaptation', 'global integration/coordination' and 'resource allocation'. The survey was conducted among a representative sample of companies chosen from the Hoppenstedt database and the SAMA (Strategic Account Management Association) Internet platform for members. The questionnaire design conformed to the requirements of causal data analysis because validation of the scale would be conducted by means of a confirmatory factor analysis. The result would be confirmation or rejection of the selected indicators. In addition the companies in question had to be categorised as international, multinational, global or transnational. This was difficult to determine, even for experts, as most were still developing; that is, few were using all the different levels of key account management (national, international and global) in tandem. Therefore it was necessary to verify the number of firms that were global or transitional and had global account management programmes.

If the chosen indicators actually measured the single dimensions, a mean value per dimension was generated and a cluster analysis was performed by means of these values. The reason for this was as follows. Because the dimensions among themselves were independent, the indicators within one dimension were highly correlated. But cluster analysis did not allow for highly correlated indicators. Therefore mean values of the dimensions' indicators had to be used. The cluster analysis enabled the companies to be designated as international, multinational, global or transnational. A discriminant analysis was undertaken to determine the discriminatory power of the typology's categories.

The qualitative analysis

Thirteen expert interviews were conducted with global account managers from different industries and countries (Austria, Germany, Switzerland and the UK). Global account managers were chosen because they would have extensive knowledge of global account selection (and therefore would be able to define what a global account was) and their company's own position (whether it was generally able to serve globally). The interviews took between half an hour and two hours. Most were conducted personally, but a few took place on the telephone- or via e-mail (for reasons of distance and cost). The interviews were divided into several parts. Then the respondents were asked for their assumed key characteristics of corporate globalisation. Afterwards, the respondents had to comment on a list of given key characteristics of corporate globalisation taken from the literature (for comparison reasons). The items mostly focused on global strategies and processes. The final part drew on key account selection criteria to find out whether or not the level of corporate globalisation was of importance to companies with global customer management.

The interviews were subsequently transcribed and the software program NVivo was used for the analysis. The tree structure developed from this research (that is, the dimensions and single items belonging to them) is described in detail in the following paragraphs.

The first node built a category called 'Respondents' orientation towards corporate globalisation'. This category consisted of the respondents' point of view describing what corporate globalisation was about in their company. Such points of view are often written down in a company's business mission, so the interviewees had been asked for details of their company's business mission during the interviews. This had frequently revealed some sort of global vision (described in the literature as an important factor in corporate globalisation), as illustrated by such statements as 'We want to become the world leader in ...' and 'We want to become the world's best ...' However global vision had mostly been associated with geographical boundaries (country markets and so on). The power structure between the headquarters and its affiliates had been of importance to a couple of interviewees. Interestingly, both extremes had been raised: on the one hand 'central power influence by the headquarters' attributed to the dimension centralisation and on the other hand 'low influence of the headquarters' attributed to the dimension decentralisation. What had not been mentioned by the interviewees was structural decentralisation. This fitted into the theoretical framework as structural decentralisation is strongly connected with multinational rather than global companies.

The node 'Corporate global strategy' included the dimensions 'Global branding', 'Standardisation of products and processes', 'Global representation' and 'Market entry mode choice' The other dimensions identified were 'High local market adaptation', 'Integration and adaptation' in balance (the balance could be detected through respondents' formulations such as 'we have an integrated global brand concept, but maintain the brand nationally adapted'), 'Coordination of activities', 'Cross-nationality geographies', 'Standardisation' and the well-known 'Decentralisation versus centralisation paradigm'. High local adaptation was operationalised through the items 'National product development', 'Nationally adapted product lines and plants' and 'Nationally adapted portfolio of services'.

In addition to the category 'Global strategy' the interviewees came up with the dimension 'Global processes', accounting essentially to the level of corporate globalisation. This node included the following factors:

'System requirements', 'Sharing of knowledge', 'Management commitment', 'Converging of culture' and 'Information and communication flow'. These factors were operationalised and included in the measurement scale.

The node 'Respondents' orientation towards globalisation' included the respondents' personal expert views on dimensions and indicators determining the degree of corporate globalisation. The following factors clearly emerged: 'Coordination', 'Standardisation of products and sales', 'Geographic orientation' (referring to financial criteria, cross-national activity and worldwide presentation), 'Standardised versus adapted strategy', 'Centralisation' (of brand strategy, product design and product sales) and 'Localisation'. Most of the factors directly related to factors named in literature. Contradictory was that integration and interdependence had not been mentioned by the interviewees when asked for their assumptions on key characteristics of corporate globalisation, but had been deemed to be important from the respondents in the given list of items taken from the literature. Both factors were included in the measurement scale because from the qualitative part of the analysis the conclusion could not be drawn that integration and interdependence did not characterise corporate globalisation or that they were unimportant.

Interestingly the interviewees had had a very strong geographical understanding of corporate globalisation (for example for some corporate globalisation had meant 'Being present in more than 10 countries', 'Doing business across borders' and so on) although in the literature geographical factors are assigned to internationalisation. Despite the latter, some items with a geographical focus were included in the analysis. This was also a good opportunity to ascertain whether geographical items had a higher discriminatory power than the other items attached to the remaining factors.

The category 'Degree of globalisation of value chain activities' included all the interviewees' statements on which value chain activities (purchasing, manufacturing, sales/distribution, marketing, finance and accounting, human resource management and so on) had been globalised by their companies. The companies could be grouped into two major clusters: cluster one comprised companies that had globalised all their value chain activities, while cluster two had only globalised single activities, such as IT, marketing, production, purchasing, sales organisation, communication, finance, controlling or process management. Interestingly, human resource management and R&D were not among the activities Rather they had retained at the control of the headquarters. This can be interpreted with the help of theories presented in the literature, including the core competencies hypothesis (Porter, 1986) and the resource-based view (Penrose, 1959; Prahalad and Hamel, 1990). Human resource management and R&D are both counted among a company's core competencies for which it strives for centralisation and central distribution to affiliates and not for worldwide integration. According to the interviewees, globalisation of these two activities seemed to be a question of willingness to take risks.

The cluster analysis also revealed that the globalisation of some activities had been accompanied by local adaptation. In the literature standardisation is associated with corporate globalisation while local adaptation is associated with multinational companies. However it seems that local adaptation is definitely of importance to global companies – this relates to the findings in literature that complex global (transnational) companies strike balance between global integration and local adaptation. The difference between local adaptation by MNEs and local adaptation by complex global companies lies – according to the findings from the expert interviews – in the fact that complex global companies tend to adapt not nationally (that is, different products, strategies, processes and so on for each country) but regionally (that is, regions with internally homogenous, needs and characteristics of its customers are segmented and the adaptations are aligned with these differences).

During the analysis it became clear that some of the items that had been mentioned were drivers of or constraints on globalisation rather than determinants of the level of corporate globalisation. As a consequence they were filtered out and transferred into the nodes 'Corporate globalisation drivers' and 'Corporate globalisation constraints'. The drivers were market saturation, technical infrastructure (especially as costs are increasing and the technical opportunities enhanced), culture (the company's own culture and the often cited convergence of culture – sometimes called 'Americanised convergence'), competitive issues ('We had to go global because our competitors did') coherence of strategy and operation, and the availability of human resources (if available in adequate quality and quantity). The main constraints were product suitability (whether the product's characteristics, benefits, design and so on were suitable throughout the whole world), capital issues (corporate globalisation is associated with a need for considerable financial resources), a restrictive company culture, risk estimation (this is of course connected with the 'capital issues' constraint above), legal and political constraints, the industry to which the company belongs (therefore 'industry' can be considered as a moderating factor on the level of corporate globalisation and should be taken into account in a quantitative analysis) and general resources.

The last two nodes were 'Reasons for using GAM' and 'Global account differentiation'. The first of these arose from questions on why and how global accounts were selected. This node supports the hypothesis that GCM is connected with the extent of corporate globalisation and the demand ('pressure') for GCM by customers as both reasons were explicitly named during the interviews. The second node, 'Global account differentiation', had several dimensions. Two groups were distinguished: those who made no differentiation and those who engaged in key account selection. For the latter the selection criteria were size of the company, financial criteria (such as total corporate revenue, customer revenue, profit generation, or customer potentials for the distinction of profitable and non-profitable customers), geographical position (business across country borders, presence all around the world, number of foreign operating units on foreign affiliates for the distinction of global customers), the strategic fit of the customer and the company, the value that could be added for the customer and generated through the customer, relationship strength (loose relationships were likely to be of short duration and uncertain profitability, and therefore constituted a risk), the reference potential of the customer, and the customer's brand perception and acceptance.

The results of the qualitative analysis were summarised into the dimensions and indicators used for the questionnaire. The companies were classified according to their degree of integration, interdependence, coordination, standardisation, centralisation and local adaptation. The resulting hypothesese are (1) simple global companies will rate highly on the interdependence, coordination and integration items, (2) complex global (also called 'transnational' companies) will rate highly on the latter and on the national differentiation items, (3) a high rate only on the national differentiation level is characteristic of MNEs, and (4) simple centralisation and standardisation are characteristics of internationalised companies. Moreover to test the hypothesis that not all value chain activities are globalised at the same time and same amount, the single activities were included for interrogation using the key dimensions described above.

Theoretical and managerial implications

The ability to measure their degree of globalisation will enable companies to (1) develop a suitable strategy for each stage of globalisation and enhance their financial performance, and (2) engage effectively in customer segmentation and conclude whether global customer management is needed. This will prevent unnecessary wastage of resources. In addition a suitable GCM strategy and programme features can be developed for each stage of globalisation. This work can also contribute to the evaluation of GCM programmes. One part of GCM performance measurement is the evaluation of the global account selection process and used criteria. The use of the presented degree of corporate globalisation as selection criterion adds positively to the quality of the whole account selection process and, therefore, to overall performance. In addition, this research contributes to the clarification of the construct 'corporate globalisation'.

Notes

1. According to Bruhn (2001, p. 9): 'Relationship marketing includes all analysis, planning, implementation and controlling methods, which serve the initiation, stabilisation, intensification and recovery of business relationships with ... the company's customers with the aim of *mutual value*.'
2. The terms global account management and global customer management are used interchangeably.
3. Many authors writing on qualitative research – for example Miles and Huberman (1994, p. 41) – endorse the proposition that qualitative data can help a quantitative study by providing conceptual development and instrumentation.
4. Different industries were chosen to gain a broad perspective of the construct 'global' and develop standard indicators to measure LoCGs in different industries.
5. As far as one can speak of 'validity' when talking about qualitative research.

References

Ashkenas, R., Ulrich, D., Jick, T. and Kerr, S. (1995) *The Boundaryless Organization* (San Francisco, CA: Jossey-Bass).
Backhaus, K., Erichson, B., Plinke, W. and Weiber, R. (2000) *Multivariate Analysemethoden: Eine anwendungsorientierte Einführung* (Berlin: Springer).
Bartlett, C. A. (1986) 'Building and managing the transnational: The new organizational challenge', in M. E. Porter, *Competition in Global Industries* (Boston, Mass.: Harvard Business School Press), pp. 367–401.
Bartlett, C. A. and Goshal, S. (1989) *Managing Across Borders: The Transnational Solution* (Boston, Mass.: Harvard Business School Press).
Beamish, P. W., Morrison, A. J., Rosenzweig, P. M. and Inkpen, A. C. (2000) *International Management: Text and Cases* (Boston, Mass.: Irwin McGraw-Hill).
Bruhn, M. (2001) *Relationship Marketing: Das Management van Kundenbeziehungen* (Munich: Vahlen).
Carmines, E. G. and Zeller, R. A. (1979) *Reliability and Validity Assessment* (London: Sage).
Churchill, G. A. (1979) 'A Paradigm for Developing Better Measures of Marketing Constructs', *Journal of Marketing Research*, vol. 16 (February), pp. 64–73.

Daniels, J. D. and Radebaugh, L. H. (1992) *International Business* (Reading, Mass.: Addison-Wesley).

Gerbing, D. and Anderson, J. (1988) 'An Updated Paradigm for Scale Development Incorporating Unidimensionality and its Assessment', *Journal of Marketing Research*, vol. 25 (May), pp. 186–92.

Goshal, S. and Bartlett, C. A. (1998) *Managing Across Borders: The Transnational Solution* (London: Random House).

Hamel, G. and Prahalad, C. K. (1997) 'Do you really have a global strategy?', in D. J. Lecraw, A. J. Morrison and J. H. Dunning (eds), *Transnational Corporations and Business Strategy* (London and New York: Routledge), pp. 123–37.

Heenan, D. A. and Perlmutter, H. V. (1979) *Multinational Organization Development – A Social Architectural Perspective* (Reading, Mass.: Addison-Wesley).

Homburg, C. (1995) *Kundennähe von Industriegüterunternehmen: Konzeption – Erfolgsauswirkungen – Determinanten* (Wiesbaden: Gabler).

Hoppenstedt (2002) Datenbank: Firmendatenbank Österreich (Vienna: Hoppenstedt and Wirtschaftsverlag)

Ietto-Gillies, G. (1998) 'Different conceptual frameworks for the assessment of the degree of internationalization: an empirical analysis of various indices for the top 100 transnational corporations', *Transnational Corporations*, vol. 7, no. 1, pp. 17–40.

Kaplan, A. (1964) *The Conduct of Inquiry* (Scranton, PA: Chandler).

Kutschker, M. and Schmid, S. (2002) *Internationales Management* (Munich and Vienna: Oldenbourg).

Leong, S. M. and Tan C. T. (1989) 'Managing Across Borders: An Empirical Test of the Bartlett and Goshal Organizational Typology', *Journal of International Business Studies*, vol. 24, no. 3, pp. 449–64.

Levitt, T. (1983) 'The globalization of markets', *Harvard Business Review*, vol. 61, no. 3, pp. 92–102.

Martinez, J. I. and Jarillo, J. C. (1989) 'The evolution of research on coordination mechanisms in multinational corporations', *Journal of International Business Studies*, vol. 20, no. 3, pp. 489–514.

Miles, M. B. and Huberman, A. M. (1994) *An Expanded Sourcebook – Qualitative Data Analysis* (Thousand Oaks, London and New Delhi: Sage).

Millman, T. F. (1999) 'From National Account Management to Global Account Management in Business-to-Business Markets', *Thexis*, no. 4, pp. 2–9.

Montgomery, D. B. and Yip, G. S. (1999) 'Statistical Evidence on Global Account Management Programs', *Thexis*, no. 4, pp. 10–13.

Montgomery, D. B. and Yip, G. S. (2000) *The Challenge of Global Customer Management*, vol. 9, issue 4 (Chicago, Ill.: American Marketing Association).

Parker, B. (1998) *Globalization and Business Practice: Managing Across Boundaries* (Thousand Oaks, London and New Delhi: Sage).

Parvatiyar, A. and Gruen, Th. (2001) *Global Account Management Effectiveness: A Contingency Mode* (Atlanta, GA: Georgia State University and Emory University).

Penrose, E. (1959) *The Theory of Growth of the Firm* (New York: Wiley).

Phatak, A. V. (1992) *International Dimensions of Management* (Boston, Mass.: PWS-Kent).

Porter, M. E. (1986) 'Changing patterns of international competition', *California Management Review*, vol. 28, no. 2, pp. 9–40.

Porter, M. E. (1997) 'Changing patterns of international competition', in D. J. Lecraw, A. J. Morrison and J. H. Dunning (eds), *Transnational Corporations and Business Strategy* (London and New York: Routledge), pp. 138–69.

Prahalad, C. K. and Hamel, G. (1990) 'The Core Competence of the Corporation', *Harvard Business Review*, vol. 68 (May/June), pp. 79–91.

Rossman, G. B. and Wilson, B. L. (1984) 'Numbers and words: Combining quantitative and qualitative methods in a single large-scale evaluation study', *Evaluation Review*, vol. 9, no. 5, pp. 627–43.

Ruigrok, W. and Wagner, H. (2000) 'Degree of Internationalization and Performance: An Organizational Learning Perspective', (paper presented at the Academy of Management Conference, Toronto).

Sera, K. (1992) 'Corporate globalization: A new trend', *Academy of Management Executive*, vol. 6, no. 1, pp. 89–96.

Sullivan, D. (1994) 'Measuring the degree of internationalization of a firm', *Journal of International Business Studies*, vol. 25, no. 2, pp. 325–42.

Sullivan, J. L. and Feldman, S. (1979) *Multiple Indicators: An Introduction* (London: Sage).

UNCTAD (1998) *World Investment Report, 1998: Trends und Determinants* (Geneva: United Nations)

Van den Berghe, D. (2001) 'Measuring corporate internationalization and performance: A conceptualization and discussion of the indicators' (paper presented at the Academy of Management Conference, Washington, DC).

Van Tulder, R. and Ruigrok, W. (1996) 'Regionalisation, Globalisation or Glocalisation: The Case of the World Car Industry', in M. Humbert (ed.), *The Impact of Globalisation on Europe's Firms and Industries* (London and New York: Pinter), pp. 22–3.

Vernon, R. (1996) 'International investment and international trade in the product cycle', *Quarterly Journal of Economics*, vol. 80, no. 2, pp. 190–207.

Werani, Th. (1998) *Der Wert von kooperativen Geschäftsbeziehungen in industriellen Märkten: Bedeutung, Messung und Wirkungen* (Linz: Universitätsverlag Rudolf Trauner).

Wilson, K. J. (1999) 'Developing Global Account Management Programs: Observations from a GAM Panel Presentation', *Thexis*, No. 4, pp. 30–5.

Wilson, K., Millman, T., Weilbaker, D. and Croom, S. (2001) *Harnessing Global Potential: Insights Into Managing Customers Worldwide* (Chicago, Ill.: Strategic Account Management Association).

Wilson, K., Speare, N. and Reese, S. (2002) *Successful Global Account Management* (London: Kogan Page).

Wührer, G. A. (1995) *Internationale Allianz- und Kooperationsfähigkeit österreichischer Unternehmen, Beiträge zum Gestaltansatz als Beschreibungs- und Erklärungskonzept* (Linz: Rudolf Trauner).

15

Measuring Involvement: Item Development from Focus Group Interview Data

Thomas Haller

Introduction

The aim of this chapter is to show how focus groups can help to develop a statement battery to measure customers' involvement with a product. It will be shown that this empirical-qualitative approach constitutes a very valuable alternative to the usual procedure of developing items for tests. The empirical-quantitative analysis will examine and corroborate the quality of the chosen method and procedure. However this chapter should not be interpreted as a definitive guide to test development. Its actual task is to illustrate the advantages and limitations of focus group interviews for the purpose.

Problem definition and the aim of the research

With the liberalisation of the Austrian electricity market on 1 October 2001 a new era for the Austrian power industry began. Goals were redefined in order to develop a clear customer orientation. The time of simple power supply had come to an end and tariffs were replaced by newly created products. Marketing executives reacted with product and price differentiation, and extended their product range with services connected with electricity.

Being informed about customers' wants, needs and involvement with the product in question are crucial to successful product planning and penetration of the market. This study uses a qualitative research method to develop items to measure private customers' involvement with electricity. The process of developing test items to measure hypothetical constructs often escapes scientific discussion because there is insufficient documentation. One cause of the latter is that the development of test items is often neglected by researchers, who see it as just a minor part of the research process. In marketing science, too, little room is given to the development of tests and items. This is exactly the problem that is dealt with in this chapter.

Methodology

Strategies for exploring data

Exploration is a systematic approach to collecting information on a research topic. Thus it prepares and supports the formulation of hypotheses and theories (Bortz and Döring, 2002, pp. 355 ff.) Contemporary scientific literature differentiates between various exploration strategies (ibid.; Lamnek, 1995; Atteslander, 2000). Bortz and Döring (2002, pp. 362 ff.) group individual exploration strategies on the basis of the most important elements of empirical social research (theory, methodology and empiricism) (Figure 15.1).

This chapter is based on an empirical-qualitative exploration. Its goal is to analyse and interpret data that were gathered by means of qualitative collection techniques. Bortz and Döring (ibid., p. 385) describe the importance of empirical-qualitative exploration as follows: due to their

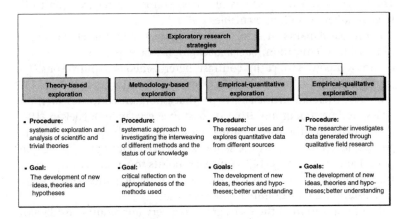

Figure 15.1 Overview of exploratory research strategies
Source: Bortz and Döring (2002), pp. 362 ff.

open form qualitative methods increase the likelihood ... to encounter new aspects of a subject. As with empirical-quantitative exploration, researchers can also use existing material (letters, minutes, advertisements, narratives and so on) for the purpose of empirical-qualitative exploration. The most important techniques of qualitative data collection are qualitative interviews[1] and observation, as well as so-called non-reactive procedures. Focus groups have become very popular in marketing research (ibid., p. 319 and ch. 3.2). The features and limitations of this method are discussed below.

Focus groups

Development and aims

The weaknesses of the individual interview technique[2] gave rise to the use of focus groups (Lamnek, 1995, p. 125; Bohnsack, 2000, p. 370). A focus group is a free discussion by participants on a certain topic, observed by the researcher and guided by moderating questions. There are two purposes of focus groups: to enable better analysis of individual opinions and to explore group opinions (see Lamnek, 1995, pp. 143–5).

Selection and number of participants

The ideal number of participants and the composition of the group, as well as the length of the discussion and the type of moderation to be used, are a matter of debate in the literature (Nießen, 1977, pp. 64 ff.; Flick, 1995, pp. 133–6; Lamnek, 1995, pp. 146–51; Morgan and Scannell, 1998). The range of research designs of focus groups is extensive due to the large number of options available.

If the participants in a focus group share substantial characteristics (for instance education, social background or experience) they form a homogeneous group. In contrast heterogeneous groups consist of participants who substantially differ from each other (Lamnek, 1995, p. 147). Moreover there are artificial groups (that is, organised for research purposes) and natural groups (that is, exist in everyday life). Nießen (1977, p. 66) advocates the use of natural groups because 'members of natural groups have more or less the same experience about the topic in question.' Lamnek (1995, p. 147), however, points to a number of problems with natural groups, including the fact that participants with a higher social standing may dominate the discussion.

The composition of the focus group is a very important consideration because heterogeneity and homogeneity among the participants both can serve either to accelerate or to restrain the discussion. Whether the participants are artificially selected or belong to an existing group is likewise crucial for the discussion process and of great importance to the outcome. The pros and cons of different group designs have to be considered in association with the research objectives. Lamnek (ibid.) points out that the choice of a specific group should be intersubjectively comprehensible.

With regard to group size there are divergent opinions in the literature. Mangold (1960) used three to twenty persons in his studies, but later recommended groups of six to ten (Mangold, 1962, p. 210). The final choice of the number of participants has to be made by the researcher him- or herself. In general the size of a focus group should be determined by the research objectives and goals and should be intersubjectively comprehensible.

Focus group discussions and the role of the moderator

Group discussions are almost always carried out with the help of a moderator.[3] The moderator starts the discussion by introducing him- or herself and making it clear that he or she will not take an active part in the discussion. Next the participants are asked to introduce themselves to each other. In this phase the moderator encourages a relaxed and open discussion (Lamnek, 1995, pp. 151–9; Krueger, 1998b). The moderator's task is to control the topics and course of the discussion, for example by asking provocative questions when the discussion becomes sluggish and restoring balance when the discussion is dominated by one participant. However the moderator has to be careful not to destroy the flow of the discussion by using directive guidance.[4] Furthermore the discussion must not take on the character of a group interview (Flick, 1995, pp. 135 f.; Lamnek, 1995, pp. 151 ff.) Lamnek (1995, p. 159) summarises this as follows: 'The moderator has to manage the process without predetermination of any results. Thus he manages directive but regarding the content he operates non-directive.

Data analysis

According to Lunt and Livingstone (1996, p. 94), 'Little is written in the technical literature on focus groups about the process of analysis or interpretation.' However this statement is contradicted by the literature in the fields of psychology, sociology and social sciences, where there are numerous publications on qualitative evaluation methods in general and the evaluation of focus group results in particular. There is, however, no doubt that evaluating focus group discussions is difficult (Pollock, 1955; Mangold, 1960; Nießen, 1977; Lamnek, 1995, pp. 159–65, 1998;

Krueger, 1998c; Titscher *et al.*, 1998; Bortz and Döring, 2002, pp. 329–37). This is not because there are insufficient methods to analyse or interpret the discussions, rather the problem lies in the appropriate application of the various methods. Data analysis is also hampered by different conceptions leading to different group dynamics, which also makes it difficult to compare research results (Flick, 1995, p. 139). Therefore, documentation of the entire research process is essential if the researcher is to counter criticisms about data collection and interpretation. It is not the process or the method of evaluation but the intersubjective comprehensibility of the results that proves the solidity of the research.

With regard to evaluation of the results, Krueger (1998c) recommends the so-called analysis continuum. This consists of four phases, that can be roughly differentiated by the level of evaluation, which is determined by the research goals in general and the researcher in particular (Figure 15.2).

The analysis continuum offers the researcher a pragmatic way of structuring and evaluating the results. Lamnek (1995, pp. 159–62) offers a more theoretical basis for the evaluation and analysis of focus group results with reference to the theory of symbolic interactionism and phenomenological sociology. Depending on the methodological and theoretical position we can identify two analysis procedures that can be roughly divided in two classes: (1) statistical-quantitative methods of analysis, which are mainly used to explore group-dynamic processes, and (2) interpretative-reductive and interpretative-explicative procedures, which focus on analysis of the content of discussion (ibid., pp. 162–5).

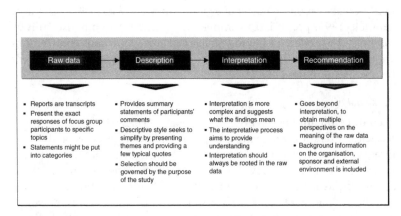

Figure 15.2   Focus group analysis continuum
Source: Krueger (1998c), pp. 27 f.

The great effort put into recording and transcribing focus group discussions and the difficulties connected with the analysis and interpretation of the transcripts make documentation of the entire research process one of the most important elements in using the instrument of focus groups. However there are software programs that facilitate the evaluation and systematisation of transcripts, and thus promote intersubjective comprehensibility.

Limitations of and perspectives on the method

For Morgan (1988, pp. 11, 21), focus groups are useful only for the generation of hypotheses because they lack a methodological basis. However Flick (1995, p. 138) insists that the results of focus groups can be used to develop theories. Bortz and Döring (2002, p. 320) concur with this and also state that focus groups can be used to test hypotheses.

The advantages and disadvantages of focus group discussions are listed in Lamnek (1995, p. 166), Flick (1995) and Morgan (1998). Focus groups:

- Offer an ideal framework to explore group-dynamic processes.
- Provide a quick overview of attitudes towards and opinions on a certain topic.
- Motivate participants to make spontaneous statements (this is due to the relaxed atmosphere).
- Enable identification of inconsistent opinions.
- Are less expensive than other methods.

However focus groups:

- Have only a limited number of participants and, therefore lack representativeness.
- Are problematic because data analysis is hindered by different group conceptions and different group dynamics, which also make it difficult to compare research results.
- Can involve an atmosphere in which individuals' statements are suppressed, so that the general outcome is distorted.

On balance, however, focus groups are an efficient research tool and can make a valuable contribution in the explorative phase of studies, that are dedicated to the development of hypotheses and theories. Supporters of mixed-method approaches would agree with Krüger (1983), who suggests that focus groups should be used to explore structures while quantitative methods should be used to test the revealed tendencies. Similarly Lamnek (1995, pp. 168–71) regards focus groups as a valuable method of detecting certain action patterns, while quantitative methods are best used to test the distribution of these patterns in reality.

Developing items to measure involvement with electricity

The research design

After pretesting the research questions, two focus groups were formed with five participants each. The participants were between 20 and 50 years of age and had their own electricity account. These characteristics were chosen after a review of empirical studies on the electricity industry and its customers. Customers in this category were characterised by a higher willingness to change their supplier and a greater than usual interest in electricity.

The subject and goal of the research permitted the selection of an artificial, heterogeneous group of participants since the pretest showed that neither ideological barriers nor varying social positions would affect active participation in the discussion. Moreover the selection of a heterogeneous group seemed to be appropriate for a vital and controversial discussion process. The heterogeneity and artificiality of the groups suggested a smaller group size. An overly large number of participants would make it more difficult for the participants to get to know each other and therefore would probably cause the group to split into several subgroups.

Before the sessions started each participants was handed a form on which to write their personal details: title, first name and surname, address, telephone number, e-mail address, age, education level and current job/profession. This procedure helped to bridge the gap between the arrival of the participants and the beginning of the focus group. Four of the participants were aged between 20 and 29, five between 30 and 39 and one was over 40. There was a uniform distribution of the sexes and the participants had a relatively high educational level.

In the first part of the group discussions, which included opening and start-up questions, the moderator formally led the group. The moderator then set the scene for the continuation of the discussion by asking the key questions. Only when there were strong deviations from the actual topic did he redirect the discussion.

The pretest had shown that the moderator alone would not be able to record all the statements and observations needed for the evaluation.

During the focus group discussions he was therefore supported by an assistant, who took notes of the participants' statements and observed individual and group behaviour. The sessions were also recorded on tape. Hence the full discussion and the reactions of the participants were documented, and on this basis meaningful transcripts could be provided. Nevertheless there were a small number of incomprehensible statements that could not be transcribed. This was mainly due to more than one participant speaking at the same time, mumbled utterances and statements in heavy dialect. This could have been avoided by stricter discussion guidance. However we decided not to interfere too much in the discussion as this could spoil the flow.

Description of the stimuli

Stimuli are tools to encourage participants to express their attitudes, motives, experiences and expectations. In our study they took the form of questions to the participants by the moderator. Stimuli that influenced the reaction of the participants but did not serve the primary research goal will not be discussed here, but they included specific effects that certain individuals had on the group and the course of discussion, the influence of the moderator and similar phenomena. The chosen questions were designed not only to encourage the participants to talk, but also to set the topics for discussion. Accordingly there were two sets of questions, the first of which helped with the creation of more suitable questions to ask the participants during the course of the discussion. The first set of questions can therefore be understood as 'programme stimuli' and the second as 'test stimuli'[5]. The questions were determined partially by the topic of the study and partially by the methods planned for its execution.

- The programme stimuli had to refer clearly to the research subject. They consisted of questions about the marketing of electricity, with special reference to issues connected with new product planning.
- The test stimuli had to be concrete enough to evoke specific reactions from the participants.
- The test stimuli had to be arranged in such a way that they would not inhibit the participants' willingness to play an active part in the discussion.

The questions were formulated on the basis of this pragmatic catalogue of criteria. As well as straight forward questions about electricity and the electricity industry, questions aimed at eliciting expectations about products and services were included in the programme stimuli:

- What are consumers' conceptions of electricity?
- How do private customers characterise the electricity industry or their own power suppliers?
- Which products and services do private customers expect of their power suppliers?
- What motivates private customers to change or stay with a supplier?
- In which ways do competitive products have to be developed/designed?
- Which value added services are desirable from the customer's perspective?

The test stimuli were ordered according to Krueger's (1998a, pp. 21–30) five-step guide for focus group moderation (Table 15.1).

Table 15.1 Operationalisation of the test stimuli

Step	Questions
1. Opening	Please tell us who you are, what you do and what you like doing when you are not working?
2. Start-up	When you think of electricity, what comes spontaneously to mind?
	How would you characterise the electricity industry in general and your power supplier in particular?
	Have you detected any differences since the liberalisation of electricity supply?
3. Bridging	Which products/services spark enthusiasm?
	What is so exciting about them, and why?
4. Theme entry	With regard to electricity, what do you consider to be important?
	What else could or should a power supplier offer?
	Which additional services would you like, and why?
	What would you tell a good friend or family member about this product?
	Imagine that electricity or a product could speak, what would it say about itself?
	What does this product need in order to be successful?
	Can you list five positive characteristics of this product, or more generally, what positive things do you associate with electrical power?
	If you were responsible for selling 1000 electricity contracts, what pursuasives arguments would you use in an advertising campaign?
	Where and/or how would you like to sign a new contract?
5. Ending	Bearing in mind all that we have discussed, which services should be included in a contract for power supply?
	Is there anything further we should discuss?

Item development

Usually test items are developed by the researcher following a detailed description of the construct, which has to be measured. The first set of items, mostly formulated as statements – often a hundred or more – is the basis for the pretest. The participants are asked to evaluate the statements. Involvement is often measured by means of Likert scales (Tigert *et al.*, 1976; Lastovicka and Gardner, 1979; Bloch, 1981; Traylor and Joseph, 1984; Laurent and Kapferer, 1985; Slama and Tashchian, 1985) and/or semantic differentials (Zaichkowsky, 1985; McQuarrie and Munson, 1986, 1991; Vaughn, 1986; Ratchford, 1987; Higie and Feick, 1988; Jain and Srinivasan, 1990). Depending on the scale used, the Likert procedure calculates the total test value of a participant as the sum of all scale values indicated by him or her. This data forms the basis of the discrimination index, which is calculated for each item. The items with the highest discrimination index make up the final test scale. The coefficient alpha after Cronbach and item to total correlations are frequently used to test the items' suitability for measuring the construct (Kroeber-Riel and Weinberg, 1999, pp. 194 f.; Berekoven *et al.*, 2001, pp. 79 f.; Bortz and Döring, 2002, pp. 222–4, 195–202). This process often goes through several loops until the final test scale is found.

In our study the purpose was to explore consumers' opinions on and attitudes towards electricity, so group phenomena such as integration, coherence and the influence of the informal group leader were ignored. The evaluation and analysis of the data focused on categorising the participants' individual statements in as detailed a manner as possible in order to detect the factors that were most important to them.

The first examination of the transcribed texts showed that the results were by no means amorphous and had been given shape by the test stimuli. Moreover the importance of certain factors, such as permanent maintenance of the power supply, was obvious simply from reading the texts. This examination provided the starting point for the formation of categories. Subsequently the data was structured by means of QSR N5. This special software package, which simplifies and systematises the coding of texts, was developed especially for the evaluation of qualitative data.

Data analysis

The text consisted of two transcripts (a total of 24 unformatted pages) and the notes taken by the moderator and his assistant. With the help of QSR N5 (Richards, 1999; Bazeley and Richards, 2000) the text was split up and central categories (tree nodes) were formed. The first task was to find out more about the concrete structure of the material by counting the total number and frequency of terms used in the discussion. This step was based on the following principle:

- If the participants' comments were similar in form, content or context and they repeated themselves with sufficient frequency, the conditions for a statistical evaluation would be met.

Based on this principle six main categories were formed:

- Associations with electricity.
- Descriptions/characteristics of the industry and individual power supply firms.
- Liberalisation.
- products and services.
- Minimum expectations of electricity supply and/or supplier.
- experiences.

Some text passages could not be easily assigned to a category as their meaning was subject to interpretation. These statements, in which certain issues were implied but not explicitly said, were counted and eventually grouped. For example, after being interpreted the following text passage was assigned to the subcategory 'Permanent maintenance of power supply': 'It is important that it [electricity] is always there. And if it is not, it is important to get it going again as soon as possible'.

During the course of the analysis several subcategories evolved within the main categories. These subcategories necessitated further ordering and systematisation of the data. The assignment of a participant's quotation/statement to a certain category was based on intersubjective comprehensibility. This rule was used as the theoretical guideline for the coding. In the next step, statements that were suitable for use as test items were extracted and formulated by the researcher. In this process, a rule-based and systematic procedure was followed to guarantee the objectification and validity of interpretations. The procedure was divided into two stages:

1. Deduction of statements (participants' comments → main categories → subcategories → items formulated as statements).
2. Validity check of the results by means of the following two questions (Bortz and Döring, 2002, p. 335):

- Is it possible to derive the statement from the transcripts (validity of the interpretation)?
- To what extent can the statement be generalised/to what extent would it hold true outside the focus group (general validity of the interpretation)?

The deduction pattern shown in Figure 15.3 explains the formation of the categories and the extraction of the statements. This pattern was adhered to throughout the process in order to ensure intersubjective transparency and comprehensibility. The transitions between the individual stages – from a simple descriptive collection of the participants' comments to the formation of the categories and deduction of the statements – were, however, not as clear as indicated by the deduction scheme. Figure 15.3 illustrates the deduction of two statements, one with an affective and one with a cognitive character.

Altogether 16 items were identified to form the final statement battery to measure the involvement of private customers with electricity:

1. A permanent power supply without any interruptions is very important to me.
2. I have already thought about changing my electricity supplier.
3. Electricity is interesting to me.
4. Electricity must always be available, everything else can be neglected.
5. I often discuss the products and offers of the various power suppliers with my friends.
6. I can't say much about electricity.
7. I have a preference for one or more brands in this product class.
8. Most of the products/offers by electricity suppliers do not differ much from each other.
9. Electricity is more of interest to me than other products used in daily life.
10. To make a choice between the different offers would be difficult for me.
11. The choice of a particular power supplier doesn't say anything about a person.
12. I am well enough informed about the different offers to make a good choice.
13. I am not interested in where and how electricity is produced.
14. At the moment changing my power supplier seems too complicated.

15. Electricity belongs to daily life, it can't be replaced and therefore it's extremely important.
16. I look closely at advertisements for electricity.

In contrast to the common way of developing items, the empirical-qualitative procedure described here offers a new approach that does not need extensive and complex calibration. The extent to which the suggested way of item development can be viewed as a useful alternative to the usual process has to be proved by empirical-quantitative analysis. The following are the minimum requirements for evaluating items and tests (Bortz and Döring, 2002, p. 221):

- Homogeneity of items: all items have to contribute to measuring the construct in question.
- Complexity of items: the items should cover a broad range of complexity.
- Discriminatory power of items: each item should be able to separate as clearly as possible persons with different attitudes.
- Objectivity of the test: clearly defined rules for the proper application of the test should guarantee objectivity.
- Reliability of the test: the number and the formulation of the items should guarantee a reliable measurement of the construct in question.
- Validity of the test: empirical proof on the basis of a theoretical concept should account for the validity of the test.

Evaluation of the quality of the developed items is discussed in the following section, which examines not only the item battery but also the process of its development.

Evaluation of the quality of the items

In April 2002, 339 private electricity customers were interviewed on the topic 'New product planning in the liberalised [Austrian] electricity market'. In the course of these interviews the abovementioned statement battery for measuring the involvement of private customers with electricity (power involvement test, PIT) underwent empirical-quantitative testing for the first time. The PIT was measured on a five-point Likert-type scale ranging from $+2$ ('I fully agree') to -2 ('I totally disagree'). For the purpose of validating the PIT, the homogeneity and complexity of the items and the coefficient alpha (Cronbach, 1951) were calculated.

The PIT is a one-dimensional instrument for measuring the construct in the given context, therefore all items have to correlate. The extent of

Participants' comments	Main category (MC)/ sub category (SC)	Statement
MF: 'It is important to me that it is there 24 hours a day.' [FG_1und2_N5 : 471–471] *ES*: 'It is really important that electricity is always there.... I mean, if it isn't there or if it doesn't work, that can be unpleasant... for example the fridge defrosts ...' [FG_1und2_N5 : 492–498] *MA*: 'Permanent maintenance of the power supply is the most important thing.... I think so too ...' [FG_1und2_N5 : 501–507]	MC: minimum expectations of electricity supply and/or supplier SC: permanent maintenance of power supply	A permanent power supply without any interruptions is very important to me.
CS: 'Comparison of the different offers is very important... it helps to make a decision... but in the end you find out that they are all the same anyway because when one thing is cheaper here it is more expensive there and vice versa...' [FG_1und2_N5 : 415–430] *GS*: 'I don't think that the product itself can get any better... but the services around the product could be improved...'[FG_1und2_N5 : 669–673] *BG*: 'They have done everything for me... they cancelled my contract with Wienstrom, and now I just pay my bills to ökostrom, that's all. But it's the same electricity that comes out of the socket, and I didn't have to change the meter or anything...' [FG_1und2_N5 : 111–125]	MC: products and services SC: electricity and more	Most of the products/offers by electricity suppliers do not differ much from each other

Figure 15.3 Pattern for the deduction of statements

mutual correlation is what we call homogeneity of the items, which should result in a total test homogeneity ranging from 0.2 to 0.4 with one-dimensional constructs (Briggs and Cheek, 1986, p. 115; Bortz and Döring, 2002, p. 220). Table 15.2 shows the item intercorrelation

Table 15.2   Item intercorrelation of the reduced PIT (8 items)

Item	3	4	5	6	7	9	12	16	TTH
3		0.43	0.32	0.27	0.11	0.42	0.16	0.34	
4	0.43		0.22	0.29	0.19	0.28	0.08	0.28	
5	0.32	0.22		0.20	0.22	0.32	0.27	0.37	
6	0.27	0.29	0.20		0.09	0.18	0.12	0.09	
7	0.11	0.19	0.22	0.09		0.12	0.24	0.19	
9	0.42	0.28	0.32	0.18	0.12		0.17	0.33	
12	0.16	0.08	0.27	0.12	0.24	0.17		0.26	
16	0.34	0.28	0.37	0.09	0.19	0.33	0.26		
IH[10]	0.29	0.25	0.27	0.18	0.17	0.26	0.19	0.27	0.23

Notes: TTH = total test homogeneity; IH = item homogeneity.

of the PIT. The homogeneity of the items was ascertained by calculating the average value of each item. The calculated average value of all item homogeneities determined the total homogeneity of the test, which was rather low at 0.12 for all 16 items. To improve the homogeneity of the test, items with low homogeneity (<0.15) were eliminated and homogeneity was thereby increased to 0.23, hence it lay within the acceptance range suggested by Briggs and Cheek (1986).

Next the complexity of the items was calculated. The aim was to identify very easy items that almost all respondents agreed upon and extremely difficult items the majority of respondents disagreed with. Such items with extreme values had to be eliminated as all items had to cover a broad range of complexity so that the PIT could help the researcher to identify respondents with different degrees of involvement (Bortz and Döring, 2002, p. 218).

The complexity of the items was calculated according to Dahl's (1971) formula. The sum of the empirically measured points (x_i) for a specific item i was divided by the theoretically calculated maximum score for this item (ibid., pp. 140 f.; Bortz and Döring, 2002, p. 218). The theoretical maximum score was calculated by multiplying the maximum sum of points, k, for item i by the number of respondents, n:

$$P_i = \frac{\Sigma_{m=1}^{n} X_{im}}{k_i \cdot n}$$

This formula allowed a range of values to be derived, ranging from 0 (the most difficult item) to 1 (the easiest item), in which 0 meant that all respondents disagreed and 1 that all agreed. In general items in the range of 0.2 to 0.8 were considered suitable for use in a test (Bortz and Döring, 2002, p. 218).

For the purpose of calculating their complexity, the items that had been measured earlier with the Likert-type scale had to be transferred to a new scale that ranged from 0 ('I totally disagree') to 4 ('I fully agree'). Then the number of respondents who answered a certain item was multiplied by the maximum value (4) in order to obtain the theoretical maximum score for this item. Finally the empirically measured points for this item were divided by the theoretical maximum score (Table 15.3).

The analysis of the complexity of the items showed that items 1 and 15 had to be eliminated due to their small information content. These items represented statements with a very high degree of agreement (0.93 and 0.84 respectively) and therefore could not contribute to the identification of groups.

As a further means of proving the validity of the PIT, the coefficient alpha (Cronbach, 1951) was calculated. All 16 statements had an alpha coefficient of 0.58. That is, the PIT measured the true value (of involvement with electricity) with a measurement error of 0.42. The degree of accuracy increased to 0.71 (measurement error = 0.29) when the coefficient alpha was only calculated for the eight items that had been selected when calculating the homogeneity of the items.

The findings were encouraging as they proved the suitability of the chosen method of developing items. The extent to which the PIT is an

Table 15.3 Complexity of the PIT statements

Item	Sample size per item	Empirically determined score	Theoretically possible score	Complexity of the item
1	337	1254	1348	0.93
2	337	595	1348	0.44
3	338	729	1352	0.54
4	337	694	1348	0.51
5	338	278	1352	0.21
6	338	744	1352	0.55
7	337	449	1348	0.33
8	335	823	1340	0.61
9	337	409	1348	0.30
10	337	813	1348	0.60
11	338	1020	1352	0.75
12	338	327	1352	0.24
13	337	365	1348	0.27
14	337	954	1348	0.71
15	338	1141	1352	0.84
16	338	393	1352	0.29

accurate instrument for measuring private customers' involvement with electricity will be the subject future investigations.

Summary

The aim of the study reported in this chapter was to use an empirical-qualitative method of collecting data to develop a test for measuring private customers' involvement with electricity. Despite possible methodological problems with focus groups, for example the selection of participants and the choice of stimuli, this method constitutes a very valuable alternative to the usual way of developing items. The empirical-quantitative analysis not only corroborated the quality of the developed test but also proved the suitability of the chosen method and procedure. Finally, it should be remarked that exploration should be reintegrated into scientific research, and this can only be achieved by following systematic procedures and documenting the entire process.

Notes

1. For types of and procedures for qualitative interviews see Spöhring (1989, pp. 147 ff.), Flick (1995, pp. 94 ff.), Lamnek (1995, pp. 35 ff.), Friebertshäuser (1997).
2. The weaknesses include problems that are caused by the situation of the interview, the interviewer or the interviewee, systematic errors caused by deviation from the interview plan, suggestive interview techniques, selective recording of answers, wrong answers resulting from faulty recall, pretentious behaviour by the interviewee, prestige and affect (Noelle-Neumann and Petersen, 1996, pp. 372–4; Berekoven *et al.*, 2001, pp. 67 f.; Bortz and Döring, 2002, pp. 246–8).
3. Apart from research projects that focus on certain group dynamics (Flick, 1995, p. 135).
4. According to Lamnek (1995, pp. 154 f.), because of their qualitative character focus groups require non-directive discussion guidance.
5. For the use and origin of the terms programme stimuli and test stimuli see Noelle-Neumann and Petersen (1996, pp. 93–102).

References

Atteslander, P. (2000) *Methoden der empirischen Sozialforschung* (Berlin and New York: de Gruyter).

Bazeley, P. and Richards, L. (2000) *The NVivo Qualitative Project Book* (London: Sage)

Berekoven, L., Eckert, W. and Ellenrieder, P. (2001) *Marktforschung: Methodische Grundlagen und praktische Anwendung* (Wiesbaden: Gabler).

Bloch, P. H. (1981) 'An Exploration into the Scaling of Consumers' Involvement with a Product Class', in K. B. Monroe (ed.), *Advances in Consumer Research*, vol. 8 (Provo, Ut.: Association for Consumer Research), pp. 61–5.

Bohnsack, R. (2000) 'Gruppendiskussion', in U. Flick, E. von Kardoff and I. Steinke (eds), *Qualitative Forschung – Ein Handbuch* (Hamburg: Rowohlt), pp. 369–84.

Bortz, J. and Döring, N. (2002) *Forschungsmethoden und Evaluation für Human- und Sozialwissenschaftler* (Berlin, Heidelberg and New York: Springer).

Briggs, S. R. and Cheek, J. M. (1986) 'The Role of Factor Analysis in the Development and Evaluation of Personality Scales', *Journal of Personality and Social Psychology*, vol. 54, no. 1, pp. 106–48.

Cronbach, L. J. (1951) 'Coefficient Alpha and the Internal Structure of Tests', *Psychometrika*, vol. 16, no. 3, pp. 297–334.

Dahl, G. (1971) 'Zur Berechnung des Schwierigkeitsindex bei quantitativ abgestufter Aufgabenbewertung', *Diagnostica*, vol. 17, no. 3, pp. 139–42.

Flick, U. (1995) *Qualitative Forschung – Theorien, Methoden, Anwendung, Psychologie und Sozialwissenschaften* (Reinbek bei Hamburg: Rowohlt).

Flick, U., von Kardoff, E. and Steinke, I. (eds) (2000) *Qualitative Forschung – Ein Handbuch* (Hamburg: Rowohlt).

Friebertshäuser, B. (1997) 'Interviewtechniken – ein Überblick', in B. Friebertshäuser and A. Prengel (eds), *Handbuch Qualitative Forschungsmethoden in der Erziehungswissenschaft* (Weinheim and Munich: Juventa), pp. 371–95.

Higie, R. A. and Feick, L. F. (1988) 'Enduring Involvement: Conceptual and Methodological Issues', in T. Srull (ed.), *Advances in Consumer Research*, vol. 16 (Provo, Ut.: Association for Consumer Research), pp. 690–6.

Jain, K. and Srinivasan, N. (1990) 'An Empirical Assessment of Multiple Operationalizations of Involvement', in M. Goldberg, G. Gorn and R. Pollay (eds), *Advances in Consumer Research*, vol. 17 (Provo, Ut.: Association for Consumer Research), pp. 594–602.

Kroeber-Riel, W. and Weinberg, P. (1999) *Konsumentenverhalten* (Munich: Vahlen).

Krueger, R. A. (1998a) *Developing Questions for Focus Groups* (Thousand Oaks, CA: Sage).

Krueger, R. A. (1998b) *Moderating Focus Groups* (Thousand Oaks, CA: Sage).

Krueger, R. A. (1998c) *Analyzing and Reporting Focus Group Results* (Thousand Oaks, CA: Sage).

Krüger, H. (1983) 'Gruppendiskussionen. Überlegungen zur Rekonstruktion sozialer Wirklichkeit aus der Sicht der Betroffenen', *Soziale Welt*, vol. 34, pp. 90–109.

Lamnek, S. (1995) *Qualitative Sozialforschung. Band 1: Methodologie. Band 2: Methoden und Techniken* (Weinheim: Beltz, Psychologie Verlags Union).

Lamnek, S. (1998) *Gruppendiskussion – Theorie und Praxis* (Weinheim: Psychologie Verlags Union).

Lastovicka, J. L. and Gardner, D. M. (1979) 'Components of Involvement', in J. C. Maloney and B. Silverman (eds), *Attitude Research Plays for High Stakes* (Chicago, Ill.: AMA), pp. 53–73.

Laurent, G. and Kapferer, J.-N. (1985) 'Measuring Consumer Involvement Profiles', *Journal of Marketing Research*, vol. 22 (February), pp. 41–53.

Lunt, P. and Livingstone, S. (1996) 'Rethinking the Focus Group in Media and Communications Research', *Journal of Communication*, vol. 46, no. 2, pp. 79–98.

Mangold, W. (1960) *Gegenstand und Methode des Gruppendiskussionsverfahrens* (Frankfurt: Europäische Verlagsanstalt).

Mangold, W. (1962) 'Gruppendiskussion', in R. König (ed.), *Handbuch der empirischen Sozialforschung*, Band I (Stuttgart: Enke), pp. 209–25.

McQuarrie, E. F. and Munson, M. J. (1986) 'The Zaichowsky Personal Involvement Inventory: Modification and Extension', in P. Andersen and M. Wallendorf (eds), *Advances in Consumer Research*, vol. 14 (Provo, Ut.: Association for Consumer Research), pp. 36–40.

McQuarrie, E. F. and Munson, M. J. (1991) 'A Revised Product Involvement Inventory: Improved Usability and Validity', in J. F. Sherry and B. Sternthal (eds), *Advances in Consumer Research*, vol. 19 (Provo, Ut.: Association for Consumer Research), pp. 108–15.

Morgan, D. L. (1988) *Focus Groups as Qualitative Research. Qualitative Research Methods* (Newbury Park, CA: Sage).

Morgan, D. L. (1998) *The Focus Group Guidebook* (Thousand Oaks, CA: Sage).

Morgan, D. L. and Scannell, A. U. (1998) *Planning Focus Groups* (Thousand Oaks, CA: Sage).

Nießen, M. (1977) *Gruppendiskussion – interpretative Methodologie, Methodenbegründung, Anwendung* (Munich: Fink).

Noelle-Neumann, E. and Petersen, T. (1996) *Alle, nicht jeder. Einführung in die Methoden der Demoskopie* (Munich: DTV).

Pollock, F. (1955) *Gruppenexperiment – Ein Studienbericht. Frankfurter Beiträge zur Soziologie*, Band 2 (Frankfurt: Europäische Verlagsanstalt).

Ratchford, B. T. (1987) 'New Insights About the FCB Grid', *Journal of Advertising Research*, vol. 27, no. 4, pp. 24–38.

Richards, L. (1999) *Using NVivo in Qualitative Research* (London: Sage).

Slama, M. E. and Tashchian, A. (1985) 'Selected Socio-economic and Demographic Characteristics Associated With Purchasing Involvement', *Journal of Marketing*, vol. 49, no. 1, pp. 72–82.

Spöhring, W. (1989) *Qualitative Sozialforschung* (Stuttgart: Teubner).

Tigert, D. J., Ring, L. R. and King, C. W. (1976) 'Fashion Involvement and Buying Behavior: A Methodological Study', in B. B. Anderson (ed.), *Advances in Consumer Research*, vol. 3 (Provo, Ut.: Association for Consumer Research), pp. 46–52.

Titscher, S., Wodak, R., Meyer, M. and Vetter, E. (1998) *Methoden der Textanalyse: Leitfaden und Überblick* (Opladen: Westdeutscher Verlag).

Traylor, M. B. and Joseph, B. W. (1984) 'Measuring Consumer Involvement With Products: Developing a General Scale', *Psychology & Marketing*, vol. 1, no. 1, pp. 65–77.

Vaughn, R. (1986) 'How Advertising Works: A Planning Model Revisited', *Journal of Advertising Research*, vol. 27, no. 1, pp. 57–66.

Zaichkowsky, J. L. (1985) 'Measuring the Involvement Construct', *Journal of Consumer Research*, vol. 12, no. 3, pp. 341–52.

16

Analysing Qualitative Data with Quantitative Methods: An Illustration Using Personalised Item Recommendation Techniques

Thomas Reutterer and Andreas Mild

Data sets collected in qualitative marketing research often represent respondents' reactions to open questions or stimuli. These responses are typically encoded as binary or frequency count entries across a set of text code categories or items, which may have to be predefined by the researcher. Given such 'pick-any' data, the analyst is frequently interested in predicting whether an item (or text code category) applies or does not apply to an individual respondent's reaction based on the remainder of her or his reaction profile and other respondents' profiles. Collaborative filtering (CF) methods, as introduced in the data mining literature, focus on a very similar task. However most of the CF algorithms have so far been applied to derive personalised item recommendations based on respondents' preference ratings.

This chapter investigates the suitability and limitations of CF methods when only binary respondent information is available. Using shopping basket data (consumers' choices/non-choices of product categories in a grocery assortment) with very similar characteristics as pick-any data encoded from qualitative interviews, in an extensive simulation experiment the effects of different similarity measures, available data points per respondent and the number of items or categories to be recommended on the relative predictive performance of a memory-based CF algorithm is studied. Using various measures to evaluate the predictive ability, we derive some recommendations for the proper parameterisation of such systems when applied to qualitative marketing research data.

Introduction

In a qualitative research framework, data are typically collected via narrative or problem-centred interviews, talking-aloud protocols or similar techniques derived from a hermeneutic or phenomenologic approach to scientific investigation. In such a set-up the data-generation process is driven by a coding and transcription scheme, as applied by the researcher to the observed material, which is typically textual or observational information. The data are then treated to further analysis or transformation and interpretation in a usually very high dimensional binary or count data format (with coding entries or count frequencies signifying the association or non-association of a specific contextual denotation).

According to data theory terminology (Coombs, 1964) such types of data can be qualified as 'pick-any/J', where the set of items can be constrained by a maximum number of (text code) categories J, or unconstrained, that is, 'pick-any'. Such data formats are no novelty in many fields of empirical social research. Consider for example marketing researchers, who are constantly analysing the multiple binary reactions of respondents to marketing stimuli, product category purchase frequencies or dichotomous responses to product image attribute statements; the perceptions-based market segmentation (PBMS) approach, as proposed by Mazanec and Strasser (2000), is just one example of how to deal with typical analytical issues associated with the latter data type. In the case of high-dimensional binary data – such as transcription code entries from qualitative interviews, multiple responses to an item set or customers' shopping baskets from retail assortments – the most common task for the analyst is to reduce complexity. This is the primary objective of exploratory data analysis in which the focus is on extracting prototypical or structural patterns out of the available data in order to reduce the dimensionality or compress the number of data points to a partition of the original data set. To make the pattern extraction, dimensionality reduction or resulting classification meaningful and convenient for further interpretation, it is desirable to perform this task with a minimum loss of information hidden in the original data. This is exactly the objective of the various data compression techniques, including cluster analysis and pattern recognition (Bock, 1974).

More formally, there are two major analytical tasks associated with data compression, both of which depend on how the observed data matrix is processed. Recalling the discussion on data characteristics (Young, 1987), the shape of a data matrix can be defined by the number of ways

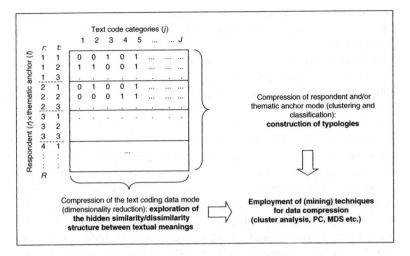

Figure 16.1 Conceptual framework for data compression of qualitative marketing data and related analytical tasks

(that is, the dimensions of the matrix), the number of modes (sets of different entities that represent the ways of the matrix – for example respondents, thematic anchors, statements, phrases and text code categories represent different data modes) and symmetry conditions (symmetric/asymmetric data). Furthermore each way of a data matrix has its own number of levels (corresponding to the number of entities in the respective object set). Thus the ways define the overall shape of a data matrix, modes determine the interpretation of the objects and the levels specify the size of the matrix (Jacoby, 1991).

High-dimensional qualitative marketing data arise in numerous ways, one being on the basis of textual statements collected from (open) qualitative interviews. After encoding and conversion to coding categories, these data can usually be made available in a two-way, three-mode data format.[1] As illustrated in Figure 16.1, the first way is an elongated or 'stacked' representation of two data modes, namely the respondent (r) and the 'thematic anchor' (t) modes of data.[2] The latter are typically respondent-specific ($r \in \{R\}$) observation entities such as sentences, text fragments or – more generally – responses to open questions or stimuli, which are mapped onto a J-dimensional (binary) vector $c_{r,t}$, with J being a predefined set of denotative or connotative text code categories (hence 'pick-any/J'). Note that the t mode of the raw data matrix in Figure 16.1 can be (but does not necessarily have to be) fixed in terms of the number of valid levels; for data derived from qualitative interviews a variable or respondent-specific number of thematic anchors (that is, $t \in \{T(r)\}$) can be expected.

From this point of view the concepts of dimensionality reduction and construction of typologies (or clustering) can be considered as formally identical problems of data compression. The only (formal) difference between the two concepts concerns the data mode(s) involved in the data reduction task. If the task is to compress the data way, including the stacked $r \times t$ responses encoded into the J text code categories via some type of cluster algorithm, the resulting set of prototypes will represent a compressed version of interactions between respondents and thematic anchors and form the basis of typology construction and response classification. The analogue applies to the task of dimensionality reduction. Here the complex interaction structure of information nodes hidden behind the redundant and ambiguous character of high-dimensional text code categories is meant to be extracted and represented in a sparse and meaningful way.

It is important to note that both the dimensionality reduction and the typology construction objective of data compression can be achieved via the employment of quite similar and well-known techniques of explorative data analysis, such as cluster analysis, principal components analysis and multidimensional scaling methods. Since the advent of the Internet and other devices for electronic data processing and exchange, it has been possible to collect the above data structures as verbal (for example e-mail or on-line discussion groups) or non-verbal items (for example click-stream data and menu choices) via interactive media such as the Web at extremely high speed and in great quantity. However very large data volumes exceed the data-processing capabilities of traditional exploratory data analysis methodology. Consider, for example, an apparently simple computation of the mean value of a specific quantity. This becomes a very costly (in terms of computing time) task for samples of several million or billion observations and even conceptually problematic if storage capabilities do not allow the necessary data to be made available (such as navigation and clicking data accruing permanently from users of on-line media).

To cope with such problems, specific 'mining' techniques have been designed, many of which are an extension of more traditional methods. In the next section a number of these techniques are briefly described. In the subsequent sections, special attention will be paid to so-called collaborative filtering (CF) methods. Like most exploratory approaches to cluster analysis, CF techniques are based on similarity matching between sequences of data patterns, such as click-stream data and coded textual statements.

CF algorithms have been applied in various fields, predominantly for deriving item recommendations based on the preferences – or more specifically, preference ratings – stated by on-line users. There is little in the literature on the predictive performance of these algorithms when applied to the binary world of qualitative marketing data. This chapter provides some evidence in this direction. In an extensive simulation experiment we study the effects of different similarity measures, available data points per user and the number of items to be recommended on the relative predictive performance of the CF approach. The experiment makes use of market basket data (product categories or items that individual consumers purchase on the same occasion) collected from a grocery retailer. Using various measures to evaluate the predictive ability, we derive some clues to the proper parameterisation of such systems. Since market basket data exhibit pick-any/*J* characteristics that are shared by most other data types in qualitative marketing research (such as binary text coding data), the findings should also provide some useful benchmarks for the complete class of binary data sets.

Data mining tools for data compression and knowledge discovery

The traditional method of turning data into knowledge relies on 'manual' or batch-mode analysis and interpretation. Due to the steady increase in the amount of data available, as indicated above, data mining (sometimes also called 'automated knowledge discovery in databases') is a way of avoiding information overload by automating the knowledge-creating process from raw data sets (Fayyad *et al.*, 1996).

While there is no generally accepted definition of data mining, most activities in the field are concerned with classification, estimation, prediction, affinity grouping (association rules) and clustering or data compression (Berry and Linoff, 2000). The first three can be subsumed under 'directed' data mining tasks, since the goal is to use the available data to build a model that is capable of predicting or explaining one or a group of particular variables. In these cases the primary task is to test a certain underlying structural model against a null hypothesis. A second group of tasks, frequently referred to as 'undirected' data mining, seek to establish an *a priori* unknown relationship among a set of variables. As opposed to the confirmatory character of directed data mining, the

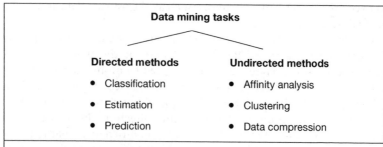

Data mining tasks

Directed methods	**Undirected methods**
• Classification	• Affinity analysis
• Estimation	• Clustering
• Prediction	• Data compression

Data mining methodology:

- **Artificial neural networks:** non-linear predictive models that learn through training and resemble the principles of information processing as assumed in biological neural networks in structure; on-line processing capabilities.

- **Decision trees:** tree-shaped structures that represent sets of decisions. These decisions generate rules for the classification of a data set. Specific decision tree methods include classification and regression trees (CART) and chi square automatic interaction detection (CHAID).

- **Genetic algorithms:** optimisation techniques that use processes such as genetic combination, mutation and natural selection in a design based on the concepts of evolution.

- **Nearest neighbour methods:** techniques that match each record in a data set based on a combination of the classes of the *k* record(s) most similar to it in a historical data set. Sometimes called *k*-nearest neighbour or filtering techniques.

Figure 16.2   An overview of tasks and methodologies associated with data mining techniques

main purpose of undirected tasks is to uncover structures hidden in the typically large amount of available data (Figure 16.2).

Irrespective of the underlying analytical task, numerous statistical techniques, methods of pattern recognition and machine learning methods are typically associated with data mining techniques. The most commonly used techniques in data mining are artificial neural networks, decision trees and nearest neighbour methods (Figure 16.2 provides an overview).

Artificial neural networks (Hertz *et al.*, 1991; Gallant, 1993; Bishop, 1995) are non-linear predictive models that mimic the way in which information is presumed to be processed by biological neural networks. Due to their on-line processing capabilities, neural networks can relatively easily be adapted to the specific analytical requirements arising from a permanent influx of data, such as from on-line retail scanning devices or navigation and clicking information through on-line media, as collected via log-file documents from Web users. Compared with statistical models, neural networks typically have many more parameters and these are strongly interconnected. Hence parameters are sometimes hard to interpret and serve as a black-box model in the favour of a high degree of choice flexibility among various types of network architecture.

Decision trees are tree-shaped structures that represent subsets of decisions. These decisions generate rules for the classification of a data set that can be easily interpreted and directly transformed into, for example, structured query language (SQL) statements. Specific decision tree methods such as CART (classification and regression trees – Breiman *et al.*, 1984), C4.5 (Quinlan, 1993) and CHAID (chi square automatic interaction detection – Kass, 1980) differ in the number of splits in each level, the way these splits are chosen and the pruning technique applied to prevent the model from over-fitting. Nearest neighbour methods, sometimes called *k*-nearest neighbour methods, are techniques that match each record in a data set based on a combination of the classes of *k* record(s) most similar to it in a historical data set. Data mining has been successfully used for such diverse applications as astronomy (Fayyad *et al.*, 1996), manufacturing (Manago and Auriol, 1996) and marketing. In the field of marketing, special attention is paid to customer segmentation, customer targeting, customer profitability, credit fraud risk analysis and market-basket analysis (for a selection of contributions to this field see Hippner *et al.*, 2001). Customer segmentation (Reutterer, 1997; Mazanec, 1999; Natter, 1999) involves subdividing a set of given customers into groups that share similar characteristics, such as purchasing behaviour or known preferences. It is usual to endeavour to find a solution that shows high degree of similarity within the group and a large dissimilarity between the groups. Market-basket analysis is aimed at discovering structures in market baskets to exploit cross-/upselling opportunities. The association rules method (Agrawal and Srikant, 1994; Buechter and Wirth, 1998) is commonly used in this regard. It explores patterns such as 'if customers buy A and B, they are likely to buy Y and Z, as well'. The use of advanced vector quantisation techniques allows a disaggregated (segment-level) representation of relationship patterns between product categories (for an application see Schnedlitz *et al.*, 2001).

In the framework of the above directed versus undirected analytical tasks, CF algorithms can be classified as hybrid approaches that both perform data compression (via similarity matching) and predict items to be recommended. In the next section the CF methodology is outlined in more detail.

Collaborative filtering methods as recommendation agents

CF methods are widely used by most of the individual-level customised recommendation systems in real-world on-line (such as amazon.com, cdnow.com and barnesandnoble.com) and off-line media (such as interactive point-of-sale information systems). In recommendation systems, CF methods mimic word-of-mouth recommendations by using data from users with similar preferences to determine a customer's preferences and recommend a list of items derived from these. From a data analytical perspective, CF algorithms have some potential to be employed for the specific requirements of qualitative text analysis. Consider, for example, the task of predicting (or recommending) a selection of specific statements or responses based on a past sequence of coded text categories of an active user or respondent and a database of other respondents. In terms of the data structure presented in the introduction to this chapter, this is equivalent to predicting the expected values of items $j \in \{J\}$ for a particular active user, a, based on the available pick-any/J observations, $c_{r,t}$. Most of the CF algorithms presented so far, however, are designed to analyse customers' preference rating data (for example the frequently cited GroupLens research project, as presented by Resnik *et al.*, 1994; Konstan *et al.*, 1997), which makes them less appropriate for the binary world of qualitative marketing data (that is, choice/non-choice of customers among product categories offered in retail assortments or text code entries of responses in a qualitative market research survey).

Following a brief outline of the basic assumptions and alternative variants of the CF methodology, we shall investigate the performance of CF methods using pick-any/J market basket data across 55 product categories. The data represent 9835 retail transactions (that is, customers' purchases of multiple product categories) collected from the point-of-purchase scanning devices of a grocery retail outlet over a one-month period. The relative predictive performance of competing model specifications is examined by experimentally varying external (data-related) conditions and model parameters that are hypothesised to be crucial for the accuracy of CF-based recommendations.

The collaborative filtering methodology

The current approaches of CF methodology can be classified into two main groups: memory-based CF and model-based CF (for a detailed overview of contemporary CF approaches see Runte, 2000). Memory-based CF algorithms are deterministic in nature. They rely on a database of previous users' preferences and perform certain calculations (similarity matching) on the database each time a new prediction is required (see for example Breese *et al.*, 1998). The most common examples are neighbour-based algorithms, where a subset of users most similar to an active user are chosen and a weighted average of their preference ratings is used to estimate the preferences of the active user for other items (Konstan *et al.*, 1997; Sarwar *et al.*, 2000). Model-based algorithms, including Bayesian clustering, Bayesian networks and other classification-based algorithms (Breese *et al.*, 1998), first develop a descriptive model of the database and then use it to make predictions for an active user.

For a given number of R customers included in the database, memory-based CF algorithms calculate the predictive value, $p_{a,j}$, for a user, a, and a specific item, j, on the basis of a weighted sum of votes of other similar users. Without loss of generality, in our subsequent empirical application the term 'item' corresponds to product category and 'vote' to a consumer's choice [0;1] among a predefined set of categories (note that 'item' could also denote a text code category and 'vote' a respondent's statement). We use a modified version of the function proposed by Breese *et al.* (1998):

$$p_{a,j} = \kappa \sum_{r=1}^{R} w(a,r)c_{rj} \tag{16.1}$$

The propensity of user a to purchase item j thus depends on the similarity, $w(a,r)$, between user a and each user r as well as the actual purchasing behaviour, c_{rj}, of each user r. κ ensures that the absolute values of the weights sum to unity. Most studies on collaborative filtering restrict themselves to the use of Pearson's correlation coefficient (Resnick *et al.*, 1994) or a measure of vector similarity (Sarwar *et al.*, 2000) based on the cosine of the angle between two vectors to calculate similarity between users. We introduce two additional measures to calculate the weights: the so-called Jaccard or Tanimoto coefficient and the Hamming distance (for brief descriptions of these proximity measures see Anderberg, 1973; Kaufman and Rousseeuw, 1990; Kohonen, 1997). In contrast to the correlation coefficient, both measures cannot take on negative values. The Tanimoto similarity between two users, a and r, is defined as

$$w(a,r) = \frac{n(c_a \cap c_r)}{n(c_a \cup c_r)} = \frac{n(c_a \cap c_r)}{n(c_a) + n(c_i) - n(c_a \cap c_r)} \tag{16.2}$$

where $n(X)$ is the number of elements in customer basket (or item set) X. As is obvious from the above description, the Tanimoto coefficient ignores the number of coinciding non-chosen elements (that is, zeros). There is very limited expected variance in similarities (using, for example, correlational measures) constructed for sparse data sets, and this might be advantageous in the case of extremely asymmetrically distributed or sparse data vectors. The Hamming distance is the most trivial measure of dissimilarity between code representations. It is simply defined as the number of different bits in sequences of equal length:

$$d_h(a, r) = \text{bitcount}\{(\hat{c}_{aj} \wedge c_{rj}) \vee (c_{aj} \wedge \hat{c}_{rj}) \; \forall j = 1,...,j\} \tag{16.3}$$

where $\hat{c}_{aj}$ is the logic negation of c_{aj}; $\vee$ denotes the logical sum and $\wedge$ denotes the logical product. The function bitcount $\{X\}$ determines the number of elements in the set $\{X\}$ with the logical value 1. For direct application, we normalise d_h to a range between 0 and 1 and calculate the similarity as

$$w(a, r) = 1 - \text{norm}(d_h(a, r)) \tag{16.4}$$

While there is an almost endless catalogue of proximity coefficients in the literature (for overviews see Gower, 1971; Anderberg, 1973; Hubalek, 1982; Kaufman and Rousseeuw, 1990), the vast majority are closely related to one of the measures included in the following experiment.

Experimental design of the simulation study and evaluation criteria

The choice of a specific proximity measure for similarity matching of customers' choice patterns is one of the (probably most important) technical factors that might affect the predictive accuracy of CF techniques. However there are several other data-related factors (such as the amount of information available from a person) that are reported to affect the performance of CF-based recommender systems (Breese *et al.*, 1998; Ansari *et al.*, 2000). In order to separate the effects and evaluate their relative importance when designing an appropriate recommendation system for (binary) market basket analysis, we shall conduct an extensive simulation study by systematically varying some hypothesised experimental design factors.

The study consists of two stages. In the first stage, for each customer–item combination a value for expression 16.1 is calculated for each cell of a complete factorial design. In the second stage, TOP-N recommendations are formulated, as follows. We first calculate the median predictive value for each item across all available customers, that is, median(p_j). Then for each customer r we calculate the difference between the predictive

Table 16.1   Experimental design variables

Factor	Levels	Used in stage
Proximity measure (1)	Correlation Tanimoto Hamming	1, 2
Number of given items (2)	54 44 34	1, 2
Sparsity of item list (3)	8 10 12	1, 2
Number of item recommendations	5 10 15	2

value of each item and the median predictor, that is, diff$(r, j)=p_{rj}-$ median$(p_{.j})$. Finally, the TOP-N list of potential item recommendations for each customer r is generated using the N largest values for diff$(r,.)$. Table 16.1 summarises the treatment variables and their respective levels, which are combined in a full-factorial design. The corresponding hypotheses to be tested are briefly commented on below.

In line with the above discussion on similarity concepts frequently used in CF and related matching techniques and the expected impact on predictive performance, the first experimental factor represents the proximity function used to calculate the similarities between customers. This brings to us our first hypothesis:

- Hypothesis 1: the choice of the proximity measure used to calculate weights $w(a, r)$ affects the predictive accuracy of the CF algorithm.

The second factor – the number of given items – is synonymous with the length of the vector, c_{rj} (that is, the number of categories), used for similarity calculation between an active customer and the database. Since the length of the item vectors used are indicative of the amount of data available from a customer and more information about a person's choice pattern is expected to be beneficial for the algorithm's predictive performance, we posit:

- Hypothesis 2: the number of given items positively affects the predictive accuracy of the CF algorithm.

While the number of given items is designed to test whether there is a trade-off between predictive accuracy and the amount of data collected per person, the third experimental factor determines the degree of sparsity of the available item list in terms of the minimum size (that is, number of items) per shopping basket included in the database for our simulation study. For example if a minimum size of eight items is required, only shopping baskets containing at least eight different items are used. Thus a smaller minimum basket size increases the sparsity of the data matrix used and forces the weights to be based on a few common items. To test this we posit:

- Hypothesis 3: the sparsity of the available item lists (minimum number of items per shopping basket) negatively affects the predictive accuracy of the CF algorithm.

In stage 2 of our experiment we vary the number of recommended items. While the probability of recommending 'correct' items (that is, items that are actually chosen) is expected to increase with an increase in Top-N recommendations, the quality of the recommendations might decrease due to smaller distances between the respective votes and the median. This suggests:

- Hypothesis 4: the number of Top-N recommendations per user affects the predictive accuracy of the CF algorithm.

In the first stage of our simulation experiment we use the mean absolute deviation (MAD $=\Sigma$ (|predicted value – choice[0,1]|)/# of observations) between the prediction and the actual choice or non-choice. In real-world applications with practical importance, however, the analyst is especially interested in the accuracy of predictions for actually chosen items. Thus we calculate the MAD for those items which have been chosen by a user, defined as $MAD_1 = \Sigma$ (|predicted value – choice[1]|)/# of observations). To measure the predictive accuracy of our TOP-N recommendations in the second stage of our experiment we proceed as follows. Analogous to the well-known construction framework used for proximity measures based on binary data (Anderberg, 1973; Hubalek, 1982; Kaufman and Rousseeuw, 1990), for each cell of the full-factorial design we evaluate the simulation outcome based on the association of chosen versus recommended items, as shown in the two-by-two contingency in Figure 16.3.

The cell denoted as a, for instance, contains the number of users who choose a specific item, j, that is also included in the list of TOP-N

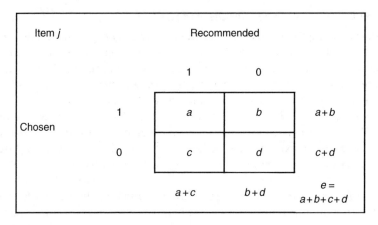

Figure 16.3 Contingency table of chosen versus recommended items

recommendations for the respective users. Hence cell *e* corresponds to the total number of users. Based on this cross-classification scheme, we define the following performance measures:

$$\text{Simple matching coefficent (SM)} = \frac{a + d}{a + b + c + d} \qquad (16.5)$$

Here the SM coefficient measures the fraction of correctly predicted items. Using this measure, actually chosen items that were recommended and non-chosen items that are not displayed in the TOP-*N* list are equally weighted. However, correctly predicted items that are actually chosen are more important. Therefore we derive two components of the Tanimoto similarity measure to account for the practically important difference between true positives and false negatives:

$$\text{HR1} = \frac{a}{a + c} \text{ and HR2} = \frac{a}{a + b} \qquad (16.6)$$

Hit rate 1 (HR1) represents the fraction of correctly predicted choices and all predicted choices, whereas hit rate 2 (HR2) expresses the fraction of correctly predicted choices and all actual choices. In the information retrieval literature, both measures are widely used performance metrics, with HR1 indicating the precision and HR2 the recall rate of an algorithm. Unlike the latter, HR1 takes into account the problem of so-called 'false-negatives' (Kowalski, 1997).

Simulation results and hypotheses tests

After running the simulations for the full-factorial experimental design using a total number of 9835 grocery retail transactions, each covering pick-any/J (choice/non-choice) market basket data across 55 product categories, we can test the posited hypotheses and study the relative impact of the design factors. With regard to the first stage of the experiment, the results of an analysis of variance (ANOVA) for the performance MAD are summarised in Table 16.2. In accordance with the treatment variables of the experimental design, (1) the proximity measure, (2) the number of items given, (3) the sparsity of the item list, (4) the choice variable, and first-order interactions are used as factors. The choice variable was introduced to capture the performance differences for all other potential (unobserved) factors between actually chosen and non-chosen items.

As can be seen, apart from the number of given items (factor 2) all the main effects are significant at the 95 per cent level, which consequently supports hypotheses H1 and H3. The small F-ratio[3] for variations of factor (2) levels is not sufficient to reject the null hypothesis of equal group means at the 95 per cent confidence level, thus hypothesis H2 is not supported by our results. This prompts the interesting conclusion that (at least for binary data) CF algorithms seem to behave relatively robustly with respect to the amount of data collected from each person

Table 16.2   Experimental stage 1: ANOVA results for the performance measure MAD

Factor	df	F-value
Constant	1	746603*
Proximity measure (1)	2	17.5*
Number of given items (2)	2	0.6
Sparsity of item list (3)	2	140*
Actual choice (4)	1	227136*
First-order interactions:		
Factors 1×2	4	0.483
Factors 1×3	4	0.442
Factors 1×4	4	129.546*
Factors 2×3	4	0.170
Factors 2×4	4	1.946
Factors 3×4	4	2057.929*
$R^2 = 0.474$		

* Significant at the 95 per cent confidence level.

and that their predictive performance is unaffected even if a considerable degree of information is missing.

The factor with the greatest impact on predictive accuracy is 'actual choice', that is, whether only actually chosen or non-chosen items are investigated. The huge difference between the MAD for actually non-chosen (MAD=0.15) and chosen items (MAD$_1$=0.58) illustrates the problem of correctly predicting chosen items. We focus our further presentation on the analysis of chosen item–customer combinations. Interestingly, there are significant first-order interactions between the proximity measure used and the choice dummy (factors 1×4), as well as between the minimum basket size (item list sparsity) and the choice variable (3×4). Figures 16.4 and 16.5 show the corresponding results (factor level means and 95 per cent confidence intervals). Even though the absolute differences are relatively small, it can be seen from Figure 16.4 that both the Tanimoto and the Hamming distance measures outperform the correlation coefficient in respect of MAD$_1$, indicating that the

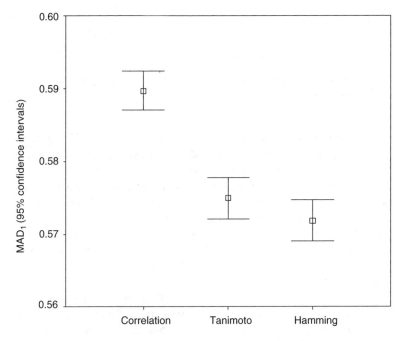

Figure 16.4 Performance measure MAD$_1$ means and confidence intervals for three different proximity measures

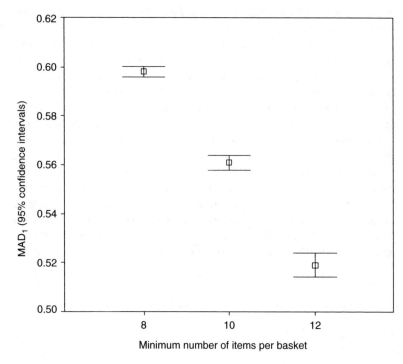

Figure 16.5 Performance measure MAD_1 means and confidence intervals for three levels of minimum basket size

frequently proposed correlation coefficient is no adequate similarity measure for relatively sparse binary data that are typically observed in market basket data analysis. Figure 16.5 shows that there is a positive impact on the MAD_1 measure of predictive accuracy when the minimum basket size is increased, thus supporting hypothesis 3. This phenomenon can be explained by the decreasing sparsity of the database, and it high-lights the sensitivity of the CF technique with respect to the correct specification of customer data with a minimum number of (common) items to achieve an acceptable degree of predictive accuracy.

Let us now turn to the results of stage 2 (TOP-*N* recommendations) of our experiment. Table 16.3 shows the results of separate ANOVAs on all three defined performance measures using the 5, 10 and 15 TOP-*N* of recommendations as factor levels (means and standard deviations indicated in brackets). While hit rates HR1 and HR2 show larger ratios with an increasing number of recommendations, SM decreases.

Table 16.3 Experimental stage 2: ANOVA results for predictive accuracy (simple matching and hit rates)

Recommendations	SM	HR1	HR2
5	0.726 (0.221)	0.156 (0.208)	0.062 (0.082)
10	0.675 (0.203)	0.165 (0.212)	0.124 (0.124)
15	0.616 (0.178)	0.170 (0.213)	0.183 (0.152)
F-value (2 df)	110.6*	1.5	356.7*

* Significant at the 95 per cent confidence level.

The declining SM values clearly show the increasing risk of wrong predictions with larger recommendation sets. Since the hit rate HR2 can be interpreted as the realised fraction of a (anything else equal) constant potential of cross-selling opportunities, augmented HR2-ratios are signalling an increasingly successful exploitation of that potential with ascending number of recommendations. On the other hand, it should be clear from the above definition that 1 – HR1 represents the fraction of recommendations that did not meet customers' needs. Hence, hit rate HR1 indicates the accuracy of recommendations, which also, however very slightly and insignificant, improves with an increasing number of recommendations. Thus with the exception of the insignificant impact that the number of TOP-N recommendations has on HR1, hypothesis 4 is supported by our findings.

Finally, Figure 16.6 shows HR2 across various product categories for an optimal combination of the design factors. It can be seen that the HR2 ratios vary strongly across product categories. Note that a value of zero does not necessarily mean that the predictions were wrong because the respective category could also have no or only few entries, that is, it was not or only rarely included the shopping baskets considered for the simulation study. Hence in practical applications the marketing analyst who wishes to utilise a CF technology-based recommendation system is advised to focus on categories with sufficiently high HR2 values.

Summary and concluding remarks

This chapter has investigated the suitability and limitations of collaborative filtering (CF) methods when only binary ('pick-any') respondent information is available. Potential applications of CF algorithms in qualitative marketing research include predicting (or recommending) a selection of encoded response items based on an observed (but possibly incomplete or missing) sequence of coded text categories for an active

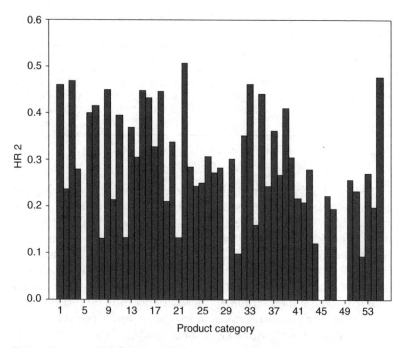

Figure 16.6   Recall rate (hit rate HR2: the fraction of actually chosen items that were correctly recommended)

user or respondent and a database of other respondents. In a simulation study the CF methodology was used to predict consumers' choices among product categories using binary market basket data collected from a grocery retailer. The simulation experiment was conducted by systematically varying hypothesised experimental design factors that are frequently reported to have a crucial effect on the predictive accuracy of recommendations.

Our findings suggest the following. For similarity matching, the often recommended correlation coefficient is outperformed (though not dramatically) by the Tanimoto coefficient and the Hamming distance measure. This result is not surprising, since the presence of binary data clearly puts the suitability of correlation measures into question. With regard to the design of CF techniques for qualitative data, further research is needed on other similarity concepts. A particularly interesting stream of research is that into the 'fuzzy similarity' concept, as introduced by Zadeh (1971) and successfully applied in models for case-based reasoning (Plaza *et al.*, 1996; Dubois *et al.*, 1997).

An important finding of our study is that CF performance is clearly harmed by database sparsity, which should draw the analyst's attention to the proper determination of useful respondent data with a minimum number of (common) items in order to achieve acceptable levels of predictive accuracy. On the other hand CF algorithms behave relatively robustly with respect to the amount of data collected from a single person; the predictive performance remains almost unaffected even if a considerable degree of information is missing. Furthermore, considerable differences in predictive performance can be observed depending on whether the prediction concerns actual item choices or non-choices. Since the former is typically the primary objective in most practical applications, including qualitative marketing data analysis (here the choice versus non-choice options would have to be replaced by the more general distinction between an item or text code category that 'applies' or 'not applies'), the raw predictive scores or votes delivered from CF algorithms should be treated with caution. Hence our findings suggest that further investigation of the effects of reasonable algorithmic modifications and/or manipulations of the predictive output should be conducted before drafting the final recommendations. Finally, it should be noted that our simulation study was based on just one binary data set. Further research should use different data sets from various (preferably on-line) data sources.

Notes

1. Of course larger numbers of ways and/or modes are possible. Examples of additional data modes are 'time' for repeated measurements and 'object' in the case of object-specific (for example product brand) measurements.
2. In conventional marketing and consumer behaviour research it is quite common to rearrange multiway, multimode data matrices by stacking two or even more data modes into one elongated data way; this is frequently called the 'extended data matrix approach' (Law *et al.*, 1984; Dillon *et al.*, 1985).
3. The F-values are the ratio of the sample variance estimated from the group means of the respective factor levels used and that estimated within these groups. Hence large F-values are indicative of substantial performance differences between factor levels. They can also serve as a score for statistically testing the null hypothesis that the group means (of factor levels) are equal in the population of simulation runs at a prespecified confidence level and for a given number of degrees of freedom (df).

References

Agrawal, R. and Srikant, R. (1994) *Fast Algorithms for Mining Association Rules* (Santiago, Chile: Morgan Kaufmann).

Anderberg, M. R. (1973) *Cluster Analysis for Applications* (New York, San Francisco and London: Academic Press).

Ansari, A., Essegaier, S. and Kohli, R. (2000) 'Internet Recommendation Systems', *Journal of Marketing Research*, vol. 37 (August), pp. 363–75.

Berry, M. and Linoff, G. (2000) *Mastering Data Mining: The Art and Science of Customer Relationship Management* (New York: Wiley).

Bishop, C. (1995) *Neural Networks for Pattern Recognition* (Oxford: Clarendon Press).

Bock, H. H. (1974) *Automatische Klassifikation* (Göttingen: Vandenhoek & Ruprecht).

Breese, J. S., Heckerman, D. and Kadie, C. (1998) *Empirical Analysis of Predictive Algorithms for Collaborative Filtering* (Madison, WI: Morgan Kaufmann).

Breiman, L., Friedman, J. H., Ohlsen, R. and Stone, C. (1984) *Classification and Regression Trees* (Belmont, CA: Wadsworth International).

Buechter, O. and Wirth, R. (1998) 'Discovery of association rules over ordinal data, A new and faster algorithm and its application to basket analysis', in X. Wu, R. Kotagiri and K. B. Korb (eds), *Research and Development in Knowledge Discovery and Data Mining* (Berlin, Heidelberg and New York: Springer), pp. 36–47.

Coombs, C. H. (1964) *A Theory of Data* (New York: Wiley).

Dillon, W. R., Frederick, D. G. and Tangpanichdee, V. (1985) 'Decision Issues in Building Perceptual Product Spaces with Multi-Attribute Rating Data', *Journal of Consumer Research*, vol. 12 (June), pp. 47–63.

Dubois, D., Esteva, F., Garcia, P., Godo, L., Lopez de Mantaras, R. and Prade, H. (1997) 'Fuzzy sets-based models in case-based reasoning', *Lecture Notes in Artificial Intelligence*, no. 1266 (Berlin, Heidelberg and New York: Springer), pp. 599–610.

Fayyad, U. M., Piatetsky-Shapiro G. and Smyth P. (1996) 'From Data Mining to Knowledge Discovery: An Overview', in U. M. Fayyad, G. Piatetsky-Shapiro, P. Smyth and U. Ramasamy (eds), *Advances in Knowledge Discovery and Data Mining* (Cambridge, Mass.: MIT Press), pp. 1–34.

Gallant, S. I. (1993) *Neural Network Learning and Expert Systems* (Cambridge, Mass.: MIT Press).

Gower, J. C. (1971) 'A general coefficient of similarity and some of its properties', *Biometrics*, vol. 27, pp. 857–71.

Hertz, J., Krogh, A. and Palmer, R. G. (1991) *Introduction to the Theory of Neural Computation* (Reading, Mass.: Addison-Wesley).

Hippner, H., Kuesters, U., Meyer, M. and Wilde, K. (2001) *Handbuch Data Mining im Marketing. Knowledge Discovery in Marketing Databases* (Wiesbaden: Vieweg).

Hubalek, Z. (1982) 'Coefficients of association and similarity, based on binary (presence–absence) data: An evaluation', *Biological Review*, vol. 57, pp. 669–89.

Jacoby, W. G. (1991) *Data Theory and Dimensional Analysis* (Newbury Park, CA: Sage).

Kass, G. V. (1980) 'An Exploratory Technique for Investigating Large Quantities of Categorical Data', *Applied Statistics*, vol. 29, pp. 119–27.

Kaufman, L. and Rousseeuw, P. J. (1990) *Finding Groups in Data. An Introduction to Cluster Analysis* (New York, Chichester, Brisbane, Toronto and Singapore: Wiley).

Kohonen, T. (1997) *Self-Organizing Maps* (Berlin, Heidelberg and New York: Springer).

Konstan, J., Miller, B., Maltz, D., Herlocker, J., Gordon, L. and Riedl, J. (1997) 'GroupLens: Applying Collaborative Filtering to Usenet News', *Communications of the Association for Computing Machinery*, vol. 40, no. 3, pp. 77–87.

Kowalski, G. (1997) *Information Retrieval Systems: Theory and Implementation* (Norwell, Mass.: Kluwer).

Law, H. G., Snyder, C. W. Jr, Hattie, J. A. and McDonald, R. P. (eds) (1984) *Research Methods for Multimode Data Analysis* (New York: Praeger).

Manago, M. and Auriol, M. (1996) 'Mining for OR', *ORMS Today*, special issue on data mining, vol. 23, no. 1, pp. 28–32.

Mazanec, J. A. (1999) 'Simultaneous Positioning and Segmentation Analysis with Topologically Ordered Feature Maps: A Tour Operator Example', *Journal of Retailing and Consumer Services*, vol. 6, no. 4, pp. 219–35.

Mazanec, J. and Strasser, H. (2000) *A Nonparametric Approach to Perceptions-Based Market Segmentation: Foundations* (Vienna and New York: Springer).

Natter, M. (1999) 'Conditional Market Segmentation by Neural Networks: A Monte Carlo Study', *Journal of Retailing and Consumer Services*, vol. 6, no. 4, pp. 237–48.

Plaza, E., Esteva, F., Garcia, P., Godo, L. and Lopez de Mantaras, R. (1996) 'A Logical Approach to Case-Based Reasoning Using Similarity Relations', *International Journal of Information Sciences*, vol. 106, pp. 105–22.

Quinlan, J. R. (1993) *C4.5: Programs for Machine Learning* (San Mateo, CA: Morgan Kauffman).

Resnick, P., Iacovou, N., Suchak, M., Bergstrom, P. and Riedl, J. (1994) *GroupLens: An Open Architecture for Collaborative Filtering of Netnews* (New York: ACM Press), pp. 219–31.

Reutterer, T. (1997) *Analyse von Wettbewerbsstrukturen mit neuronalen Netzen – Ein Ansatz zur Kundensegmentierung auf Basis von Haushaltspaneldaten* (Vienna: Service Fachverlag).

Runte, M. (2000) *Personalisierung im Internet. Individualisierte Angebote mit Collaborative Filtering* (Wiesbaden: DUV).

Sarwar, B., Karypis, G., Konstan, J. and Riedl, J. (2000) *Analysis of Recommendation Algorithms for E-commerce* (New York: ACM Press), pp. 158–67.

Schnedlitz, P., Reutterer, T. and Joos, W. (2001) 'Data-Mining und Sortimentsverbundanalyse im Einzelhandel', in H. Hippner, U. Kuesters, M. Meyer and K. Wilde (eds), *Handbuch Data Mining im Marketing. Knowledge Discovery in Marketing Databases* (Wiesbaden: Vieweg), pp. 951–70.

Young, F. W. (1987) 'Theory', in F. W. Young and R. M. Hamer (eds), *Multidimensional Scaling: History, Theory, and Applications* (Hillsdale, NJ: Lawrence Erlbaum), pp. 42–158.

Zadeh, L. A. (1971) 'Similarity relations and fuzzy orderings', *Information Sciences*, vol. 3, pp. 177–200.

Index

HF 5415.13 .A664 2004

Applying qualitative
 methods to marketing
 management research

ⵏⴻ ⴻⴰⴰⴻ ⴰⵣ   ⴰⴰⴰ ⴰⴰⴰⴰ